SO YOU WANT TO SING LIGHT OPERA

So You Want to Sing

Guides for Performers and Professionals

A Project of the National Association of Teachers of Singing

So You Want to Sing: Guides for Performers and Professionals is a series of works devoted to providing a complete survey of what it means to sing within a particular genre. Each contribution functions as a touchstone work not only for professional singers but also for students and teachers of singing. Titles in the series offer a common set of topics so readers can navigate easily the various genres addressed in each volume. This series is produced under the direction of the National Association of Teachers of Singing, the leading professional organization devoted to the science and art of singing.

SO YOU WANT TO SING LIGHT OPERA

A Guide for Performers

Linda Lister

Allen Henderson
Executive Editor, NATS

Matthew Hoch
Series Editor

A Project of the National Association of
Teachers of Singing

ROWMAN & LITTLEFIELD
Lanham • Boulder • New York • London

Published by Rowman & Littlefield
A wholly owned subsidary of
The Rowman & Littlefield Publishing Group, Inc.
4501 Forbes Boulevard, Suite 200, Lanham, Maryland 20706
www.rowman.com

Unit A, Whitacre Mews, 26-34 Stannary Street, London SE11 4AB

British Library Cataloguing in Publication Information Available

Library of Congress Cataloging-in-Publication Data

Names: Lister, Linda.
Title: So you want to sing light opera : a guide for performers / Linda
  Lister.
Description: Lanham : Rowman & Littlefield, [2018] | Series: So you want to
  sing | Includes bibliographical references and index.
Identifiers: LCCN 2017031663 (print) | LCCN 2017032537 (ebook) | ISBN
  9781442269392 (electronic) | ISBN 9781442269385 (pbk. : alk. paper)
Subjects: LCSH: Singing—Instruction and study. | Operas—Instruction and
  study.
Classification: LCC MT820 (ebook) | LCC MT820 .L7712 2018 (print) | DDC
  782.1/143—dc23
LC record available at https://lccn.loc.gov/2017031663

Printed in the United States of America

CONTENTS

LIST OF FIGURES

SERIES EDITOR'S FOREWORD

Compared to previous volumes in the So You Want to Sing series, *So You Want to Sing Light Opera* is unique. After a long succession of books that dealt with a plethora of contemporary commercial music (CCM) genres—including rock 'n' roll, jazz, country, gospel, folk music, and barbershop—we are devoting a book to what is considered by many to be a "classical" genre. Why are we doing this? Is such a book really necessary?

Yes, it is, and without question. Light opera remains one of the most frequently performed genres among students of classical singing and community theater groups. These works are regularly programmed by colleges and universities, as well as professional opera companies. This is perhaps surprising. What could be more dated than the Victorian stuffiness of *The Pirates of Penzance* and *HMS Pinafore*? Or more of an anachronism than the staunchly Viennese, waltz-infested strains of *Die Fledermaus* or *Die lustige Witwe*? Why do these period pieces seem to endure generation after generation, their popularity showing no sign of waning?

This book attempts to answer these questions, as well as many more. In the following pages, Linda Lister guides the reader through the many facets of light opera, from a repertoire overview to training requirements, acting style, dancing, stylistic considerations, auditioning, and vocal technique. In addition to being a seasoned performer of light opera herself, Dr. Lister is also a successful and experienced director, and she addresses the art form from both perspectives. Helpful and exhaustive appendixes help to round out the volume. A book like this has never before been written, and it is long overdue. The aspiring performer and teacher of light opera will come away from these pages with many tools to use in the studio and onstage.

Although light opera is a permanent fixture in the theatrical canon, it too often falls into a "no man's land" among resources for voice pedagogy. Classical singing teachers have tended to regard this repertoire as "not worthwhile" or "less legitimate" than the traditional operatic canon. Likewise, music theater specialists have disregarded Gilbert and Sullivan or Victor Herbert as "too classical," instead favoring more contemporary repertoire. Light opera—clearly its own unique art form—falls somewhere between these two genres. Hence the need for a book devoted exclusively to it. Light opera is a unique and important genre worthy of study in its own right.

Like other books in the So You Want to Sing series, several additional chapters round out this volume. One important contribution comes from Christopher Webber, author of *The Zarzuela Companion* and one of the world's foremost experts on this unique Spanish-language form of light opera. This volume would be incomplete without discussing zarzuela alongside its European and American cousins, and we are grateful to him for writing this chapter. Additional "common chapters" include a discussion of voice science by Scott McCoy, as well one on vocal health by Wendy LeBorgne. These chapters help to bind the series together, ensuring consistency of fact when it comes to the most essential matters of voice production.

The collected volumes of the So You Want to Sing series offer a valuable opportunity for performers and teachers of singing to explore new styles and important pedagogies. I am confident that voice specialists, both amateur and professional, will benefit from Linda Lister's important resource. It has been a privilege to work with her on this project. *So You Want to Sing Light Opera* is an invaluable resource for any performer or teacher interested in exploring this fascinating repertoire.

Matthew Hoch

FOREWORD

So You Want to Sing Light Opera by Dr. Linda Lister is the latest book in the So You Want to Sing series published by the National Association of Teachers of Singing (NATS) and Rowman & Littlefield. This book is an invaluable resource for voice teachers, vocal coaches, professional and amateur singers and actors, and educators seeking to know more about the vast history and repertoire of light opera. When most people think of light opera, they immediately turn to the W. S. Gilbert and Arthur Sullivan works, such as *The Mikado* or *The Pirates of Penzance*, or the great German operettas—*Die Fledermaus* by Johann Strauss II or *Die lustige Witwe* by Franz Lehár. However, there are a rich variety of other works spanning centuries and countries. This book sheds light on the earliest history of light opera and details works from the Italian tradition of *intermezzi*, German *Singspiel*, French *opéra bouffe*, and Spanish zarzuela through English works from the late nineteenth century and into American operetta. All of these subgenres helped influence the great American musicals of the twentieth century and beyond.

In addition to gaining an understanding and scope of light opera and its impact on our popular Broadway and West End musicals of today, this volume explores the proper technical demands and requirements to sing and perform this repertoire. Chapters on music, spoken dialogue, dance, and performance traditions are included to give teachers, coaches, and performers the tools necessary to prepare for auditions and performances. As with other volumes in this series, this book details ways to maintain proper vocal health while singing. Examples of audition pieces for each voice type are included as well.

As a performer, teacher, and director, Dr. Lister brings firsthand knowledge, experience, and expertise to give the reader an immersive and detailed look into light opera and operetta. Not only have Dr. Lister and I had the opportunity to perform together, but we also share a love and admiration for this popular genre of stage works. This book will be a valuable asset for every performer, educator, vocal teacher, and coach interested in understanding the history and performance tradition of light opera.

Keith Jameson
Opera Singer

ACKNOWLEDGMENTS

I would like to thank the opera professionals who shared their insights via phone, e-mail, and in-person interviews, especially F. Paul Driscoll, James Mills, David Weiller, Ann Marie Wilcox-Daehn, and Heather Nicole Winter. I also want to thank contributing author Christopher Webber for sharing his wealth of knowledge in the chapter on zarzuela. Finally, I owe a huge debt of gratitude to Matthew Hoch for being such a supportive editor, and to my husband, Nate Bynum, a theater professional himself, for being so patient as I spent time working on this book.

INTRODUCTION

Why Light Opera?

Light opera is a multifaceted art form. It could be described, like the quintet from Leonard Bernstein's *Candide*, as "the best of all possible worlds." Combining the operatic tradition of classical singing with theatrical high jinks, comedic spoken dialogue, stylized dance forms, exotic locales, and lavish production values, light opera provides ample rewards for both audience members and performers. For the audience, light opera consistently delivers comic relief with nonsensical plots, often involving mistaken identity or amusing disguises. For fans of *verismo* or Wagner, it may be an acquired, or never acquired, taste. But for those willing to suspend disbelief and accept the genre's charming absurdity, light opera can offer a wealth of lighthearted but not insignificant entertainment. In simpler terms, it's fun! There is great pleasure to be taken in a frothy *Fledermaus* or a rollicking *Ruddigore*. For the singer, light opera offers the opportunity, like music theater, to be a triple-threat performer. The genre demands the classically trained voice of an opera singer, the precise comedic timing and clear speaking voice of a trained actor, and the dance ability to execute choreography such as a grapevine or waltz step. ♪

With Puccini and Verdi often considered bread-and-butter repertoire, why would opera companies want to produce light opera? Lighter fare, such as operettas and musicals, is thought to help boost ticket sales, drawing in audience members who might not normally attend opera. When opera companies program music theater, they may encounter newfound challenges in casting, since many musicals require singers to have facility in contemporary commercial music, or CCM, singing technique. For instance, when Wagnerian soprano Deborah Voigt portrayed Annie Oakley in Glimmerglass Opera's 2011 production of *Annie Get Your Gun*, she reportedly tried to avoid belting[1] while singing the role created by legendary belter Ethel Merman. Although singers like Kristin Chenoweth and Audra McDonald are able to successfully switch from a belt mix to an operatic *chiaroscuro* resonance, most opera singers are not so nimble across techniques and genres. In operetta, opera singers can usually employ their familiar vocal technique and maintain stylistic viability. Therefore, programming light opera is a more natural fit, and many opera companies continue to include operetta as part of their seasons. From 2011 to 2016, light opera composers Johann Strauss II, Jacques Offenbach, and Emmerich Kálmán ranked number 8, 11, and 14, respectively, worldwide on the Operabase list of most performed composers. (In Austria, Strauss is second after Wolfgang Amadeus Mozart, while Franz Lehár and Kálmán rank number 1 and 2 in Hungary.) On their list of most commonly performed works, Strauss's *Die Fledermaus* was number 11 worldwide (number 4 in Austria) while Lehár's *Die lustige Witwe* ranked number 19 globally (number 1 in Hungary) and Kálmán's *Die Csárdásfürstin* was number 22 (number 2 in Hungary).[2] According to statistics by Opera America, *Candide* is number 4 on the listing of most produced North American works.[3]

In addition to professional opera companies, university opera programs often find light opera to be appropriate and appealing repertoire. While most collegiate singers are not yet ready to tackle roles such as Aida or Scarpia, the Pirate King or La Périchole could be an ideal vehicle for showcasing their burgeoning talents. The generally smaller-sized orchestras of light opera works are agreeable to student singers and instrumentalists alike. While there are important musical nuances essential to perform operetta well, the lighter orchestration does not put undue demands on young voices and is more feasible for a university symphony.

Despite its strong position in the operatic repertory, light opera still demands some different skills not always asked of the mainstream opera singer. Therefore, the training requirements for a singer of light opera encompass singing, acting, and dancing. Chapter 2 will explore the singing techniques and voice types used in light opera, as well as an introduction to repertoire suggestions. In chapter 3, the acting training needed for light opera will be addressed, while chapter 4 will delve into dance forms and steps frequently encountered in operetta.

Besides showcasing classical voice, comedy, and choreography, light opera transports the audience to a number of opulent settings both real and imaginary. While operettas have been set in famous cities including Paris (*Die lustige Witwe*, Herbert's *Mlle. Modiste*, Offenbach's *La vie parisienne*), Venice (Sullivan's *The Gondoliers*, Offenbach's *Le pont des soupirs*, Strauss's *Eine Nacht in Venedig*, Millán's *La Dogaresa*), Vienna (Strauss's *Wiener Blut*, Noël Coward's *Bitter Sweet*), and New Orleans (Herbert's *Naughty Marietta*, Romberg's *The New Moon*), many take place in fictional places that almost sound real but always sound entertaining. Only in light opera can you meet characters from Pontevedro (*Die lustige Witwe*) or Barataria (*The Gondoliers*) and travel to Karlsberg (Romberg's *The Student Prince*) or Utopia (Sullivan's *Utopia, Limited*).

Figure Intro.1.   Bristol Riverside Theatre's 2013 production of *The Pirates of Penzance*. Photo by BRT Staff

Light opera's striking and sumptuous locales provide ample creative outlets for scenic, lighting, and costume designers and thus abundant visual delights for the audience. In addition, the foreign and/or fictitious milieus embolden one of the key elements of light opera: satire. Amid the absurd plots and places, light opera often divulges biting societal satire veiled by unusual locations (Japan in Sullivan's *The Mikado*, Morocco in Romberg's *The Desert Song*) and droll characters. So while light opera may seem light and frivolous, it can offer rich opportunities for performers to show their wit and explore political issues past and present. For instance, Offenbach's *Orphée aux enfers* satirized Napoleon Bonaparte, disguised as the Roman god Jupiter. A modern updating of the operetta could use the mythological setting to parody a more recent political leader. Sullivan's *Princess Ida* is a ripe choice for a contemporary production with its exploration of feminism and the role of women in society. So while light opera affords lighthearted entertainment, it can also offer the singer the chance to be a shrewd satirist or clever comedian. With "flowing champagne, ceaseless waltzing, risqué *couplets*, Graustarkian uniforms and glittering ballgowns, romancing and dancing! Gaiety and lightheartedness, sentiment and *Schmalz*,"[4] why *not* light opera! This delightful genre, like Lehár's beloved operetta *Das Land des Lächelns*, is the Land of Smiles. ♪

NOTES

1. Daniel J. Wakin, "Opera Star Tries Doin' What Comes Naturally," *The New York Times*, http://www.nytimes.com/2011/07/15/arts/music/deborah -voigt-stars-in-annie-get-your-gun.html. Accessed December 22, 2016.

2. http://operabase.com. Accessed December 22, 2016.

3. http://operaamerica.org/applications/NAWD/index.aspx. Accessed May 4, 2017.

4. Richard Traubner, *Operetta: A Theatrical History* (Garden City, NY: Doubleday & Company, Inc., 1983), ix.

ONLINE SUPPLEMENT NOTE

So You Want to Sing Light Opera features an online supplement courtesy of the National Association of Teachers of Singing. Visit the link below to discover additional exercises and examples, as well as links to recordings of the songs referenced in this book.

www.nats.org/So_You_Want_To_Sing_Book_Series.html

A musical note symbol ♪ in this book will mark every instance of corresponding online supplement material.

❶

DEFINING LIGHT OPERA

Matthew Hoch

They are some of the most enduring tunes in the canon of Western music: the famous can-can from Jacques Offenbach's *Orpheus in the Underworld* . . . the Watch Duet from Johann Strauss's *Die Fledermaus* . . . "I Am the Very Model of a Modern Major-General" from Gilbert and Sullivan's *The Pirates of Penzance* . . . "Ah! Sweet Mystery of Life" from Victor Herbert's *Naughty Marietta* . . . and so many more! What a wonderful and electric list this is. Can this collective mix of styles from both sides of the Atlantic really have a common thread, representing the same genre through different countries, languages, and composers? What is "light opera" anyway, and how do we define it? Does it have anything in common with opera and music theater, and how is it unique? This introductory chapter will attempt to define light opera, discuss the history of the genre, outline its various forms, and provide a basic overview of the repertoire. ♪

WHAT'S IN A NAME?

Light opera is an umbrella term encompassing a variety of subgenres, including Italian *intermezzi*, German *Singspiel*, French *opéra bouffe*,

Viennese operetta, English comic opera, American operetta, and Spanish zarzuela. In many circles, the term light opera is used interchangeably with operetta. This is widely accepted but also potentially confusing, because operetta—like many musical terms—has both a specific and broader definition. In the narrow musicological sense, the term operetta usually refers to the waltz-based Viennese genre of the late nineteenth century, as exemplified in the works of Johann Strauss II (1825–1899) and Franz Lehár (1870–1948). However, operetta is also commonly used in a wider, "catch-all" sense referring to any form of light opera in any language. This is a very similar phenomenon to the way we use the term "classical music," which can refer to the art music canon as a whole, as well as the specific Viennese period during which Joseph Haydn (1732–1809), Wolfgang Amadeus Mozart (1756–1791), and Ludwig van Beethoven (1770–1827) composed. In this publication, we have made the decision to use light opera when discussing the genre as whole, believing it to be a slightly better catch-all term. Labels for specific subgenres, the terminology of which is discussed below, will also be used with frequency. Sometimes—especially when quoting other sources—the term operetta is also used interchangeably with light opera when referring to the repertoire as a whole.

DEFINING LIGHT OPERA

When discussing light opera, one of the most troublesome matters is perhaps also the most basic. How does one define light opera? Not really full-fledged opera but also not quite music theater (at least in the contemporary sense of the term), operetta finds itself somewhere in between the two genres, and the definition can be slippery. In the following passage, Thomson Smillie offers a humorous distinction between opera (which he refers to as "grand opera") and its "lighter" cousin (which he labels "operetta"):

> People get very hung up on the difference between an opera and an operetta, and between a "grand opera" and a *grand opéra*. And no wonder—the subject is mind-bogglingly complex. But more important, it doesn't matter! But more for amusement than erudition, let's spend a moment on this unnecessarily vex subject. The word "opera" is Italian,

but derives from the Latin plural of "opus" and means "the works," a reference to the fact that it is an amalgam of several arts. *Grand opéra* (with the French pronunciation) refers to those mighty five-act monsters produced for the Paris Opéra on deeply serious subjects, lasting for hours, with huge choruses and orchestras and the mandatory ballet in the fourth act—like Gounod's *Faust*, for example. Operetta usually means a piece on a lighter comic subject with dialogue. Oh, like *The Magic Flute*? Well, not exactly, because *The Magic Flute* deals with such elevated themes that "operetta" hardly describes it. . . . And operas with dialogue (as opposed to those composed all the way through) can hardly be counted as really "grand" operas, can they? Well, what about *Fidelio*? It deals with the noblest subjects, political injustice, the transcendent power of married love—they don't come any grander than that—surely! Again, it is not a grand opera, as it has dialogue. Well, what is it? Comic opera? *Singspiel*? *Opéra comique* (*not* the same as "comic opera")? *Carmen* is an *opéra comique*, but it is not especially humorous. And what about Wagner and his music dramas? And how do you describe Verdi's *Don Carlos*, written in five acts for the Paris Opéra, and later revised in four acts for Milan? And are you saying that because Verdi's *Aida*, the grandest opera of them all, is only in four acts, it is not a grand opera? Wouldn't it be simplest to say that to be a grand opera, a thing must be very long, on a grand scale, with a tragic theme, and have no dialogue? There! That's settled. We conclude that *The Phantom of the Opera* is a grand opera, and Beethoven's *Fidelio* is not.[1]

Dialogue and lighthearted humor are indeed major hallmarks of light opera, but Smillie rightly points out that some of the opera canon's most enduring works contain these elements as well. In another essay on the topic, Peter Gammond echoes these sentiments, offering a quintessentially British description of the conundrum:

You can really only distinguish an operetta from an opera by its flavour; just as you might tell a light wine from a heavier one. There is not a lot in their appearance to tell them apart. An opera probably has more notes to the page and operettas tend to have some passages of spoken dialogue (but so do some operas). Operettas set out to be tuneful and entertaining, but *Le nozze di Figaro* is both of these things. We still recognize it as an opera while *Die Fledermaus* is quite definitely an operetta. Is it simply that operettas refuse to be taken seriously; that they are incurably frivolous and lighthearted; made up of isolated melodies rather than serious musical development? The recipe is a mixture of all these elements. Operetta is quite simply entertainment music in operatic form. Like all good light music, it chases you rather than asking, as good serious music does, that you shall come and chase it.[2]

And in the Naxos *History of Opera*, Richard Fawkes weighs in with some thoughts that might offer the clearest distinction (or—at the very least—the least muddy one):

> What is the difference between operetta and opera? Operetta is an Italian word that meaning literally "little opera," but that's hardly a definition applicable to what we understand by the term today. Operetta has spoken dialogue between the numbers, but then so too does *Carmen* or Mozart's *The Magic Flute*, neither of which could remotely be called operetta. Operetta contains romance. So too do many operas. Operetta is lighthearted. So are some operas. Operetta can be frivolous. So too can opera. It is really rather pointless to try to define operetta too closely, but it's been said that operetta is a piece of music theater written to pull in audiences, while opera is written with one eye very firmly on the future. That seems as good a definition as any. Operetta is a lighthearted look at the world, containing melody, glamour, comedy, and romance. It is escapist entertainment designed to send people out of the theater happier than when they went in.[3]

No matter how one attempts to define it, light opera was born out of a desire to have a lighter form of theatrical entertainment. Although most light operas are sung in a classical style—with the exception of some character roles, just like in opera—one can reasonably think of the genre as a primary forerunner of music theater, in the case of *Singspiel*, extending all the way back to the late eighteenth century. Acknowledging light opera as the music theater of its day—music for the masses "designed to send people out of the theater happier than when they went in"—is perhaps the best way to think of the genre.

Alyson McLamore, in her excellent study of the history of music theater, traces the lineage of the genre all the way back to Mozart's *Bastien und Bastienne* through Offenbach's *Orphée aux enfers*, Strauss's *Die Fledermaus*, Gilbert and Sullivan's *The Pirates of Penzance*, Lehár's *Die lustige Witwe*, Herbert's *Babes in Toyland* and *Naughty Marietta*, and

Friml's *Rose-Marie* and *The Vagabond King* before arriving at Kern's *Show Boat* and the birth of the modern era of music theater.[4] Such a sequence and timeline acknowledge the common thread and role of light opera in the theatrical canon. In spite of its myriad subgenres, all forms of light opera offer escapist entertainment sung in a classical style.

SUBGENRES OF LIGHT OPERA

As mentioned above, the world of light opera is divided into many subgenres, and these labels and distinct stylistic differences speak directly to three criteria for categorization: where the work was written (i.e., in which country), in which time period (i.e., when), and the specific musical characteristics of that particular subgenre. Obviously, certain composers are also inextricably linked with specific forms of light opera as well. The following paragraphs will give a historical overview of the repertoire and its primary composers as well as articulate the distinct stylistic features of each flavor of light opera.

Italian *Intermezzi*

The Italian *intermezzo* is a short, Italian comic opera (*opera buffa*) that was originally written to be performed "in the middle" (hence its name) of a longer, serious opera. Many of these *intermezzi* eventually came to be divorced from the original operas that framed them, becoming independent theatrical works in their own right. *Intermezzi* are entirely sung and have no dialogue; like other full-length operas of the era, recitative takes place between the numbers. Since dialogue is an essential feature of virtually all light operas, grouping them alongside other subgenres discussed in this chapter is slightly problematic. Nevertheless, this lighthearted comic alternative to the Italian operas of the eighteenth century make the *intermezzo* an important forerunner of light opera, foreshadowing what was to develop in Germany and France over the course of the next century. Pergolesi's *La serva padrona* (1733) is by far the most famous example of an *intermezzo*, first performed between the acts of Pergolesi's opera seria *Il prigionier superbo* (1733).

Figure 1.1. *Shepherd Piping to a Shepherdess* (c. 1747–1750) by François Boucher (1703–1770). **Such pastoral scenes were the subject matter of many eighteenth-century German Singspiels.** *Creative Commons (CCBY-SA 3.0)*

German *Singspiel*

One could argue that the story of light opera begins with *Singspiel*, a German-language form of light opera dating back to the mid-eighteenth century. In *Singspiels*, spoken dialogue alternates with songs and ensemble numbers. Settings are usually in rural or exotic places. Many composers in Germany and Austria tried their hand at writing *Singspiels*, but the most famous examples of the genre include four composed by Wolfgang Amadeus Mozart: *Bastien und Bastienne* (1768), *Die Entführung aus dem Serail* (1782), *Der Schauspieldirektor* (1786), and *Die Zauberflöte* (1791). Out of these four works, however, only *Bastien and Bastienne* and *Der Schauspieldirektor* are typical of the genre. The other two are built on a much grander scale and in many ways resemble full-scale operas with the exception that dialogue is inserted between musical numbers. Other important composers of *Singspiel* include Johann Adam Hiller (1728–1804), Jiří Antonín Benda (1722–1795), and Carl Ditters von Dittersdorf (1739–1799).

French *Opéra Bouffe*

Opéra bouffe is a form of French light opera that emerged in the mid-nineteenth century. An *opéra bouffe* was a comical and satirical work that was also often quite bawdy in nature. The genre derived its name from the Bouffes Parisiens, where many of the first *opéra bouffe* productions were premiered. The *opéra bouffe* was invented by the French composer Louis Auguste Florimond Ronger (1825–1892)—better known to history as Hervé—but the genre achieved popularity with the works of Jacques Offenbach (1819–1880). Offenbach's *Orphée aux enfers* (1858), which satirizes the Greek myth of Orpheus, is considered to be the quintessential *opéra bouffe*. It is no accident that Offenbach chose this myth—the same one chosen by Claudio Monteverdi (1567–1643) and Christoph Willibald Gluck (1714–1787)—for his subject; the possibilities for satire could not have been richer.

While Offenbach never surpassed the popularity of *Orphée aux enfers*—better known in the English-speaking world as *Orpheus in the Underworld*—with any subsequent work, he continued to compose prolifically and contributed many other important works to the genre. Examples of other well-known *opéra bouffes* by Offenbach include *La belle Hélène* (1864), *La vie parisienne* (1866), *La Grande-Duchesse de Gérolstein* (1867), and *La Périchole* (1868). When Offenbach's popularity waned, other French composers who composed in the *opéra bouffe* tradition included Charles Lecocq (1832–1918), Robert Planquette (1848–1903), Edmond Audran (1840–1901), and André Messager (1853–1929).

It should be noted that there is sometimes a tendency to confuse *opéra bouffe* with another closely related genre, *opéra comique*. Like *opéra bouffe*, *opéra comique* is also a nineteenth-century sung French work with dialogue. However, although *opéra comique* literally translates as "comic opera," the plot of an *opéra comique* is not necessarily comical; more often, it is serious or dramatic. These works are given their name because of their venue: they were often performed at the Opéra-Comique, a Parisian opera company that still exists. *Carmen* (1875) by Georges Bizet (1838–1875)—an *opéra comique* that is not at all humorous—is the most well-known example of the genre that is still in the repertory today. While *opéra comique* certainly had some influence on the invention of *opéra bouffe* as a subsequent "spin-off" theatrical form

Figure 1.2. Theatrical poster by Jules Chéret (1836–1932) for *Orphée aux enfers* at the Bouffes Parisiens (1866). *Creative Commons (CCBY-SA 3.0)*

(particularly in the use of dialogue in both genres), the two terms are distinct from one another and should not be used interchangeably.

Viennese Operetta

Viennese operetta is a waltz-based form of light opera that emerged in Vienna during the 1870s. Developed after *opéra bouffe*, it is a more formal, refined, and "cleaner" version of its bawdy French cousin. Like most light operas, Viennese operetta features dialogue, dancing, and memorable tunes. The genre's libretti usually feature members of the aristocracy who embark on comical romps of nonsense and infidelity only to have it all work out in the end.

Die Fledermaus (1874)—translated as "The Bat"—by Johann Strauss II, represents the apotheosis of Viennese operetta and heralds the golden age of the genre. In the 1880s and 1890s, public demand for Viennese operetta was at its zenith. Somewhat waning in popularity by the beginning of the twentieth century, operetta was almost single-handedly revived by *Die lustige Witwe* (1905) by Franz Lehár. This work ushered in a new "silver age" of Viennese operetta. When *Die lustige Witwe* was revived two years later in New York City, it was immensely popular, and the 1907 American production of *The Merry Widow* (the English translation of *Die lustige Witwe*) is credited with the birth of merchandizing through souvenirs—*Merry Widow* cigars, chocolates, scarves, and so forth—a practice that has been a staple commercial practice of the Broadway industry ever since. The popularity of these two works has never waned; today, *Die Fledermaus* and *Die lustige Witwe* remain the only two works from the light opera repertory that are regularly staged by major opera companies across the globe. Germany, Austria, and Hungary still mount numerous productions of *Die Fledermaus* as an annual New Year's Day tradition.

Both Strauss and Lehár contributed many works to the genre. In addition to *Die Fledermaus*, some of Strauss's most famous Viennese operettas include *Eine Nacht in Venedig* (1883), *Der Zigeunerbaron* (1885), and *Wiener Blut* (1899). Lehár's most popular works beyond *Die lustige Witwe* include *Der Graf von Luxemburg* (1909), *Der Zarewitsch* (1927), and *Das Land des Lächelns* (1929). Other significant composers of Viennese operettas include Franz von Suppé (1819–1895), Carl Millöcker (1842–1899), Oscar Straus (1870–1954), Leo Fall (1873–1925), Robert Stolz (1880–1975), Emmerich Kálmán (1882–1953), Walter Goetze (1883–1961), and Eduard Künneke (1885–1953). Although the repertoire is vast, few Viennese operettas are performed today outside of Germany, Austria, and Hungary. The significant exceptions are *Die Fledermaus* and *Die lustige Witwe*, which continue to receive hundreds of international performances each year.

English Comic Opera

Much of late nineteenth-century British music is now forgotten, but the one area in which England made its mark on musical and theatrical history was in the genre of light opera. The distinct twist on the genre, known as English comic opera, rests almost entirely on the achievement of two men: the librettist William Schwenck Gilbert (1836–1911)

and the composer Arthur Sullivan (1842–1900). The thirteen surviving comic operas of these two men—known, of course, as the famous
duo Gilbert and Sullivan—exemplify the genre. These works were so
popular that the Savoy Theatre was built in the West End of London
for the sole purpose of staging Gilbert and Sullivan's comic operas.
Therefore, the collective body of "G&S" works are often referred to
as the "Savoy operas."

English comic operas usually featured a two-act structure with dialogue. The librettos generally satirize some aspect of Victorian British
society, and excessive confusion and mayhem are almost always resolved
neatly (although not always logically) in the final moments of the evening. Essential to the Gilbert and Sullivan formula was their own set of
stock characters: the attractive ingénue (the soprano); the pining tenor
(her love interest); the bad bass; the uglier and older mezzo-soprano;
and—most idiomatically to Gilbert and Sullivan—the patter baritone,
who is usually the central comic figure of the work.

The thirteen surviving Gilbert and Sullivan comic operas are *Trial
by Jury* (1875), *The Sorcerer* (1877), *HMS Pinafore* (1878), *The Pirates of Penzance* (1879), *Patience* (1881), *Iolanthe* (1882), *Princess
Ida* (1884), *The Mikado* (1885), *Ruddigore* (1887), *The Yeomen of
the Guard* (1888), *The Gondoliers* (1889), *Utopia, Limited* (1893),
and *The Grand Duke* (1896), and almost all of them enjoy frequent
revivals. They stand alongside *Die Fledermaus*, *Die lustige Witwe*, and
Orphée aux enfers as some of the only examples of light opera that
have never fallen out of the repertoire, remaining perennial favorites
among audiences across the globe.

Needless to say, Gilbert and Sullivan's works are unapologetically
dated even as they still enjoy frequent revivals. In contemporary productions, there is a tradition of updating certain comic references to
relatively obscure Victorian places, institutions, and conditions so that
they now refer to local situations that are immediate to the particular
audience. For example, Knightsbridge becomes Brooklyn for a New
York audience, and Josephine's reference to Gillows becomes Filene's
Basement when performed in Boston. Along the same lines, directors
and performers often write new final verses, with local or contemporary
references, to some of the comic patter songs, for example, "I Am the
Very Model of a Modern Major-General."

Figure 1.3. Sketch by David Henry Friston (1820–1906) of a scene from Gilbert and Sullivan's *Trial by Jury* (1875). *Creative Commons (CCBY-SA 3.0)*

The comic operas of Gilbert and Sullivan hail from the Victorian era of Britain, referring to the reign of Queen Victoria, who was the longest reigning monarch of Great Britain until Queen Elizabeth II surpassed her in 2015. Victoria reigned from 1837 until her death in 1901. One generation later, a body of work sometimes referred to as Edwardian comic operas succeeded Gilbert and Sullivan's Victorian works, but these comic operas have never secured a permanent place in the light opera repertory. The term Edwardian refers to Victoria's successor, King Edward VII, who reigned from 1901 until 1910. Thus, English comic operas written before 1901 are often referred to as "Victorian" comic operas, and ones composed in 1901 or later as "Edwardian" comic operas. Principal composers and librettists of Edwardian comic opera, which is still a kind of English comic opera, include Ivan Caryll (1861–1921), Lionel Monckton (1861–1924), and Sidney Jones (1861–1946). The popularity of Edwardian comic operas was short-lived, however, and by World War II they had fallen completely out of fashion. Today, these works are only performed in England, and abroad they are kept alive primarily through preservation societies such as the Ohio Light Opera in Wooster, Ohio.

American Operetta

American operetta is a European-style form of light opera that emerged in New York City during the first several decades of the twentieth century. American operetta is a repertory distinct from Viennese operetta and English comic opera, distinguished by the composers who wrote them as well as more flexible and less formulaic compositional structures. The principal composers of American operetta were Victor Herbert (1859–1924), Rudolf Friml (1879–1972), and Sigmund Romberg (1887–1951), all of whom lived and worked in New York. Ironically, none of these composers were born in the United States: Herbert was born in Ireland, Friml in Czechoslovakia, and Romberg in Hungary. Herbert's operettas appeared first, during the first decade of the twentieth century; his most famous works include *Babes in Toyland* (1903), *The Red Mill* (1906), and *Naughty Marietta* (1910). Friml's star rose after Herbert's, during the 1920s; his most famous works—*Rose-Marie* (1924), *The Vagabond King* (1925), and *The Three Musketeers* (1928)—all date from this period. Romberg was the most European of the three, and his most popular works—*The Student Prince* (1924), *The Desert Song* (1926), and *The New Moon* (1928)—are very much in the style of Viennese operetta.

Zarzuela

Of all the subgenres addressed in this introductory chapter, zarzuela is unquestionably the most varied. Zarzuela is a form originally developed in Spain but has since spread to other countries in which Spanish is spoken. Although the earliest examples of this genre were written for the court of King Philip IV in the seventeenth century, zarzuela achieved popularity and international recognition in the nineteenth century, as well as a huge number of recordings in the twentieth. Zarzuela literally translates as "bramble bush," but its name derives from the name of the palace of King Philip IV (1621–1665)—La Zarzuela. The genre became established and flourished in the cosmopolitan public theaters of Madrid, gradually absorbing some characteristics of other forms of opera and light opera—French *opéra comique* and Italian *opera buffa* in particular. Important composers of zarzuela have included Sebastián Durón (1660–1716), Francisco Asenjo Barbieri (1823–1894),

Federico Chueca (1846–1908), Ruperto Chapí (1851–1909), Amadeo Vives (1871–1932), and Pablo Sorozábal (1897–1988). One subgenre of zarzuela is the *tonadilla escénica*, a one-act satirical zarzuela that reached the height of its popularity in the mid-eighteenth century and which contributed to the classic nineteenth-century *género chico*, the most popular one-act form of zarzuela, which featured more dialogue, Spanish urban dances such as the *chotis*, and a working-class perspective. In chapter 8 of this book, zarzuela expert Christopher Webber provides a thorough introduction to this unique genre of Spanish theater.

LIGHT OPERA AS NOSTALGIA FOR A BYGONE ERA

By the 1940s, light opera had largely fallen out of fashion, and few original works were created after this time. This change in public taste had much to do with World War I and II (and the Great Depression, which took place between them), but light opera was also largely replaced by the musical, a new era of Broadway theater that began around 1943 with the advent of *Oklahoma!* by Richard Rodgers and Oscar Hammerstein II. *Oklahoma!* signaled a new kind of music theater writing, one that merged aspects of operetta with the musical comedy tradition of the 1930s.[5] These two genres—along with the revue—comprised the vast majority of Broadway shows prior to the 1940s, but after *Oklahoma!* musicals became the norm, and pure operettas suddenly sounded "dated" to theatergoers, harkening back to a bygone era.[6]

Thus, light operas are unashamed period pieces, cherished relics from our fondly remembered past. Thomson Smillie provides a fitting conclusion to this introductory chapter when he writes:

> What is it, we might ask, about these grand old waltzes, polkas, and ma-
> zurkas that makes us feel nostalgic for an era that was dead or dying be-
> fore our grandparents were born? Psychologists tell us that we tend to feel
> greatest nostalgia not of our youth, but of our parents' youth. But what
> explains nostalgia for the music of our great-great-grandparents? One rea-
> son may be the great watershed of the first World War, which in addition
> to so much else swept away what we now think of as an age of glamour.
> Enduring love for the waltzes of Johann Strauss and his contemporaries
> . . . the autumnal glow of Merchant-Ivory films . . . the interest in anything

to do with the Titanic . . . all these are symptoms of a remembrance of things past sometimes called the "nostalgia industry."[7]

Many people tend to think of the past as a "golden era." We buy in to the notion that our best times are behind us. Film director Woody Allen brilliantly explores this human inclination in his humorous and poetic film *Midnight in Paris* (2011). Perhaps it is this very nostalgia for a bygone era that keeps light opera alive, perennially remaining in our repertoire and warming our hearts even after many listenings. There is every reason to believe that audiences one hundred years from now will still be charmed by the music of Jacques Offenbach, Johann Strauss II, Arthur Sullivan, Franz Lehár, and so many other voices from this golden age. If the past is any prediction of the future, the distinct voice of light opera will always remain an important cornerstone of the classical singer's repertoire.

NOTES

1. Thomson Smillie, *Opera Explained: Johann Strauss's "Die Fledermaus"* (United States: Naxos Audiobooks, 2003).

2. Peter Gammond, liner notes for *Die Fledermaus* (EMI records, 1972).

3. Richard Fawkes, *The History of Opera* (United States: Naxos Audiobooks, 1999).

4. Alyson McLamore, *Musical Theater: An Appreciation* (Upper Saddle River, NJ: Pearson Prentice Hall, 2004).

5. *Show Boat* (1927), with music by Jerome Kern (1885–1945) and book and lyrics by Oscar Hammerstein II (1895–1960), also has a strong claim to being the first musical, but this work was an outlier in its time and failed to inaugurate a new era of Broadway theater. During the 1930s, the Great Depression hit Broadway hard, and many composers and lyricists found work in Hollywood instead of New York. Most of the Broadway shows written during this decade were musical comedies in the style of Cole Porter's *Anything Goes* (1934).

6. These three "premusical" genres are explored exhaustively in Gerald Bordman's trio of studies *American Operetta: From H.M.S. Pinafore to Sweeney Todd* (1981), *American Musical Comedy: From Adonis to Dreamgirls* (1982), and *American Musical Revue: From The Passing Show to Sugar Babies* (1985).

7. Smillie, *Opera Explained*.

②

SINGING LIGHT OPERA

Light opera offers singers some of the most beautiful and singable melodies to showcase their vocal beauty and range, not to mention a plethora of patter songs to challenge the agility of their articulation. Most often, light opera is performed without amplification for the singers, as is the common practice in opera houses around the world. Thus, the singer must project over the orchestra through the use of vocal resonance consistent with classical singing technique. While microphones are often used in operettas produced by theater companies, operatic productions usually only use amplification for dialogue, if at all. So singers crossing over to light opera from music theater may need to think about singing "on the voice" and cultivating more consistent vibrance, whereas a *spinto* soprano might need to think of singing with less vocal weight when venturing into the realm of operetta. The 1970s rock star Linda Ronstadt famously "crossed over" and adjusted her vocal technique to sing Mabel in *The Pirates of Penzance* on Broadway and in the 1983 film version. Most singers will not sing light opera exclusively, so it is helpful to examine the repertoire and vocal requirements for each voice type so that performers can successfully approach the genre regardless of whether they are primarily singers of Richard Strauss, Johann Strauss, or Charles Strouse. ♪

VOCAL CHARACTERISTICS AND
REPERTOIRE RECOMMENDATIONS

Soprano

In light opera, the soprano is typically required to sing with elegant lyricism. Not surprisingly, head voice predominates. Sweetness of timbre and purity of legato are essential for the sweeping melodies such as Josephine's aria "Sorry Her Lot" from *HMS Pinafore* and "Ah! Sweet Mystery of Life" from *Naughty Marietta*. At times, the soprano will also have wordy text to deliver as in many Offenbach *couplets* or in the verses of Yum-Yum's "The Sun, Whose Rays Are All Ablaze" from *The Mikado*. Some light operas have two major soprano roles (Rosalinda and Adele in *Die Fledermaus*, Hanna and Valencienne in *Die lustige Witwe*, Marianne and Julie in *The New Moon*), with a fuller lyric soprano as the leading lady and a lighter lyric or lyric coloratura soprano as her maid, friend, or sidekick. But often the coloratura soprano herself is the main female character. Much of the repertoire requires substantial vocal agility, with an abundance of staccato singing, fioritura, and playful musical figures.

Appendix C will list more examples, but here are some light opera repertoire recommendations for sopranos:

1. "Poor Wandering One" from *The Pirates of Penzance*: coloratura, staccato
2. "A Simple Sailor Lowly Born" from *HMS Pinafore*: recitative, aria
3. "Es lebt' eine Vilja" from *Die lustige Witwe*: storytelling strophes, lyrical refrain
4. "Klänge der Heimat" from *Die Fledermaus*: faux-Hungarian tour de force
5. "Mein Herr Marquis" from *Die Fledermaus*: staccato, high Ds
6. "Glitter and Be Gay" from *Candide*: many runs and high E♭s
7. "Lover, Come Back to Me" from *The New Moon*: lyrical line, soft dynamics
8. "Italian Street Song" from *Naughty Marietta*: melismas and tongue twisters
9. "Je suis nerveuse" from *Le voyage dans la lune*: cadenza, playful dotted rhythms

10. "Au chapeau je porte une aigrette" from *Les brigands*: trills, patriotic feel

In examining the repertoire, it is helpful to mention a few prominent operetta singers of both past and present. Marie Geistinger (1833–1903) was the original Rosalinda in *Die Fledermaus* and the so-called Queen of Operetta, performing in numerous Offenbach operas in Vienna. The queen of operetta on the silver screen was Jeanette MacDonald (1903–1965), although to modern ears her vibrato may sound a bit fast. With her silvery, clear tone, Barbara Cook (1927–2017) became a star after creating the role of Cunegonde in the original production of *Candide* (1956). More recently, Tony Award–winner Kelli O'Hara (b. 1976) ventured from Broadway to the Metropolitan Opera to play Valencienne in the 2014–2015 production of *The Merry Widow*. Like these four famous singers, the light opera soprano needs to have a voice of mellifluousness and sophistication, able to sing with seamless legato as Princess Ida or effortless coloratura as Adele. ♪

Mezzo-Soprano

For mezzo-sopranos, light opera is replete with plum roles. You can play a fairy queen, a duchess, a Russian prince, or Helen of Troy. Instead of soprano sweetness, the voice should display a warm, burnished quality and a hint of sass without heaviness. Some songs require a lyrical legato, while others feature lively musical articulation with a teasing or coquettish quality. To achieve this sound, and to help project in the middle register, a bit of chest voice may be used, especially for comedic effects.

1. "Cheerily Carols the Lark" from *Ruddigore*: an operetta mad scene
2. "My Lord, a Suppliant at Your Feet" from *Iolanthe*: recitative, *sostenuto* song
3. "When a Merry Maiden Marries" from *The Gondoliers*: tuneful melody, play on words
4. "Ah! Quel dîner" from *La Périchole*: the so-called Tipsy Waltz
5. "Amours divins" from *La belle Hélène*: graceful entrance aria

6. "Ah! Que j'aime les militaires" from *La Grande-Duchesse de Gérolstein*: comedic word repetition, martial energy
7. "Chacun à son goût" from *Die Fledermaus*: high onsets, upward leaps
8. "Alles mit Ruhe geniessen" from *Der Graf von Luxemburg*: strophic mazurka
9. "If Love Were All" from *Bitter Sweet*: languorous, nostalgic ballad
10. "A Widow Has Ways" from *The Red Mill*: witty waltz by a young widow

Gilbert and Sullivan wrote a number of mezzo roles for Jessie Bond (1853–1942), who progressed from small parts like Hebe in *HMS Pinafore* to the title role in *Iolanthe*. Similarly, Offenbach was inspired by Hortense Schneider (1833–1920), who starred in *La belle Hélène* and *La Périchole*. The charming light lyric mezzo of Frederica von Stade (b. 1945) was well suited to Offenbach as well, while Susan Graham (b. 1960) played both the Grand Duchess of Gerolstein and Prince Orlofsky. Both divas even sang the soprano role of Hanna in Metropolitan Opera productions of *The Merry Widow*, von Stade in 2000 and Graham in 2015 alternating with Renée Fleming. So in light opera, mezzos don't always play second fiddle. Often the leading ladies (or leading men in pants roles), they maintain a degree of vocal refinement befitting their status in the genre. ♪

Contralto

Contralto roles are less common in light opera, especially in the Viennese tradition, which favored the model of two soprano principals. For these secondary but key roles, vocal beauty is not as important as vocal color. Instead of soprano sweetness or mezzo sassiness, the light opera contralto should have a hint of brashness to distinguish her from the ingénue. A more speech-like vocal quality and the use of more chest voice help portray characters of greater age or less glamour. Instead of the young songbird, the contralto plays buxom Buttercup (*HMS Pinafore*), the earthy gypsy Czipra (*Der Zigeunerbaron*), or the older Dame Hannah (*Ruddigore*).

Figure 2.1.   Jessie Bond as Mad Margaret in *Ruddigore* (1887). *Creative Commons (CCBY-SA 3.0)*

1. "When Frederic Was a Little Lad" from *The Pirates of Penzance*: moderato strophic song with the key pilot/pirate plot point
2. "Alone and Yet Alive" from *The Mikado*: dramatic recitative, melodramatic chorus
3. "Silvered Is the Raven Hair" from *Patience*: amusing reflection on aging
4. "On the Day When I Was Wedded" from *The Gondoliers*: jaunty, wordy up-tempo piece
5. "Come Bumpers-Aye, Ever So Many" from *The Grand Duke*: a jaunty drinking song
6. "Oh Foolish Fay" from *Iolanthe*: the Fairy Queen's staid cautionary tale
7. "Bold-Faced Ranger" from *Utopia, Limited*: Lady Sophy's loquacious lecture
8. "I Am Easily Assimilated" from *Candide*: teasing tango, Spanish accent
9. "'Neath the Southern Moon" from *Naughty Marietta*: slow, beautiful ballad
10. "Bald wird man dich viel umwerben" from *Der Zigeunerbaron*: a gypsy song with a climactic high A ending

Maria Duchêne-Billiard (1884–?), the original quadroon slave Adah in *Naughty Marietta*, also sang Verdi and Wagner at the Metropolitan Opera, implying a voice of considerable heft. British contralto Anne Collins (1943–2009) performed Wagner at Covent Garden but went on to sing Gilbert and Sullivan with the English National Opera. In a production of *Patience*, she played cello onstage as part of her portrayal of Lady Jane, which is an interesting parallel to Patti LuPone's playing of the tuba as Mrs. Lovett in the 2005 Broadway revival of *Sweeney Todd*. LuPone (b. 1949) also appeared as the Old Lady in the 2004 New York Philharmonic *Candide* concert broadcast on PBS. The contralto characters of Bernstein and Sondheim owe their lineage to the Savoy contraltos, thus it is not surprising that Angela Lansbury (b. 1925) excelled as both Mrs. Lovett and Ruth (*The Pirates of Penzance*). While contraltos may not be the stars of light opera, they are still granted chances to highlight both dramatic and comedic vocal effects in their cameo moments. ♪

Tenor

The tenor is most often the romantic lead in light opera. In the Gilbert and Sullivan repertoire, the sweet-voiced and sweet-natured Nanki-Poo epitomizes the paradigm with his "dreamy lullaby." A honeyed vocal timbre is essential to win over the hearts of the leading lady and the audience. Like with the light opera soprano repertoire, soaring high notes and climactic cadenzas show off tenor range and flexibility, as well as the ability to sing softly with great dynamic control. In Gilbert and Sullivan's *Princess Ida*, two tenors are featured: the hero, Hilarion, and his sidekick Cyril, who sings a drunk and charmingly repetitious arietta, "Would You Know the Kind of Maid?" Offenbach's *Orphée aux enfers* has multiple tenor roles: Orpheus, Pluto, Mercury, and John Styx. Some roles created by tenors are now sometimes sung by high baritones or *Zwischenfach* singers, namely Eisenstein (*Die Fledermaus*) and Danilo (*The Merry Widow*), depending on the casting preferences of the company. And there are a few *comprimario* character roles for tenor, like the stuttering *Spieltenor* Dr. Blind in *Die Fledermaus* or pig farmer Zsupán in *Der Zigeunerbaron*, but overall, the tenor reigns as the male star of light opera.

1. "Oh Is There Not One Maiden Breast?" from *The Pirates of Penzance*: amusing, lyrical plea with cadenza
2. "Oh, Gentlemen, Listen, I Pray" from *Trial by Jury*: the defendant's wordy and clever aria
3. "Take a Pair of Sparkling Eyes" from *The Gondoliers*: aptly Italianate barcarolle
4. "Dein ist mein ganzes Herz" from *Das Land des Lächelns*: the operetta tenor's gold standard
5. "Gern hab' ich die Frau'n geküßt" from *Paganini*: flirtatious and charming, another famous so-called *Tauberlied*
6. "O mes amours, ô mes maitresses" from *Les brigands*: up-tempo with yodel and falsetto effects
7. "Heureuses divinités" from *Orphée aux enfers*: playful aria quoting the famous can-can
8. "Pour découper adroitement" from *La vie parisienne*: spirited couplets requiring nimble diction

9. "Serenade" from *The Student Prince*: uber-romantic song with a wide range
10. "The Time and the Place and the Girl" from *Mlle. Modiste*: waltz with a climactic high A

Lehár was inspired by the voice of Austrian tenor Richard Tauber (1891–1948), writing roles for him in his operettas *Giuditta* and *Paganini*, to name a few. Like Marni Nixon did in many movie musicals, Mario Lanza provided the singing voice for the character of Prince Karl in the film version of *The Student Prince* (while actor Edmund Purdom lip-synched). Modern performers excelling at the repertoire include German tenor Philip Lüsebrink, frequenting the Hamburger Engelsaal (the so-called Theatre of Light Entertainment), and American tenor Keith Jameson, who has been a regular with the New York Gilbert and Sullivan Players and New York City Opera as Nanki-Poo and Candide. ♪

Baritone

While tenors are the leading men in most Gilbert and Sullivan operas, baritones tend to be the romantic leads in American operetta. With a warm, resonant timbre, the lower voice type brings more machismo and romantic richness to the characters. In the Savoy opera repertoire, there are a few leading lyric baritones (Captain Corcoran, the Pirate King), but primarily the patter baritone prevails. While in Offenbach's operas, the comedic baritone must also display agile articulation, often involving onomatopoeia or nonsense syllables. To sing these parts, the singer should always be certain to train the articulators for clear and rapid enunciation.

Lyric baritone:

1. "Da geh' ich zu Maxim" from *Die lustige Witwe*: replete with rubato, a sentimental paean to the Parisian restaurant
2. "Fair Moon, to Thee I Sing" from *HMS Pinafore*: straightforward lyrical piece with ascending scalar lines
3. "Oh, Better Far to Live and Die" from *The Pirates of Penzance*: the Pirate King's macho manifesto

4. "One Alone" from *The Desert Song*: a reflective ballad containing repeated intervals
5. "Pretty as a Picture" from *Sweethearts*: conversational verse, followed by a lilting refrain including a laughing interjection

Nelson Eddy (1901–1967) sang operatic roles such as Harlekin and Wolfram before becoming Jeanette MacDonald's partner in their multiple movie adaptations of operettas. Kevin Kline brought a resonant vocal presence and robust physical presence to his portrayal of the Pirate King in the 1983 *Pirates of Penzance* film. Similarly, modern day "barihunks" Rodney Gilfry (b. 1959) and Nathan Gunn (b. 1970) have both become regulars as Danilo, with Gilfry also appearing as Robert in *The New Moon* and Falke in *Die Fledermaus*. ♪

Comic baritone:

1. "I Am the Very Model of a Modern Major-General" from *The Pirates of Penzance*: the quintessential patter song
2. "I've Jibe and Joke" from *The Yeomen of the Guard*: a patter song with more melodic shape
3. "On a Tree by the River" a.k.a. "Titwillow" from *The Mikado*: a rare slow piece for the patter baritone
4. "À cheval sur la discipline" from *La Grande-Duchesse de Gérolstein*: a charming piece with fast text and reiterations of "pif-paf-pouf"
5. "V'lan, V'lan, je suis V'lan" from *Le voyage dans la lune*: entrance *couplets* with more repetitive word play, this time employing the character's own name

Amable Courtecuisse, known onstage as Désiré (1823–1873), became a regular in Offenbach operas, creating more than twenty roles ranging from M. Choufleuri (Mr. Cauliflower) to Madame Madou in *Mesdames de la Halle*. At the D'Oyly Carte Opera Company, Sir Henry Lytton (1865–1936) became the resident patter baritone, singing a multitude of parts over fifty years. Both Désiré and Lytton are precursors to vocal wordsmiths such as Danny Kaye and Nathan Lane.

To excel at operetta patter, you should challenge yourself with tongue twisters. For instance, Jack Point's song from *The Yeomen of the Guard*

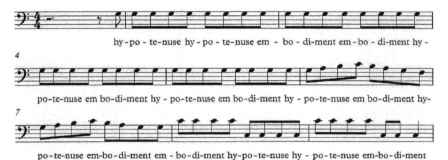

hy-po - te-nuse hy-po - te-nuse em - bo - di-ment em-bo - di-ment hy -

po-te-nuse em bo-di-ment hy - po-te-nuse em bo-di-ment hy - po-te-nuse em bo-di-ment hy-

po-te-nuse em-bo-di-ment em - bo-di-ment hy-po-te-nuse hy - po-te-nuse em-bo-di-ment

Figure 2.2. Patter exercise. *Vocalise by Linda Lister after Gilbert and Sullivan*

has many examples of onomatopoeia that can be strung into an exercise
to challenge the articulators: *jibe, joke, quip, crank.* Try saying that quickly
ten times without sounding like Elmer Fudd. You can also try the above
sung exercise combining words from patter songs sung by the Major-
General (*The Pirates of Penzance*) and Lord Chancellor (*Iolanthe*).

You might start just with the first line, intoning the two words on one
pitch, before taking the words up and down the scale and the octave. Or
use other fun words from patter songs, such as *tautology* (*The Sorcerer*)
and *philanthropist* (*Princess Ida*), or whatever words may be tripping
your tongue. Practice first at a moderate pace and then try to accelerate
the tempo to an impressive vivace. ♪

Bass-Baritone/Bass

Befitting the deepest voice type, bass roles in light opera are often
darker characters, like Dick Deadeye (*HMS Pinafore*), Sir Despard
Murgatroyd (*Ruddigore*), and Mars, the god of war (*Orphée aux enfers*). The lower tessitura helps depict characters of authority such as
policemen, guards, or elders (Professor Martini in *Giuditta*), as well as
individuals of a seemingly exotic background (Ali Ben Ali in *The Desert
Song*). There are not a lot of bass operetta arias, with the characters
participating more in ensemble numbers. While the bass never gets the
leading role, he can create great comic and dramatic effects with his low
notes and vocal color. ♪

1. "When a Felon's Not Engaged in His Employment" from *The Pirates of Penzance*: the sergeant's song, with a dramatic downward
   octave leap at the end of each verse

2. "When All Night Long a Chap Remains" from *Iolanthe*: a rumination on politics, followed by *fa-la-la*s
3. "Oh, Why Am I Moody and Sad?" from *Ruddigore*: melodramatic character piece
4. "He Is an Englishman" from *HMS Pinafore*: the Boatswain jokes about other countries and finishes with a cadenza
5. "Let Love Go" from *The Desert Song*: *misterioso*, pseudo-Moroccan song

Ensemble Numbers of Note

Ensemble numbers from light opera are appealing repertoire for symphonic concerts, opera galas, and opera workshop programs. There are many familiar favorites but also numerous unexplored gems. While most everyone is familiar with "Three Little Maids" from *The Mikado*, "Three Little Maids" from *Blossom Time* is less familiar but also good fun. So the recommendations below strive to include some popular selections along with some more obscure options.

Duets

Well-known:

1. "Dieser Anstand, so manierlich" or the Watch Duet (ST or SB) from *Die Fledermaus*: classic flirtatious duo with Eisenstein typically resting his ear on the bosom of the Hungarian countess (Rosalinda in disguise)
2. "Il m'a semblé sur mon épaule" or the Fly Duet (SB) from *Orphée aux enfers*: Jupiter is disguised as a fly, thus he and Eurydice join in buzzing vocalization on the sibilant [z]
3. "Were You Not to Ko-Ko Plighted" (ST) from *The Mikado*: Yum-Yum and Nanki-Poo sing about how they would never kiss, while proceeding to kiss repeatedly
4. "We're Called Gondolieri" (TB) from *The Gondoliers*: Italianate gondolier buddy duo between Marco and Giuseppe
5. "Lippen schweigen" (ST or SB) from *Die lustige Witwe*: romantic waltz finally reuniting Hanna and Danilo

Worthwhile:

1. "Now Wouldn't You Like to Rule the Roast?" (MC) from *Princess Ida*: Melissa and her mother, Lady Blanche, commiserate
2. "Rapture, Rapture" (CB) from *The Yeomen of the Guard*: jaunty duet showcasing the lower voices of Dame Carruthers and Sergeant Meryll
3. "Prithee Pretty Maiden" (SB) from *Patience*: wooing wordplay between Patience and Archibald Grosvenor
4. "C'est le ciel qui m'envoie" or Duo du rêve (MT) from *La belle Hélène*: sexy scene with Paris and Hélène
5. "You Can Never Tell about a Woman" (BB) from *The Red Mill*: innkeeper Willem and burgomaster Jan bemoan their inability to understand the opposite sex

Trios

Well-known:

1. "Here's a How-de-do" (STB) from *The Mikado*: Yum-Yum, Nanki-Poo, and Ko-Ko sing this classic trio with modulating sections and a spoken final line
2. "Never Mind the Why and Wherefore" (SBB) from *HMS Pinafore*: Josephine, Captain Corcoran, and Sir Joseph reflect joyfully on love leveling rank and station
3. "So muss allein ich bleiben" (SST or SSB) from *Die Fledermaus*: Adele, Rosalinda, and Eisenstein try to be secretive but cannot curtail their excitement over Orlofsky's ball
4. "Quiet" (SCT) from *Candide*: the Governor tries to silence Cunegonde and the Old Lady
5. "Go to Sleep, Slumber Deep" (SSB) from *Babes in Toyland*: a fairy serenades siblings Alan and Jane to sleep in the vein of Hansel and Gretel and the Sandman

Worthwhile:

1. "I Am a Maiden, Cold and Stately" (TTB) from *Princess Ida*: Hilarion, Cyril, and Florian dress *en travesti* in search of Hilarion's betrothed

2. "The Music Lesson" (STB) from *The Serenade*: *primo tenore* Colombo and his daughter, Yvonne, give Gomez a much-needed voice lesson
3. "Je suis le joli géolier" or "Trio of the Jolly Jailer" (MTB) from *La Périchole*: Piquillo and La Périchole try to distract the jailer, really the Viceroy of Peru in disguise, in order to escape the dungeon
4. "Lorsque la Grèce est un camp de carnage" or "Trio Patriotique" (TBB) from *La belle Hélène*: featuring Ménélas, Agamemnon, and Calchas, this patriotic trio is a parody of Rossini's *Guillaume Tell*
5. "Like a Real, Real Man" (SSS or SSM) from *The Lady of the Slipper*: Punks and Spooks sympathize with Cinderella in this mostly unison piece

Quartets

1. "Ladies of the Town" (SSSS or SSMM) from *Bitter Sweet*: Lotte, Freda, Hansi, and Gussie sing this unison up-tempo selection
2. "The World Is But a Broken Toy" (STTB) from *Princess Ida*: lyrical piece in which Ida, Hilarion, Cyril, and Florian share a rare serious moment
3. "Strange Adventure" (SCTB) from *The Yeomen of the Guard*: madrigalesque, mostly a cappella number sung by Kate, Dame Carruthers, Fairfax, and Sergeant Meryll
4. "Live for Today" (SCTB) from *Naughty Marietta*: lilting waltz sung by Marietta, Adah, Captain Dick, and Etienne
5. "Jeanette and Her Wooden Shoes" (STBB) from *Sweethearts*: a novelty number, inviting obvious shoe choreography, featuring Liane backed by the trio of Slingsby, Caniche, and Von Tromp

Quintets

1. "The Flowers That Bloom in the Spring" (SMTBB) from *The Mikado*: Yum-Yum, Pitti-Sing, Nanki-Poo, Ko-Ko, and Pooh-Bah join in *tra-la*s as they strategize against Katisha
2. "Try We Lifelong" (SCTBB) from *The Gondoliers*: after arriving from the sunny Spanish shore, Casilda, Luiz, Don Alhambra, and the Duke and Duchess of Plaza-Toro ponder their puzzling situation

3. "The Woman of the Wisest Wit" (SCTTB) from *Princess Ida*: Melissa tries to convince Lady Psyche to soften her feminism after falling in love with Hilarion, who is as always flanked by his sidekicks Cyril and Florian
4. "Strange the Views Some People Hold" (SCTBB) from *The Grand Duke*: Julia, Lisa, Ernest, Notary, and Ludwig sing multiple bell-like *ding-dong* effects in this piece, which is followed directly in the show by another quintet, "Now Take a Card and Gaily Sing"
5. "Ein Scheck auf die englische Bank" (TTBBB) from *Der Graf von Luxemburg*: the penniless Count René commiserates with the unison quartet of Basil, Pawlowtisch, Mentschikoff, and Pélégrin until all break into five-part harmony for the final line

Sextets

1. "Tell Me What Your Eyes Were Made For" (SSSMMC) from *Madame Pompadour*: Madame de Pompadour, her maid Madeleine, and the Comtesse Mariette commiserate with the maids
2. "A Nice Dilemma We Have Here" (STBBBB) from *Trial by Jury*: after an a cappella opening, this sextet builds as the chorus joins the principals (Plaintiff, Defendant, Learned Judge, Counsel, Foreman) and is finally silenced by the Usher
3. "Comme elle ressemble à sa soeur" from *Giroflé-Girofla:* Giroflé, Paquita, Aurore, Marasquin, Boléro, and Mourzouk try to decipher the betrothals of the twin sisters
4. "Assieds-toi là" (SSCTBB) from *Les p'tites Michu*: Blanche-Marie, Marie-Blanche, Madame Michu, Michu, Aristide, and Gaston unravel the true parentage of the supposed twin sisters
5. "Make Our Garden Grow" from *Candide*: this famous finale soars and inspires in a sextet with Candide, Cunegonde, Maximillian, Paquette, Pangloss, and the Old Lady, joined in the climax by the chorus

Septets

1. "Wie die Weiber man behandelt" (TTBBBBB) from *Die lustige Witwe*: Danilo, St. Brioche, Cascada, Zeta, Kromow, Bogdan-

owitsch, and Pritschitsch celebrate the merits of women in this famous march septet

2. "Ihr Toren, ihr wollt hassen mich" (SMMCBBB) from *Boccaccio*: another march septet, this piece features barber Scalza commenting as Beatrice, Isabella, and Peronella read love notes written by Boccaccio, Lotteringhi, and Lambertuccio

3. "Je défendrai mon enfant" (SSTTBBB) from *Mesdames de la Halle*: this fun and theatrical septet features both pants and skirt roles

4. "Minos, Eaque et Rhadamante!" (TTTTBBB) from *Orphée aux enfers*: this Septour du Tribunal features multiple mythological characters

5. "It Has Reached Me a Lady Named Hubbard" (SSMCTBB) from *The Rose of Persia*: Dancing Sunbeam, Scent of Lilies, Honey of Life, Heart's Desire, Yussuf, Hassan, and Aballah try to come up with a story for the sultan, but keep resorting to nursery rhymes

Octets

1. "Farewell, My Own" (SMCTBBBB) from *HMS Pinafore*: Sir Joseph sends Josephine's beloved Ralph to the dungeon as Cousin Hebe, Dick Deadeye, the Boatswain, and the Carpenter observe, and Buttercup begins her confession

2. "The Sultan's Executioner" (SSSMCTBB) from *The Rose of Persia*: the sultan's harem anticipates the arrival of the executioner with the fearful repetition, "What will become of us, us, us, us, us, us, us, us, us, us, us, us?"

Larger Group Numbers

1. "List and Learn" from *The Gondoliers*: this opening *scena*, sung both in English and Italian, begins with the Contadine chorus, features several solos for supporting characters, and continues with the introduction of the principals, Marco, Giuseppe, Gianetta, and Tessa

2. "Stout-Hearted Men" from *The New Moon*: a macho rallying cry for the men's ensemble

3. "Why Did We Marry Soldiers?" from *The Desert Song*: the playful French military marching song sung by Margot and the ladies
ensemble and eventually the soldiers
4. "Drink! Drink! Drink!" from *The Student Prince*: the student-
chorus drinking song evolves into a concerted number featuring
Kathie and her high Cs
5. "Im Feuerstrom der Rebe" from *Die Fledermaus*: the act II celebration of champagne is an ideal group number, especially for
opera galas serving bubbly

While light opera is entertaining because of its spectacle and schmaltz,
the main reason for its appeal is the singing. Light, beautiful voices in
sweeping melodies and comedic rapid-fire banter provide something for
everyone to enjoy. ♪

3

ACTING AND DIALOGUE

To sing light opera, you can't just fit the vocal requirements of the role, you must fit the character as well. In line with the operatic system of *Fach*, or vocal categorization, your voice must have the timbre that matches the character. Furthermore, to be believable theatrically, you need to suit the character type.

STOCK CHARACTER TYPES

As in the theatrical realm, there are stock character types that permeate light opera, some tracing back to the *commedia dell'arte* tradition. Descended from the Italian Isabella, the ingénue is almost always a soprano, helping to portray her youth and sweetness (Yum-Yum). She is usually the typical Victorian heroine, with an angelic disposition (Angelina) and perhaps rosy cheeks. In fact, she may be named Rosa, Rose-Marie, or Rose Maybud (not unlike *The Mystery of Edwin Drood*'s Rosa Bud). In many operettas, the ingénue is the romantic female lead. In a number of Gilbert and Sullivan operas, there is a cameo ingénue role, which is an ideal training ground for a young singer or for the understudy/cover to the lead ingénue. Throughout the Viennese repertoire, the lead soprano is more leading lady than ingénue, still young but with more gravitas or sophistication. In this tradition, there is often a secondary soubrette soprano in line with *commedia*'s Colombina. She could be a pert Peep-Bo or Bo-Peep. In contrast with the ingénue's sweetness and the leading lady's elegance, the soubrette will demonstrate sassiness and spunk and may also express herself through dance. (For more on this topic, skip to chapter 4.) While we typically associate them with mezzo-sopranos, pants roles are sometimes assigned to the higher *Fach*; Offenbach in particular had a predilection for soprano breeches roles. One dream soprano role might be the dual-title role of twin sisters in Lecocq's *Giroflé-Girofla*, played by one performer (as in television soap opera tradition). Another plum part is in Herbert's *The Fortune Teller*, which specifies that one soprano should play fortune teller Musette, ballet student Irma, and Fedor, Irma's twin brother.

Soprano Roles

Leading Ladies: Rosalinda (*Die Fledermaus*), Hanna (*Die lustige Witwe*), Eurydice (*Orphée aux enfers*), Geneviève (*Geneviève de Brabant*), Denise (*Mam'zelle Nitouche*), Madame Chrysanthème (*Madame Chrysanthème*), Eva (*Eva*), Giuditta (*Giuditta*), Gräfin Zedlau (*Wiener Blut*), Angèle (*Der Graf von Luxemburg*), Mascha (*Der Zarewitsch*), Annina (*Eine Nacht in Venedig*), Lisa (*Das Land des Lächelns*), Ilona (*Zigeunerliebe*), Josepha (*Im weißen Rößl*), Anna Elisa (*Paganini*), Saffi (*Der Zigeunerbaron*), Marie (*Der Karneval in Rom*), Mariza (*Gräfin Mariza*), Sarah (*Bitter Sweet*), Katherine (*The Vagabond King*), Sylva (*Die Csárdásfürstin*), Princess Fedora (*Die Zirkusprinzessin*), Juliska (*Der Zigeunerprimas*), Odette (*Die Bajadere*), Jutta (*Das Hollandweibchen*), Mary (*Der Herzogin von Chicago*), Leontine (*Der Teufelsreiter*), Josephine (*Kaiserin Josephine*), Madame de Pompadour (*Madame Pompadour*), Lona (*Arizona Lady*), Estrella (*El barberillo de Lavapiés*), Luisa (*Luisa Fernanda*), Maria (*La tempranica*), Maravillas (*La calesera*), Doña Pepita (*Pan y toros*), Katiuska (*Katiuska*), Ascensión (*La del manojo de rosas*), Zobeida (*El asombro de Damasco*).

Ingénues: Aline and Constance (*The Sorcerer*), Angelina, the Plaintiff (*Trial by Jury*), Josephine (*HMS Pinafore*), Mabel (*The Pirates* *of Penzance*), Patience (*Patience*), Phyllis (*Iolanthe*), Yum-Yum (*The Mikado*), Rose Maybud (*Ruddigore*), Elsie and Kate (*The Yeomen of the Guard*), Gianetta and Casilda (*The Gondoliers*), Ida (*Princess Ida*), Zara and Nekaya (*Utopia, Limited*), Julia (*The Grand Duke*), Sonja (*Der Zarewitsch*), Fiametta (*Boccaccio*), Marie (*Der Vogelhändler*), Pauline (*Waldmeister*), Marianne (*The New Moon*), Margot (*The Desert Song*), Ottilie (*Maytime*), Kathie (*The Student Prince*), Musette and Irma (*The Fortune Teller*), Yvonne (*The Serenade*), Fifi (*Mlle. Modiste*), Tina (*The Red Mill*), Rose-Marie (*Rose-Marie*), Nina (*The Firefly*), Sylvia (*Sweethearts*), Marietta (*Naughty Marietta*), Mitzi (*Blossom Time*), Jane and Mary (*Babes in Toyland*), Estrelda (*El Capitain*), Ciboulette (*Mesdames de la Halle*), Fiorella (*Les brigands*), Gabrielle (*La vie parisienne*), Giroflé and Girofla (*Giroflé-Girofla*), Irma (*Le grand mogol*), Blanche-Marie and Marie-Blanche (*Les p'tites Michu*), Anina (*Der Teufelsreiter*), Juliette (*Kaiserin Josephine*), Bonita (*Arizona Lady*), Alice (*Die Dollarprinzessin*), Nadina (*Der tapfere Soldat*), Galathée (*Die schöne Galathée*), Francisquita (*Doña Francisquita*), Rosaura (*Los gavilanes*), Rosa (*El rey que rabió*), Rosalía (*La bruja*), Princess Sofia (*Black, el payaso*), Angela (*La tempestad*), Lina (*Las golondrinas*), Cossette (*Bohemios*), Maruxa (*Maruxa*), Margot (*Don Manolito*), Catalina (*La del soto del Parral*), Isidra (*El santo de la Isidra*), Susana (*La verbena de la Paloma*), Asia (*Agua, azucarillos y aguardiente*), Mari-Pepa (*La revoltosa*).

Cameo Ingénues: Phylla (*Utopia, Limited*), Celia (*Iolanthe*), Zorah (*Ruddigore*), Fiametta (*The Gondoliers*), Lady Ella (*Patience*), Manja (*Gräfin Mariza*), Jeanne (*Waldmeister*).

Soubrettes: Adele (*Die Fledermaus*), Valencienne (*Die lustige Witwe*), Cunegonde (*Candide*), Julie (*The New Moon*), Liane (*Sweethearts*), Tina (*The Red Mill*), Diane (*Orphée aux enfers*), Pauline (*La vie parisienne*), Wanda (*La Grande-Duchesse de Gérolstein*), Ernestine (*Monsieur Choufleuri*), Zanetta (*La princesse de Trébizonde*), Princess Bengaline (*Le grand mogol*), Freda (*Waldmeister*), Anita (*Giuditta*), Sonja (*Der Zarewitsch*), Princess Mi (*Das Land des Lächelns*), Marie (*Zar und Zimmermann*), Fanchette (*Mlle. Modiste*), Oyouki (*Madame Chrysanthème*), Clairette (*La fille de Madame Angot*), Rose-in-Bloom (*The Rose of Persia*), Peep-Bo (*The Mikado*), Bo-Peep (*Babes in Toyland*), Isabel

(*El Capitain*), Juliette (*Der Graf von Luxemburg*), Bella (*Paganini*), Zorika (*Zigeunerliebe*), Pipsi (*Eva*), Arsena (*Der Zigeunerbaron*), Countess Falconi (*Der Karneval in Rom*), Lisa (*Gräfin Mariza*), Stasi (*Die Csárdásfürstin*), Sári (*Der Zigeunerprimas*), Mabel (*Die Zirkusprinzessin*), Franzi (*Ein Walzertraum*), Elly (*Das Hollandweibchen*), Marietta (*Die Bajadere*), Princess Rosemarie (*Der Herzogin von Chicago*), Sophie (*Der Teufelsreiter*), Nelly (*Arizona Lady*), Daisy (*Die Dollarprinzessin*), Mascha (*Der tapfere Soldat*), Christel (*Der Vogelhändler*), Ottilie (*Im weißen Rößl*), Duchess Carolina (*Luisa Fernanda*), Rosario (*La chulapona*), Clarita (*La del manojo de rosas*), Catalina (*Black, el payaso*), Fahima (*El asombro de Damasco*), Olga (*Katiuska*), Casta (*La verbena de la Paloma*), Soledad (*La revoltosa*).

Pants Roles: Fedor (*The Fortune Teller*), Cupidon (*Orphée aux enfers*), Amoroso (*Le pont des soupirs*), Fragoletto (*Les brigands*), Croûte-au-pot (*Mesdames de la Halle*), Bavolet (*La jolie parfumeuse*), Fortunato (*Madame l'archiduc*), Duke of Parthenay (*Le petit duc*), Xaver (*Gold gab ich für Eisen*), Marosi (*Tatárjárás*), Roberto (*La tempestad*), the King (*El rey que rabió*), Abel (*La tabernera del puerto*), Carlos (*La viejecita*).

Mezzo-Soprano Roles

In light opera, the mezzo-soprano roles seem to share the same paradigm as the soprano roles. There are a few leading ladies, sometimes even title characters in Offenbach operettas. However, a greater dramatic spectrum is available to the mezzo, perhaps owing to the sexy, scheming *commedia* character Vittoria. One of the juiciest mezzo roles in Gilbert and Sullivan is the love-crazed Mad Margaret (who might be considered a precursor to the Beggar Woman in *Sweeney Todd*). While sopranos get the mad scenes in bel canto operas, the mezzo is the madwoman here. Mezzos also get to play narrator-type personages (L'Opinion Publique), alluring café singers (Manon), and of course, princes (Orlofsky, Caprice, etc.). They also get to play soubrettes, most often as the ingénue's sidekick in both English and American light opera. While Viennese operetta may not often include mezzo roles,

Jacques Offenbach, Arthur Sullivan, Victor Herbert, and Sigmund Romberg give the mezzo-soprano many opportunities.

Leading Ladies: Hélène (*La belle Hélène*), La Grande-Duchesse (*La Grande-Duchesse de Gérolstein*), La Périchole (*La Périchole*), Juno and L'Opinion Publique (*Orphée aux enfers*), Métella (*La vie parisienne*), Amaranthe (*La fille de Madame Angot*), Manon (*Bitter Sweet*), Dolores (*The Serenade*), Olga (*Die Dollarprinzessin*), Isabella (*Boccaccio*), Mad Margaret (*Ruddigore*), Iolanthe (*Iolanthe*), Paloma (*El barberillo de Lavapiés*), Cecilia (*Las golondrinas*), Adriana (*Los galivanes*), Manuela (*La chulapona*), Princess de Luzán (*Pan y toros*), Blanca (*La bruja*), Elena (*La calesera*), Duchess of Medina (*Jugar con fuego*), Carmona (*La pícara molinera*).

Cameo Mezzo: Countess Kokozow (*Der Graf von Luxemburg*), Clementina (*The Desert Song*).

Soubrettes: Pitti-Sing (*The Mikado*), Tessa (*The Gondoliers*), Lisa (*The Grand Duke*), Kalyba (*Utopia, Limited*), Melissa (*Princess Ida*), Phoebe (*The Yeomen of the Guard*), Lady Angela (*Patience*), Leila (*Iolanthe*), Susan (*The Desert Song*), Bertha (*The Red Mill*), Nanette (*Mlle. Modiste*), Lizette (*Naughty Marietta*), Huguette (*The Vagabond King*), Paquette (*Candide*), Regina (*La princesse de Trébizonde*), Aurora (*Doña Francisquita*).

Pants Roles: Prince Orlofsky (*Die Fledermaus*), Orèste (*La belle Hélène*), Prince Caprice (*Le voyage dans la lune*), Friday (*Robinson Crusoé*), Daphnis (*Daphnis et Chloé*), Prince Raphael (*La princesse de Trébizonde*), Roland (*Les bavards*), Pedro (*Giroflé-Girofla*), Boccaccio (*Boccaccio*), Ganymed (*Die schöne Galathée*), Grabié (*La tempranica*), Carlos (*La viejecita*).

Contralto Roles

Some of the most enjoyable roles in light opera belong to the contralto. She can revel in the melodramatic displays of Katisha or the comedic machinations of the Duchess of Plaza-Toro. As discussed previously, these parts portray women of higher station (Countess, Baroness) or greater maturity (Old Lady). Thus, the singer playing these roles needs to have a mature presence onstage, or the appropriate age makeup.

Women of Age or Rank: Buttercup (*HMS Pinafore*), Ruth (*The Pirates of Penzance*), Lady Jane (*Patience*), Katisha (*The Mikado*), Dame Hannah (*Ruddigore*), Dame Carruthers (*The Yeomen of the Guard*), Duchess of Plaza-Toro and Inez (*The Gondoliers*), Lady Sophy (*Utopia, Limited*), Lady Blanche (*Princess Ida*), Queen of the Fairies (*Iolanthe*), Baroness von Krakenfeldt (*The Grand Duke*), Lady Sangazure and Mrs. Partlett (*The Sorcerer*), Dancing Sunbeam (*The Rose of Persia*), Old Lady (*Candide*), Dolores (*The Serenade*), Adah (*Naughty Marietta*), Madame Cécile (*Mlle. Modiste*), Princess Marghanza (*El Capitain*), Madame Michu (*Les p'tites Michu*), Paola (*La princesse de Trébizonde*), Aurore (*Giroflé-Girofla*), Queen Clémentine (Offenbach's *Barbe-Bleue*), Madame Prune (*Madame Chrysanthème*), Mirabella and Czipra (*Der Zigeunerbaron*), Donna Sofronia (*Der Karneval in Rom*), Countess de Laplace (*Paganini*), Obersthofmeisterin Salina (*Das Hollandweibchen*), Carla (*Die Zirkusprinzessin*), Aurelia (*Der tapfere Soldat*), Friederike (*Ein Walzertraum*), Peronella (*Boccaccio*), Doña Francisca (*Doña Francisquita*), Rita (*La verbena de la Paloma*), Venustiana (*La chulapona*), Magdalena (*La bruja*), Doña Simona (*Agua, azucarillos y aguardiente*), Pelagia (*Bohemios*).

Tenor Roles

The tenor is surely the romantic lead in Gilbert and Sullivan and most Offenbach. In American operettas, his name may be Karl or Carl, but he draws on the *commedia dell'arte* lovers Flavio or Lélio. The Viennese operettas have some prime tenor roles, although some have been usurped by baritones, perhaps due to tessitura and orchestration. But as a singing actor, a tenor has a wide range of roles to explore, as long as he has the dramatic range to match. As a leading man, he needs to have realistic romantic chemistry with his leading lady. If he is the secondary tenor, he may be more sweet and less heroic than the principal. The rich repertoire of *Spieltenor* or buffo roles is enviable indeed. For instance, a character tenor like Gaston in Herbert's *Mlle. Modiste* gets two songs with hilarious titles and ripe comic potential: "Love Me, Love My Dog" and "Ze English Language." There is truly a role for every type of tenor in light opera. Notably *Die Fledermaus* is replete with tenor roles: Italiante divo Alfred, buffo Blind, and the *Zwischen* leading man/funny man Eisenstein.

Note: In the following sections, an asterisk (*) denotes a role sometimes sung by a baritone, a double asterisk (**) denotes skirt roles.

Leading Men: Alfred (*Die Fledermaus*), Karl (*The Student Prince*), Etienne (*Mlle. Modiste*), Fairfax (*The Yeomen of the Guard*), Box (*Cox and Box*), Marco (*The Gondoliers*), Nanki-Poo (*The Mikado*), Ralph (*HMS Pinafore*), Frederic (*The Pirates of Penzance*), Alexis (*The Sorcerer*), Edwin, the Defendant (*Trial by Jury*), Dauntless (*Ruddigore*), Fitzbattleaxe (*Utopia, Limited*), Hilarion (*Princess Ida*), Ernest (*The Grand Duke*), Candide (*Candide*), Carl (*Bitter Sweet*), Barbe-Bleue (Offenbach's *Barbe-Bleue*), Orphée (*Orphée aux enfers*), Falsacappa (*Les brigands*), Paris (*La belle Hélène*), Fritz (*La Grande-Duchesse de Gérolstein*), Piquillo (*La Périchole*), Malatromba (*Le pont des soupirs*), Gardefeu (*La vie parisienne*), Joquelet (*Le grand mogol*), Pierre (*Madame Chrysanthème*), Lancelot (*La poupée*), Ange-Pitou (*La fille de Madame Angot*), Tsarevich (*Der Zarewitsch*), Prince Sou-Chong (*Das Land des Lächelns*), Guido (*Eine Nacht in Venedig*), Paganini (*Paganini*), Octave (*Eva*), Octavio (*Giuditta*), Barinkay (*Der Zigeunerbaron*), Edwin* (*Die Csárdásfürstin*), Mister X (*Die Zirkusprinzessin*), Laczi (*Der Zigeunerprimas*), Radjami (*Die Bajadere*), Graf Tassilo (*Gräfin Mariza*), Prince Sandor Boris (*Der Herzogin von Chicago*), Sandor (*Der Teufelsreiter*), Napoleon Bonaparte (*Kaiserin Josephine*), Roy (*Arizona Lady*), Fredy (*Die Dollarprinzessin*), Bumerli (*Der tapfere Soldat*), Niki (*Ein Walzertraum*), Leopold (*Im weißen Rößl*), Pygmalion (*Die schöne Galathée*), René (*Madame Pompadour*), Fernando (*Doña Francisquita*), Javier (*Luisa Fernanda*), Paolo (*La Dogaresa*), Julián* (*La verbena de la Paloma*), Ricardo (*La del manojo de rosas*), Antonio (*La fiesta del San Antón*), Don Gil de Alcalá (*Don Gil de Alcalá*), Roberto (*Bohemios*).

Secondary Tenor Leads: Luiz (*The Gondoliers*), Verrada (*El Capitain*), Karl (*Sweethearts*), Lopez and Colombo (*The Serenade*), Pimpinelli (*Paganini*), Camille (*Die lustige Witwe*), Armand (*Der Graf von Luxemburg*), Ottokar (*Der Zigeunerbaron*), Gaston (*Der Zigeunerprimas*), Napoleon (*Die Bajadere*), Karl (*Der Teufelsreiter*), Bernard (*Kaiserin Josephine*), Chester (*Arizona Lady*), Alexius (*Der tapfere Soldat*), Gustav (*Das Land des Lächelns*), Otto (*Im weißen Rößl*), Ménélas (*La belle Hélène*), Gontran (*La vie parisienne*), Aristide (*Les p'tites Michu*), Cardona (*Doña Francisquita*), Don Luis (*El barberillo de Lavapiés*), Fernando (*La viejecita*).

Buffo Roles: Eisenstein* and Blind (*Die Fledermaus*), Adam* (*Der Vogelhändler*), Caramello (*Eine Nacht in Venedig*), Josef (*Wiener Blut*), Duke of Dunstable (*Patience*), Cyril (*Princess Ida*), Count (*Das Land des Lächelns*), Dagobert (*Eva*), Boni* (*Die Csárdásfürstin*), Bobinet* (*La vie parisienne*), Madame Poiretapée** (*Mesdames de la Halle*), Mercury and Pluto (*Orphée aux enfers*), Gaston* (*Mlle. Modiste*), Zsupán (*Der Zigeunerbaron*), Kolomán (*Gräfin Mariza*), Bondy (*Der Herzogin von Chicago*), Honorius (*Der Teufelsreiter*), Hans (*Die Dollarprinzessin*), Gangarilla (*La calesera*), El chalina (*La chulapona*), Mateo (*La tempestad*), Marat (*Black, el payaso*), Capó (*La del manojo de rosas*), Gorón (*La leyenda del beso*).

Baritone Roles

Baritones play a gamut of characters in light opera. There are macho men like the Pirate King and amorous or adulterous charmers like Danilo and Eisenstein. In American operettas, they are usually the romantic lead. If they aren't the lead, there are numerous supporting baritone roles, sometimes even within a single show (*The Merry Widow*, *The Mikado*, *Bitter Sweet*). Gilbert and Sullivan operettas of course offer patter baritones special showcases in multiple shows, while Offenbach offers opportunities to play a god, a fly, or a woman.

Note: In the following sections, a dagger (†) denotes a role sometimes sung by a tenor, a double asterisk (**) denotes skirt roles.

Leading Men: Captain Corcoran (*HMS Pinafore*), the Pirate King (*The Pirates of Penzance*), Grosvenor (*Patience*), Strephon (*Iolanthe*), Cox (*Cox and Box*), Dr. Daly (*The Sorcerer*), Pierre/Red Shadow (*The*

Desert Song), Robert (*The New Moon*), Jim (*Rose-Marie*), Alan (*Babes in Toyland*), Dick (*Naughty Marietta*), Prince Franz (*Sweethearts*), Alvarado (*The Serenade*), Medigua (*El Capitain*), Villon (*The Vagabond King*), Rácz (*Der Zigeunerprimas*), Louis XV (*Madame Pompadour*), Gaston (*Les p'tites Michu*), Choufleuri (*Monsieur Choufleuri*), Prince Mingapour (*Le grand mogol*), Bobinet[†] (*La vie parisienne*), Danilo[†] (*The Merry Widow*), Eisenstein[†] (*Die Fledermaus*), René[†] (*Der Graf von Luxemburg*), Count Peter Homonay (*Der Zigeunerbaron*), Rafaeli (*Der Karneval in Rom*), Joaquín (*La del manojo de rosas*), Juan (*La tabernera del puerto*), Juan (*Los gavilanes*), Juan Pedro (*La rosa del azafrán*), Vidal (*Luisa Fernanda*), Don Luis (*La tempranica*), Lamparilla[†] (*El barberillo de Lavapiés*), El Caballero de Gracia (*La Gran Vía*), Rafael (*La calesera*), Don Manolito (*Don Manolito*), Puck (*Las golondrinas*), Prince Alberto (*Molinos de viento*), Felipe (*La revoltosa*).

Lyric Baritone Buddies: Falke and Frank (*Die Fledermaus*), Cascada, Zeta, and St. Brioche (*Die lustige Witwe*), Prunelle (*Eva*), Lambertuccio and Lotteringhi (*Boccaccio*), Florian (*Princess Ida*), Samuel (*The Pirates of Penzance*), Ludwig (*The Grand Duke*), Romero (*The Serenade*), Maximillian (*Candide*), Maximin (*La poupée*), Frick (*La vie parisienne*), Yves (*Madame Chrysanthème*), Lorenzo (*Doña Francisquita*), Putifar (*La corte de Faraón*), Stok (*Molinos de viento*), Victor (*Bohemios*), Cándido and Atenedoro (*La revoltosa*).

Comedians: the Duke of Plaza-Toro (*The Gondoliers*), Jack Point (*The Yeomen of the Guard*), John Wellington Wells (*The Sorcerer*), the Learned Judge and Counsel (*Trial by Jury*), Sir Joseph Porter (*HMS Pinafore*), Major-General Stanley (*The Pirates of Penzance*), Bunthorne and Major Murgatroyd (*Patience*), Lord Chancellor (*Iolanthe*), Ko-Ko, Pish-Tush, and Pooh-Bah (*The Mikado*), Robin Oakapple (*Ruddigore*), Tarara and Scaphio (*Utopia, Limited*), King Gama (*Princess Ida*), the Grand Duke (*The Grand Duke*), Hassan (*The Rose of Persia*), Benjamin Kidd (*The Desert Song*), Gaston (*Mlle. Modiste*), Pangloss/Voltaire (*Candide*), Michu (*Les p'tites Michu*), Jupiter (*Orphée aux enfers*), Don Andrès (*La Périchole*), Madame Madou** and Madame Beurrefondu** (*Mesdames de la Halle*), Black (*Black, el payaso*), Don Hilarión (*La verbena de la Paloma*), Ansúrez (*La patria chica*), Miccone (*La Dogaresa*).

Bass/Bass-Baritone Roles

As expected, basses and bass-baritones play priests, military figures, and other authority figures. They are descendants of the *commedia* character types such as Il Dottore, Il Capitano, and Pantalone. It is not only their deep voices that should aid in the characterizations. They should deliver a different energy onstage than the more manic patter baritones to help distinguish a Duke of Plaza-Toro from a Don Alhambra or Ko-Ko from the Mikado. *Princess Ida* has a wealth of bass and bass-baritone roles, so distinguishing them from each other in expression and demeanor is essential.

Mars (*Orphée aux enfers*), Calchas (*La belle Hélène*), General Boum (*La Grande-Duchesse de Gérolstein*), Cornarino (*Le pont des soupirs*), Général des Ifs (*Les p'tites Michu*), Sarmiento and Cristobal (*Les bavards*), Monsieur Sucre (*Madame Chrysanthème*), Bouncer (*Cox and Box*), Sir Marmaduke (*The Sorcerer*), Usher (*Trial by Jury*), Dick Deadeye and Boatswain (*HMS Pinafore*), Sergeant (*The Pirates of Penzance*), Colonel Calverley (*Patience*), Private Willis (*Iolanthe*), the Mikado (*The Mikado*), Sir Richard (*The Yeomen of the Guard*), Don Alhambra del Bolero (*The Gondoliers*), Phantis and Captain Edward Corcoran (*Utopia, Limited*), King Hildebrand, Scynthius, Arac, and Guron (*Princess Ida*), Abdallah (*The Rose of Persia*), Ali Ben Ali (*The Desert Song*), Etienne (*Naughty Marietta*), Gomez and the Duke of Santa Cruz (*The Serenade*), Bartucci (*Paganini*), Iwan (*Der Zarewitsch*), Count Lothar (*Ein Walzertraum*), Shep Keyes (*Golden Dawn*), Don Matías (*Doña Francisquita*), Don Pedro (*El barberillo de Lavapiés*), Don Jorge and Guillermo (*Don Manolito*), Roberto (*Las golondrinas*), Calatrava (*La calesera*), White (*Black, el payaso*), the Grand Pharaoh (*La corte de Faraón*), the Grand Vizier (*El asombro de Damasco*), Duke of Albuquerque (*Jugar con fuego*), Doge of Venice (*La Dogaresa*), Don Basilio (*Me llaman la presumida*), Pascual (*Marina*), Simpson (*La tabernera del Puerto*), Bruno Brunovich (*Katiuska*), Carracuca (*La rosa del azafrán*), Carrasquilla, the Governor, and Father Confessor (*Don Gil de Alcalá*), King Clodomiro (*La generala*), Rufo (*Maruxa*), David (*La villana*), Count of Arenal (*El juramento*).

Spoken Roles

Not everyone in light opera sings! There are a number of key roles that involve no singing. These characters may have pointed humorous moments or special dance numbers. Even amid beautiful singing, these actors can steal the show with perfect timing and/or physical comedy.

Frosch (*Die Fledermaus*), Njegus (*Die lustige Witwe*), Grand Duke (*Der Zarewitsch*), Mayor of Vienna (*Der Ziegeunerbaron*), Countess Dobruja (*Die Herzogin von Chicago*), Wilhelm (*Im weißen Rößl*), Die Gräfin von Irini (*Der Zigeunerprimas*), Benjamin Lloyd (*Der Herzogin von Chicago*), Pedro (*Les bavards*), the Marquis (*La Périchole*), the Marquis of Shayne (*Bitter Sweet*), Uncle Barnaby and the Master Toymaker (*Babes in Toyland*), Baron and Baroness of Thunder-Ten-Tronck (*Candide*), Calynx (*Utopia, Limited*), Viscont Mentone (*The Grand Duke*), Miguel (*La tempranica*), El paseante (*La Gran Vía*), the Year 1889 (*El año pasado por agua*).

Silent Roles

Yes, there are even a few nonsinging, nonspeaking roles in light opera in the vein of the silent servant in the intermezzo *La serva padrona*. Reportedly W. S. Gilbert himself made cameo appearances as the Associate in *Trial by Jury*.

Associate (*Trial by Jury*), Mr. Bunthorne's Solicitor (*Patience*), the Headsmen (*The Yeomen of the Guard*).

SPOKEN DIALOGUE

Obviously, a primary distinction between opera and light opera is spoken dialogue. With a few exceptions (notably *Fidelio*, the *Singspiel Die Zauberflöte*, the original version of the *opéra comique Carmen*), there is no speaking in opera, only singing. The words of the libretto are all set to music, be it via arias, ensembles, or recitatives. In operetta, musical

Figure 3.1. Theatrical poster for the D'Oyly Carte Opera Company. _Creative Commons (CCBY-SA 3.0)_

pieces alternate with spoken dialogue. This provides a number of challenges for singers, especially those trained to sing opera. In opera, the composer has made many decisions for the singer on how to deliver the text, predetermining the pitches and rhythms. There is some freedom of expression when it comes to cadenzas and other ornaments, but the vocal range and the rate at which text is delivered are both set. In spoken dialogue, suddenly it is up the singer/actor to decide the pitch level and the speech rate, just as an actor would in a spoken play. Singers are known for obsessing about their sound ("la voce"), but many have not thought at all about their speaking voices. Delivering dialogue can seem like a daunting or even terrifying experience, inducing anxiety like many people feel when they have to give a speech.

In addition, the sung portions of light opera are typically performed with a classical vocal technique, which differs greatly in resonance (and often tessitura) from standard speaking. This can seem like an abrupt shifting of registers and approaches. In modern music theater, singers use a more speech-like approach to vocal production, thus the switch from singing to speaking is less drastic and more natural sounding. In general, male singers will find less of an adjustment is necessary, since they sing more in their modal voice than woman do. For female singers, the trick is to find an optimal speech range that need not match her singing range exactly but will have a close proximity. If a high soprano speaks at too high a pitch, her voice could become cloying (think the Powerpuff Girl Bubbles). Likewise, if a high soprano speaks at too low a pitch level (think Kathleen Turner or Beatrice Arthur), she may be indistinguishable from the contralto in the show.

The modern proliferation of women speaking on the edge of vocal fry (blame Kim Kardashian) is something else to be avoided in light opera. Unless the production is somehow updated to a contemporary setting, operettas are not set in modern times. Since most were written in the nineteenth and early twentieth century, light opera is not about naturalism or realism, therefore a larger-than-life approach to speech is necessary for style (more on this in chapter 5) and projection. While regional theater or music theater companies producing operettas may perform them with amplification, many opera houses may not. Most opera companies are not well versed in using microphones since their use is typically eschewed in the opera world. For the 2014–2015 Metropolitan Opera production of *The Merry Widow* (by Broadway director Susan Stroman), the singers wore body mics like Broadway singers, but supposedly they were only on during the dialogue. More often, floor mics are used, but they can be problematic as they require the blocking to bring singers downstage and they catch the noise of high heels on the stage floor. Assume you won't have amplification, so try to get some training in Voice for the Actor. The Linklater Voice method is a popular and well-regarded approach used by many theater programs. You could also reverse the old Italian adage "Si canta come si parla" to "Si parla come si canta," applying the principles of placement and breath management from singing to your speaking voice. If for whatever reason you don't have access to a voice or acting class, why not try out for a play? A play, not a musical or opera or operetta. The experience of preparing an entirely spoken role can only strengthen your background as an actor and your comfort level with spoken dialogue.

Now, many light opera productions will require the use of various foreign accents. Perhaps you are Rosalinda affecting her best fake

Hungarian dialect ("from 'Ungary") in *Die Fledermaus*, or you are doing a Gilbert and Sullivan production in England and need to match
your British-born castmates. This is where your training as an opera
singer will help you, if that training included the International Phonetic Alphabet (IPA). Fluency in IPA will help you shape your diction
to the needs of the production. In the United States, some light opera
productions will employ a standardized American accent despite any
exotic settings. Others will use accents for comedic effect (*El Capitain*), to make class distinctions (Cockney Dick Deadeye and highbrow
Sir Joseph), or to imply a foreign setting when the show is translated
into English (*La vie parisienne*).

Another common practice in the United States is for productions to
have the sung portions in the original language but the spoken dialogue
in English. This custom attempts to preserve the composer's word
setting and intent but presumes that the dialogue needs to be in the
audience's native tongue to help accessibility and plot comprehension.
Switching from singing in German to speaking in English while playing
the same character presents a unique undertaking for the singing actor.
Balancing these almost bipolar constructs behooves the actor to find
a bilingual basis for the character, a base that defies language and is
based in true intent. It is also challenging to shift from English prose to
German verse. Here is an example from *Die Fledermaus* of a character
shifting from English dialogue (translation by Amanda Johnston, author
of *English and German Diction for Singers: A Comparative Approach*,
2nd ed.) to the original libretto, sung in German:

ORLOFSKY.
Listen to me! Above all, I must acquaint you
with some of my national peculiarities.
Ich lade gern mir Gäste ein, man lebt bei mir recht fein.

After smoothly transitioning from spoken English to sung German,
the singer playing Prince Orlofsky also has the task of changing briefly
to French with the aria's motto and title, the expression "Chacun à son
goût." So sometimes performing light opera is an exercise in macaronics,
making a mixture of multiple languages.

For most singers, the greatest challenge is delivering spoken dialogue in foreign languages. If you are in a European production of a light opera, no doubt the dialogue will be in the original language, so *La belle Hélène* will be all *en français* and *Gräfin Mariza* will be entirely *auf Deutsch*. Sounding idiomatic in French or German is more difficult in speech rather than in song, because again the composer helps you by setting the word stress and shaping the pace of the language. When it comes to foreign spoken dialogue, this daunting task faces the nonnative speaker. Again, IPA will help tremendously, but it is imperative to seek input from native speakers and diction coaches so as to prevent any embarrassing errors in syllabic stress. If you plan a career in light opera and want to sing abroad, then focusing on becoming proficient in French and German is necessary because acting in a foreign language adds another layer of difficulty to the process. Here's an example of the first spoken lines from act I of *Orphée aux enfers* (libretto by Ludovic Halévy):

EURYDICE.
Mon mari!

ORPHÉE.
Ma femme! Imbécile! Dépêchons-nous de crier avant
qu'elle commence. Ah! Je vous y prends, madame.

EURYDICE.
À quoi, je vous prie?

ORPHÉE.
À quoi? Mais à qui donc jetiez-vous ces fleurs, s'il vous plaît?

EURYDICE.
Ces fleurs? Au vent! Et vous, mon tendre ami, à qui jetiez-vous
ce chant passionné de votre crin-crin?

ORPHÉE.
À la lune . . .

EURYDICE.
Fort bien! Savez-vous ce que je conclus de tout cela, mon bon chéri?
C'est que si j'ai mon berger, vous avez votre bergère. Eh bien!
Je vous laisse votre bergère, laissez-moi mon berger.

ORPHÉE.
Allons! Madame, cette proposition est de mauvais gout!

EURYDICE.
Pourquoi donc, je vous prie?

ORPHÉE.
Parce que . . . parce que . . . Tenez! Vous me faites rougir!

EURYDICE.
Vraiment! Eh bien! Si cette couleur-là vous déplaît,
nous tâcherons de vous en trouver une autre.

ORPHÉE.
Eurydice! Ma femme?

EURYDICE.
Ah! Mais, c'est qu'il est temps de s'expliquer, à la fin! Et il faut qu'une
bonne fois je vous dise votre fait, maître Orphée, mon chaste époux, qui
rougissez! Apprenez que je vous déteste! Que j'ai cru épouser un artiste
et que je me suis unie à l'homme le plus ennuyeux de la création. Vous
vous croyez un aigle, parce que vous avez inventé les vers hexamètres!
Mais c'est votre plus grand crime à mes yeux! Est-ce que vous croyez
que je passerai ma jeunesse à vous entendre réciter des songes
classiques et racler l'exécrable instrument que voilà?

ORPHÉE.
Mon violon! Ne touchez pas cette corde, madame!

This dialogue sets up the acrimonious relationship between Orphée
and Eurydice, where neither is hiding their adulterous activities and Eurydice is definitely not hiding her disdain for her husband's violin. Note
the verbose mini-monologue for Eurydice. Unfortunately, there is no
Nico Castel volume in his Libretti Series to guide singers through Offenbach or Viennese operetta; although he had plans to complete them,
they were thwarted by his death in 2015. So the careful work of translat-
ing and transcribing must be done on your own, with the help of good
coaching. After completing the word-for-word translations and phonetic
transcriptions for the dialogue, just as they would for any sung elements
of their roles, the singing actors preparing a scene like this would then
be ready to delve into scene analysis. They could try acting out the scene
in English with their own paraphrased translation so that the objectives

and subtext are clear to them in their native tongue before attempting the scene in the original language. Using modern vernacular for this exercise helps make the material more relatable. Here's an example using just the first two lines from the scene:

EURYDICE.

Text from the libretto:	Mon mari!
Translation:	My husband!
Possible paraphrase:	Hi sweetie!

ORPHÉE.

Text from the libretto:	Ma femme! Imbécile!
Translation:	My wife! Imbecile!
Possible paraphrase:	Hey babe! Idiot!

So if you want to be a believable actor in light opera, familiarize yourself not just with the beautiful music of operetta but with their libretti. Most French and German operettas are in public domain, so libretti are legally obtainable on the Internet, and you are just a few clicks away from being able to practice reading them aloud. Similarly, the complete works of Gilbert and Sullivan are easily accessible, especially on the excellent and thorough website of the Gilbert and Sullivan Archive.

CHARACTER ANALYSIS

Regardless of language, prepare your role as an actor. Of course, as a singer you need to learn all of the notes and rhythms and prepare the role vocally, linguistically, and musically. But also study the libretto without the music. Read it like a play. Speak all of your text as dialogue, regardless of whether it will be sung or spoken in the final production. Once you're familiar with the work, then it's time to make your character analysis. Identify who your character is and then as the character, ask yourself: "What do I want? What's in my way? What will I do to overcome this?" These basic elements can help you determine your character's objectives, obstacles, and actions. Your character's overall goal in life is the superobjective, then there are smaller objectives the character pursues in each scene. Here's a sample character analysis for Nanki-Poo from *The Mikado*:

Character: Nanki-Poo, son of the Mikado, disguised as a wandering minstrel

Age: 22

Superobjective: To be with my lover, Yum-Yum.
Scene objectives: To not marry Katisha (Act I).
                   To not be executed (Act II).
Obstacles: Yum-Yum's engaged to Ko-Ko, the Lord High
                   Executioner.
                   I'm supposed to marry Katisha.
Actions: I try to commit suicide.
                   I make a deal with Ko-Ko.
                   I marry Yum-Yum in secret.

Figure 3.2. Courtice Pounds as Nanki-Poo in *The Mikado* (1885). *Creative Commons (CCBY-SA 3.0)*

You can use whatever format or methodology you like, of course (using first person or third person), but do a scene-by-scene analysis so that your character's intention is always clear, whether in song or in speech. Another detail to refine your acting is the use of subtext. For instance, in the act I trio "So muss ich allein bleiben" from *Die Fledermaus*, Rosalinda, Adele, and Eisenstein all talk about their miserable situation while singing joyful, spirited music. Their words do not match their true sentiment, thus their subtext contradicts what they are actually saying. Similarly, in the previous scene excerpts from *Orphée aux enfers*, Orphée and Eurydice may seem at first to be sharing affectionate greetings when their subtext is actually mutual disdain. Subtext is a great tool for an actor, but it always needs to fit the character. Shrewd soubrettes may have a subtext that differs from their spoken intent, but some more straightforward, simple characters may be in complete alignment (think Forrest Gump). After you've determined your character's objectives, obstacles, actions, and any subtexts, write these in your score. These elements should be an integral part of the notes you take in your score, alongside your blocking. ♪

Now, light opera plots are notoriously far-fetched and unrealistic, but that is part of their charm. Regardless of the absurdity, as an actor the singer must fully commit to clear-cut character choices to make the show work. Of course, movement is a big element of an actor's characterization in operetta, and the importance of dance and movement in light opera is the focus of chapter 4. But through determining their appropriate character archetype and doing a detailed character analysis, singers are on their way to being viable singing actors of light opera. Most often, the spoken dialogue will take serious preparation and practice but will only aid in creating a multifaceted portrayal and providing another means for singers to connect with the audience.

4

DANCE AND MOVEMENT

One of the key elements of light opera is dance. Ballet was a featured component of French grand opera, but overall choreographed movement did not play a huge role in opera. In addition, ballets were typically performed by a separate troupe of trained ballet dancers, not the opera singers. In contrast, dance seems to permeate the genre of operetta. Operettas frequently showcase a variety of dance steps and styles, including the waltz, the can-can, and folk dances such as the *cachucha* and the polka. Not surprisingly, dance can be intimidating to opera singers, who are not normally trained in dance and movement. When asked what she found to be the greatest challenge in performing her first operetta, Metropolitan Opera star Renée Fleming said, "The dancing. Oh those wonderful waltzing lessons from Susan [Stroman]."[1] Singers spend years in voice lessons and coachings perfecting their vowels, their cadenzas, and other important details of vocal production. But those interested in performing light opera should consider pursuing basic dance training. While not expected to be professional-caliber ballet dancers, singers in light opera should be able to execute simple dance steps such as a box step or jazz square and a grapevine. This chapter is designed to familiarize singers with some of the basic dance styles they may encounter while performing operetta.

WALTZ

As the Stephen Sondheim song asks, "Do I Hear a Waltz?" If it's a Viennese operetta, then the answer most likely is yes. The waltz flourished in nineteenth-century Vienna led in large part by the Strauss family. Johann Strauss (1804–1849) began the family tradition, which was continued by his sons, Josef Strauss (1827–1870), Eduard Strauss (1835–1916), and of course the Waltz King, Johann Strauss II (1825–1899). The waltz found its way into light opera through Johann Strauss the Younger and Austro-Hungarian composers Franz Lehár (1870–1948) and Emmerich Kálmán (1882–1953). With a triple meter (3/4 time), this popular ballroom dance form is typically performed by a male and female partner. There are many different types of waltzes, but the basic waltz footwork usually involves a box step.

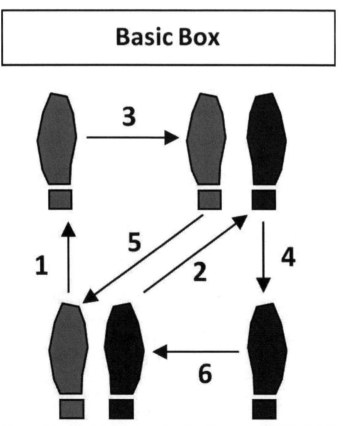

Figure 4.1.   Basic box step. *Creative Commons (CCBY-SA 3.0)*

In a more advanced waltz, sometimes the box step turns. The male partner is the leader and thus moves forward while the female partner moves backward, inspiring the famous quip about Ginger Rogers doing everything Fred Astaire did backwards and in heels. Dance steps are notoriously hard to learn by just reading about them, so it's best to take a ballroom class if you can. There are also a number of helpful online videos breaking down the steps so that you can execute each element and then put them together by yourself and then with a partner. Check this book's online resources for some suggestions. ♪

The waltz is an elegant, romantic dance that epitomizes the grace and allure of light opera. It even plays a part in the plot of many operettas. For instance, Alfred uses the waltz in act I's "Trinke Liebchen" as a flirtatious way to persuade Rosalinda to dance in *Die Fledermaus*. And when Danilo and Hanna finally unite in their climactic *Merry Widow* waltz, "Lippen schweigen," the sealing of their romance provides the denouement for the show. The waltz in effect becomes a means of flirtation and union between romantically linked characters. Besides these two well-known examples, here are some other notable operetta waltzes:

1. "Sweetheart Waltz" from *Der Zigeunerbaron*
2. "Sie geht links, er geht rechts" from *Der Graf von Luxemburg*
3. "Tanzen möcht ich" from *Die Csárdásfürstin*
4. "Deep in My Heart, Dear" from *The Student Prince*
5. "Au mont Ida," Paris's waltz from *La belle Hélène*

Due to the huge influence of the Viennese waltz, the waltz made its way across the ocean to America. The primary composers of American operetta all had European roots: Victor Herbert worked as a cellist in Vienna, while Rudolf Friml and Sigmund Romberg were both born in the Austro-Hungarian Empire. Still, it could be argued that "Herbert never captured the Viennese lilt of Strauss or Lehár; his waltzes plod conscientiously through all three beats of the measure, and never seem to get off the ground."[2] Nevertheless his waltz "Kiss Me Again" from *Mlle. Modiste* became popular, as did the similarly themed "One Kiss" from Romberg's *The New Moon* and Huguette's Waltz from Friml's *The Vagabond King*. While the Viennese waltz was typically a romantic duet, the waltz seems to become a sentimental solo for the female lead in American light opera.

Figure 4.2. *The Last Waltz* (1912) by Clarence F. Underwood (1871–1929). *Creative Commons (CCBY-SA 3.0)*

There are a number of light operas so inspired by the waltz that it is part of the title. Oscar Straus (1870–1954), who dropped an *s* from his last name so as not to be confused with the famous Strauss family, composed the operettas *Ein Walzertraum, Der letzte Walzer, Drei Walzer*, and *Ihr erster Walzer*. For the ultimate waltz inspiration, watch George Balanchine's ballet *Vienna Waltzes* for its sweeping sophistication. Be it a classic by Strauss or Straus, the waltz is undoubtedly the cornerstone of dance in light opera. ♪

CAN-CAN

While the waltz may be the most familiar dance featured in light opera, certainly its most colorful is the can-can. The high-kicking can-can became de rigueur in Parisian music halls in the mid-nineteenth century. Drawing on the partner dance the quadrille, it is characterized by a kick line of female dancers with long skirts, which are lifted to execute the dance's signature moves and reveal colorful petticoats and undergarments. Although first considered quite scandalous, it is one of the tamer routines still performed alongside the topless numbers at the Moulin Rouge cabaret in Paris.

The most familiar can-can music is the "Galop Infernal" from act IV of Offenbach's *Orphée aux enfers*. In typical operetta fashion, it is a rather absurd insertion of French popular dance within a show supposedly set in mythological Greece. But the spirited, petticoat-flashing moves help portray the fourth act's bacchanal. Another famous operetta can-can is featured in *The Merry Widow*. From his first entrance, Danilo sings fondly of the Grisettes at Maxim's, and by act III Hanna hosts a party where Valencienne joins them in their can-can (Grisetten-Lied: "Ja, wir sind es, die Grisetten"). Lehár was so smitten with the Grisettes that he made one the star of one of his light operas, *Clo-Clo*. Not surprisingly, the finale of *La vie parisienne*, with its duple meter and C major key signature, looks like his Orpheus can-can. Offenbach even works a can-can into his Peruvian setting in *La Périchole* ("Eh bonjour monsieur le mari"). Noël Coward pays his homage to the dance with the Prater Girls in act II of *Bitter Sweet*. And of course, it is the inspiration for Cole Porter's musical *Can-Can* (1953). ♪

Figure 4.3. *The Can-Can* (1889–1890) by Georges Seurat (1859–1891). *Creative Commons (CCBY-SA 3.0)*

Artful execution of the can-can takes substantial flexibility and leg extension, not to mention some gymnastic ability. Here are the major steps that comprise the can-can:

(1) *Battements*, or high kicks, (2) *ronde de jambe*, a quick movement of the lower leg with the knee and skirt raised, (3) *port d'armes*, the rotat-

ing on one leg, meanwhile grasping the other leg at the ankle, held up vertically, (4) cartwheel, and (5) *grand écart*, a flying up then landing in a jump split. Typically, screaming and yelling are optional, and modern variations include backflips in addition to traditional cartwheels. The final gesture (6) has the girls bend over, to flash their backside underwear to the audience.[3]

The unbridled energy and impressive choreography of the can-can make it a surefire audience pleaser. Its vigor and "naughtiness" provide perfect contrast from the more formal and refined waltz. But again, it is not a dance for beginners! It is very easy to pull a hamstring doing this fast-paced and demanding dance, so be sure to warm up and work on building strength and suppleness in your leg muscles before cartwheeling into can-can splits.

FOXTROT

Another dance that appears often in light opera is the foxtrot. The foxtrot resembles a waltz except that it is in a 4/4 meter. The footwork pattern involves a walk-walk-step side-step together sequence done in a slow-slow-quick-quick pace. While its exact origin is not clear, the foxtrot became popular during the jazz era and remains a classic ballroom dance. A foxtrot appears in the song "Student Life" from *The Student Prince* and the wonderfully titled "Fräulein, bitte, woll'n Sie Shimmy tanzen" from *Die Bajadere*. Not to be confused with the Broadway sensation *Hamilton*, the light opera *Lady Hamilton* by Eduard Künneke tells the story of Lord Nelson's mistress and includes two foxtrots: "Jedem Abend tönt der Gong" and "Kommt mit nach Madrid." And the German operetta *Im weißen Rößl* presents a so-called French foxtrot in "Tout bleu: Fox-trot de l'Operetta *L'Auberge du Cheval Blanc*." In homage to its American setting, *Der Herzogin von Chicago* opens with a Charleston ("Charleston, Charleston, tanzt man heut") and ends with a foxtrot as its act III finale, "Ein kleiner Slowfox mit Mary bei Cocktail und Sherry, das wär' so mein Ideal!" So besides the waltz and the can-can, those who want to sing light opera should also learn the foxtrot. ♪

FOLK DANCE

The Austro-Hungarian Empire existed from 1867 to 1918, during the prime years of the development of light opera in Europe. Therefore, it is not surprising that there were strong Hungarian influences on Viennese operetta. Composers such as Franz Lehár and Emmerich Kálmán both found inspiration in Hungarian folk music, as well as the influences of gypsy culture from the Romani Hungarian tradition.

One famous Hungarian folk dance with gypsy origins is the *csárdás*. This partner dance is typically in a duple meter, beginning at a slow pace and then accelerating into a brisk tempo with the whirl of a colorful skirt. A virtuosic violin part usually sets up the dance and accompanies its acceleration. ♪

In *Zigeunerliebe*, Lehár includes an ensemble *csárdás* in act I ("Se traska, liebe Gäste") and a climactic solo *csárdás* for Ilona in act III ("Hör' ich Zimbalklänge"). His *Wo die Lerche singt* is also set in Hungary, while Kálmán wrote four light operas set in his home country: *Tatárjárás*, *Der Zigeunerprimas*, *Die Csárdásfürstin*, and *Gräfin Mariza*. In *The Countess Maritza*, Count Tassilo ends his song "Komm, Zigány" with a *csárdás*, and it fittingly defines Sylva, the title character in *The Csárdás Princess*. The *csárdás* appears in zarzuela as well, notably in Pablo Sorozábal's *Black, el payaso*. The Hungarian dance even plays a part in *Die Herzogin von Chicago*, which depicts "the conflict between an East European crown prince who insisted on waltzes and *csárdáses* and a visiting American millionairess who wants to sing and dance only the Charleston and the fox-trot."[4] Viennese-born Johann Strauss II was not immune to the influence of the *csárdás*. His operetta *Der Zigeunerbaron* is set in Hungary and features the dance in Saffi's act I "Zigeunerlied" and Count Homonay's act II "Werberlied." And of course, he wrote perhaps the best-known operetta *csárdás* for Rosalinda in act II of *Die Fledermaus*.

Other Eastern European folk dances find their way into light opera, particularly the Czech polka and the Polish mazurka. Lehár even wrote an operetta titled *Die blaue Mazur*, or *The Blue Mazurka*, while Johann Strauss II called *Der Karneval in Rom* his so-called polka opera. In *Gold gab ich für Eisen*, Kálmán calls one of his act II duets the Zeppelin Polka. While the polka is in duple time, the mazurka is a lively dance with a triple meter. Sometimes these two dances are combined into a polka-mazurka, as in Strauss's "Da nickten die Giebel" from *Die Göttin der Vernunft*. Act II of *Der Graf von Luxemburg* features two polka-mazurkas as well as a *Polkatänzer-Duett*. The faux folk dance from the imaginary Pontevedro seen in act II of *The Merry Widow* also draws on Eastern European folk style. One even finds the so-called Umbrella Mazurka in Federico Chueca's zarzuela *El año pasado por agua*.

Turning to other foreign locations, at least two operettas choose Peru as their setting. Offenbach's *La Périchole* has two séguedilles ("Vous a t'on dit souvent" and "Un roi se promenant") and John Philip Sousa's *El Capitain* is inflected throughout with Spanish-inspired rhythms. Lehár chose Spain as the setting for his operetta *Frasquita*. Curiously, two light operas set in Venice both highlight Spanish dances. Offenbach's *Le pont des soupirs* features a bolero ("C'est un coin tout petit") while Gilbert and Sullivan's *The Gondoliers* has a call to "Dance a Cachucha." In Hervé's operetta *Chilpéric*, there is a bolero ("À la sierra morena"), which was immortalized in a famous painting by Henri de Toulouse-Lautrec. The bolero is "a sultry, hip-swaying national dance suited to an adagio beat" with "dips, crossovers, and pivots on the ball of the foot and closed on a posed duo."[5] While the bolero may be somewhat familiar due to its portrayals in popular culture, the *cachucha* is less so, although it is similar: "Executed in 3/4 or 3/8 oom-pah-pah time, the tempestuous cachucha earned the title of the Spanish waltz. The skipping steps emulated the bolero by gradually increasing speed and emphasis on brisk footwork."[6] Again, it is best to learn these dances under the aegis of a trained ballroom dancer to understand the nuances of these wonderful Spanish dances. ♪

Gilbert and Sullivan did not completely overlook their own country's folk dances. The hornpipe has a special moment in act I of *Ruddigore*, since as Sir Joseph Porter states in *HMS Pinafore*, "All sailors should dance hornpipes." This jaunty duple-meter dance is characteristically performed in hard-soled shoes. Speaking of hard-soled shoes, Dutch clogs provide the inspiration for the wooden-shoe "Sabot Dance" in *Sweethearts*, not to mention Kálmán's *Das Hollandweibchen*, or *The Little Dutch Girl*. ♪

American square dance doesn't seem to play a large role in operetta (although it does appear in Kurt Weill's folk opera *Down in the Valley*

Figure 4.4. Marcelle Lender dancing the bolero in *Chilpéric* **(1895–1896) by Henri de Toulouse-Lautrec (1864–1901).** *Creative Commons (CCBY-SA 3.0)*

and Aaron Copland's *The Tender Land*). Interestingly it is an operetta set in America but written by a Hungarian that features a prominent square dance: "Rechts herum, links herum" from Kálmán's *Arizona Lady*. But the square dance is followed immediately by a waltz duet, returning to typical light opera tradition.

DANCE ROLES

A number of roles in light opera were written with dancers in mind. Within a show like *The Merry Widow*, some may be for singers who can dance (Valencienne) or dancers who can sing (the Grisettes). Other times it may be a speaking role that requires dancing or acrobatics but no singing (Njegus). And sometimes directors add dance elements not originally indicated by the librettist. For instance, I directed an *Orpheus in the Underworld* in which I had Mercury tap dance during his entrance because the tenor happened to be a tap dancer. And I played Adele in a production of *Die Fledermaus* in which she was an aspiring dancer, finishing her audition aria with a full split. Movement can enhance characterization and create great comedic moments. Gilbert and Sullivan ensemble numbers frequently involve clever choreography that will not necessarily demand balletic flexibility but will challenge singers to coordinate singing with specific gestures, poses, or footwork. In a number of light operas, the characters are actually portraying dancers, while others are café singers, circus performers, or waltzers at a ball. So light opera can require dance and movement skills of singers whether they are chorus can-can girls (*Die lustige Witwe, Bitter Sweet*) or the title character (Clo-Clo, Katja, Fanny Elßler). Here are some examples of roles for dancers in operetta: ♪

1. Njegus (usually a nonsinging role) in *Die lustige Witwe*
2. The Grisettes (Lolo, Dodo, Jou-Jou, Frou-Frou, Clo-Clo, Margot) in *Die lustige Witwe*
3. The Prater Girls (Lisa, Trude, Fritzi, Toni, Greta, Elsie) in *Bitter Sweet*
4. The Can-Can Girls in *Orphée aux enfers*
5. The Policemen in *The Pirates of Penzance*
6. Juliette, a dancer in *Der Graf von Luxemburg*
7. Franziska Cagliari, a dancer in *Wiener Blut*
8. Fedora, a dancer in *Der Opernball*
9. Gretel, a dancer in *Die blaue Mazur*
10. Clo-Clo, a revue star in *Clo-Clo*
11. Sonja, a dancer in *Der Zarewitsch*
12. Mercedes del Rossa, a ballerina in *Schön ist die Welt*
13. Fanny Elßler, a ballerina in *Die Tänzerin Fanny Elßler*
14. Fanny Pichler, a ballerina in *Drei Walzer*
15. Beltramini, the ballet master in *Drei Walzer*
16. Katja Karina, a cabaret dancer in *Katja, die Tänzerin*

17. Lollette, Clochette, and Fleurette, dancers in *Das Veilchen von Montmarte*
18. Anina Miramonti, a dancer in *Der Teufelsreiter*
19. Bonita, a Mexican dancer in *Arizona Lady*
20. Bebe, a dancer with the Folies Bergère in *Mlle. Modiste*
21. La Frivolini, a dancer in *La cigale et la fourmi*
22. Suzanne, a tightrope walker in *Les saltimbanques*
23. Cabriolo, a tightrope walker in *La princesse de Trébizonde*
24. Mister X, a tightrope walker in *Die Zirkusprinzessin*
25. Sonja, Betty, Lilly, Suzanne, and Daisy, dancers of the Circus Stanislawski in *Die Zirkusprinzessin*
26. Théa, a dancer in *Les fêtards*
27. Baladon, a dancing master in *Vert-Vert*
28. Zaza, a ballerina in *Der kleine König*
29. First Dancer and Second Dancer in *Die Herzogin von Chicago*
30. Desirée Loree, a dancer in *Miss Underground*
31. Lulu and Margot, dancers with the Folies Bergère in *Miss Underground*
32. Tilly, a dancer in *Marinka*
33. Lisette, a ballerina in *The Girl in Pink Tights*
34. Azuri, a dancing girl in *The Desert Song*
35. Irma, a ballet student in *The Fortune Teller*
36. Fresco, the ballet master in *The Fortune Teller*
37. Irene, Trina, and Ruth, ballet students in *The Fortune Teller*
38. Dancing Master in *The Queen's Lace Handkerchief*
39. Soledad, a dancer in *Los sobrinos del capitán Grant*
40. Lina, a singer-dancer in *Las golondrinas*

More and more, opera workshop courses are providing movement training to singers as part of the curriculum. Otherwise, singers need to seek out classes in ballroom dance and perhaps basic ballet or jazz to build their vocabulary of dance steps and styles. Those wanting to sing light opera should do what they can to master the waltz and attempt a high kick, even if only for comic effect!

NOTES

1. Ryan McPhee, "Opera with High Kicks: *The Merry Widow's* Renée Fleming and Susan Stroman on Bringing Broadway Flair to the Met," Broadway World, accessed January 27, 2017, www.broadway.com/buzz/179119/opera -with-high-kicks-the-merry-widows-renee-fleming-susan-stroman-on-bring ing-broadway-flair-to-the-met/.

2. Glenn Litton and Cecil A. Smith, *Musical Comedy in America: From "The Black Crook" to "South Pacific," from "The King and I" to "Sweeney Todd"* (London: Routledge, 2013), 83.

3. Richard C. Norton, "Baby, You Can Can-Can Too," Operetta Research Center, September 2, 2015, accessed January 29, 2017, http://operetta-research-center.org/afghan-afghanistan-can-baby-can-can-can/.

4. Jessie Wright Martin, "A Survey of the Operettas of Emmerich Kálmán" Louisiana State University Major Papers (2005), 18.

5. Mary Ellen Snodgrass, *The Encyclopedia of World Folk Dance* (Lanham, MD: Rowman & Littlefield, 2016), 28.

6. Ibid., 33.

5

STYLISTIC CONSIDERATIONS

Inhabiting the realm between opera and music theater, light opera is both progeny and progenitor but stands alone in terms of its distinctive style. In the words of tenor and stage director Philip Lüsebrink, "Operetta plays with language, character, history, and social issues. The genre offers emotions of all kinds, it is frivolous, political, and a mirror of society past and present. For me, operetta can do all of this better than musical comedy or opera."[1] Light opera essentially encompasses a particular historical era, from the middle of the nineteenth century to the middle of the twentieth century. From Hervé to Leonard Bernstein, composers of light opera were commenting on the times in which they lived. Despite their mythological settings, Jacques Offenbach's *Orphée aux enfers* and *La belle Hélène* satirized the Second French Empire, while W. S. Gilbert and Arthur Sullivan parodied the mores of Victorian England even when their operettas were set in Japan (*The Mikado*) and Italy (*The Gondoliers*). Thus, to sing light opera successfully, one should explore the relevant historical context and any antediluvian references, as well as the idiomatic nature of the genre's musical style and its performance tradition on stage and screen.

HISTORICAL CONTEXT

The era of operetta spans a number of significant historical periods over one hundred years: La Belle Époque, the Austro-Hungarian Empire, the Victorian and Edwardian eras, and the Gilded Age, to name a few. Social customs of these times vary greatly from those of the twenty-first century, thus it behooves singers to research the context of the epoch in which an operetta was written.

In early nineteenth-century France, the operations of the theatrical community were strictly regulated by a decree from Napoleon I enacted in 1807. Because of these restraints, "Paris theatres in those days were officially restricted in number and governed by ordinance as to the sort of entertainment they purveyed."[2] During this time, operettas were limited to a one-act format and a three-person (later four-person) cast. Despite these restrictions, Offenbach still managed to find ample room for satire on a number of levels. Today, when we hear of the Bataclan, we think of the Parisian theater tragically attacked by terrorists in 2015. The theater is actually named after Offenbach's *Ba-ta-clan* (1855). In English, the title means something akin to "the whole shebang" or "the whole kit and caboodle." Aptly, the work parodies both French government (Emperor Napoleon III) and French grand opera (Meyerbeer's *Les Huguenots*). A so-called *chinoiserie musicale*, its pseudo-Chinese setting provided a way for the German-born Jewish composer to lampoon his adopted French homeland indirectly. When the limitations on Parisian theaters were lifted a few years later, Offenbach was finally able to present a full-length operetta. An *opéra féerie* or fairy-tale opera, *Orphée aux enfers* (1858) allowed Offenbach to employ a large cast for the first time while continuing his familiar political commentary on the imperial regime. ♪

Across the channel in London, Gilbert and Sullivan also took great pleasure in highlighting the sometimes illogical and inconsistent social customs of their country. Their later works often have foreign settings, like many operettas; but their early collaboration, *Trial by Jury* (1875), is set squarely in Great Britain, specifically at the Court of the Exchequer. With that in mind, the "rather surprising thing about *Trial by Jury* is that it suggests . . . the hypocrisy behind Victorian bourgeois respectability," not to mention "legal incapability and the achievement of position not through merit but through 'jobbery,'" in quite a direct manner.[3] The allegedly Learned Judge unabashedly reveals in his entrance aria that he earned his judicial position through nepotism, exploitation, and bamboozlement, despite the Victorian era's supposedly strict moral code of behavior. Perhaps even modern audiences can easily relate to spoofing judges and attorneys, since lawyer jokes still seem to be standard fare. Furthermore, the postfeminist era does not look kindly upon characters such as the Judge, who uses a woman to gain money and power, all along planning to abandon her. Fittingly, *Trial by Jury* was originally performed alongside Offenbach's *La Périchole*; both *Trial by Jury*'s unscrupulous Judge and *La Périchole*'s womanizing Viceroy exhibit questionable moral character and a penchant for hypocrisy, especially in their romantic endeavors. Although the Plaintiff and La Périchole are somewhat trapped within the confines of acceptable behavior for nineteenth-century women, both manage to improve their rank (Angelina gets engaged to the Judge) and finances (La Périchole is permitted to keep the Viceroy's gift of jewelry) in the denouements of the operas. So it seems the operetta heroine is typically able to overcome the obstacles of society in spite of position and politics. ♪

Figure 5.1.   Sketch by Félix Nadar (1820–1910) of a scene from Offenbach's
Ba-ta-clan **(ca. 1855).** *Creative Commons (CCBY-SA 3.0)*

Overall, Viennese operetta appears less focused on political satire. Still, Johann Strauss II did include a political focus in his first operetta, *Indigo und die vierzig Räuber* (1871), with the veil of the Turkish locale from the folk tale of Ali Baba and the Forty Thieves. As with Offenbach and Gilbert, the exotic setting serves to distance the opera from the subject of its satire, but clearly Strauss mocks "economic policy-making . . . new-found wealth" and "the Austrian army."[4] The military commentary proved somewhat problematic for Strauss and his first operetta. Thus, his later works seem to soften the political parody. While "the satirical tone never disappeared entirely from Viennese operetta, the genre began to emphasize the romantic and sentimental vein"[5] in homage to the city of Vienna and its fêted waltz. In fact, a true nationalistic bent pervades Viennese operetta in its reverence for the homeland and its native musical style. Austro-Hungarian Franz Lehár continued this musical nationalism with his first operetta, *Wiener Frauen* (1902). In his later works, such as *Der Graf von Luxemburg* (1909), he celebrates Vienna obliquely by making social commentary on the perceived values of other cultures, such as Parisian hedonism and Russian deception. In the light operas of Hungarian Emmerich Kálmán, the nationalistic perspective extends to Hungary, with the celebration of gypsies and Hungarian folk dance, especially the *csárdás*. Be it in *Die Csárdásfürstin* (1915), set in Vienna, or *Gräfin Mariza* (1924), set in Hungary, Kálmán honors the Austro-Hungarian legacy, even alluding to previous Viennese operettas. In *Gräfin Mariza*, he named a character (Baron Kolomán Zsupán) after a character in Strauss's *Der Zigeunerbaron* (Kálmán Zsupán), who also shared part of his own name. ♪

So an overview of historical context reveals the importance of political satire and nationalism in European operetta. But researching context is only part of the process. Light opera performers must meld their knowledge of the historical period with their character analysis, for "as interesting as understanding the world of a particular style may be, it is of little use to us as actors unless we can convert the attitudes and values implicit in that style into objectives and tactics."[6] Besides broader historical references inherent in the genre, singers of light opera should also become aware of the mores of the late nineteenth and early twentieth century, especially in terms of romantic relationships and the interaction between men and women. Romance plays a huge role in Viennese operetta, and its impact continued as European composers brought operetta to America. For instance, Rudolf Friml brought his romantic *Rose-Marie* to Broadway in 1924. The work emulates the Viennese style despite its Canadian setting. To perform American operettas by Czech-born Friml and German-raised Victor Herbert, singers should take into consideration the European lineage of the genre. For instance, in rehearsing *Rose-Marie* one should remember that in "European operetta, the codes of behavior between men and women were chivalrous and courtly. Knowing this will allow the singer to treat Rose-Marie appropriately by bowing before her, lowering himself, deferring to her physically. Having discovered a vocabulary of movement and vocal possibilities, you can work freely within them to play these actions and win the fight for her love."[7]

Thus, the historical context of American operetta draws on its European ancestry but also delineates some different parameters. American light opera maintains the predilection for foreign locales but seems to abandon the Hungarian gypsy influences. In fact, when compared "with the Viennese school of operetta, the American works disclose some strikingly independent, and perhaps surprising, characteristics" that are "resolutely aligned with the older order of comic opera, rather than with the relatively more worldly, chic, and gay atmosphere of the Viennese school."[8] But the waltz does remain in American operetta, perhaps a little less grandiose than its Viennese counterpart but still lilting, romantic, and stylistically emblematic of the genre.

REFERENCES

For modern performers, one of the challenges is understanding the references specific to the period or culture. If you've ever traveled to the United Kingdom, you probably noticed that some words have different meanings there than in the United States despite the fact that both countries speak English. For instance, what Americans call the trunk of a car is what Brits call the boot. Chips can mean French fries in Britain and potato chips in America (which are what Brits would call crisps). Linguistic idioms and idiosyncrasies are only part of the equation, since cultural references may also go over the heads of uninformed contemporary singers venturing into the realm of operetta.

Luckily, when it comes to Gilbert and Sullivan, there are a number of helpful resources to enlighten the uninitiated. We have Ian Bradley to thank for his comprehensive annotated guide to the full oeuvre of Gilbert and Sullivan. Bradley argues that "half the charm of the Savoy Operas is that they are so dated. They seem to breathe the innocence, the naïvety and the fun of a long-vanished age."[9] Of course, you can't breathe life into charming innocence if the text makes no sense to you. For example, a modern performer might easily misconstrue Edwin's line from *Trial by Jury*—"Be firm, my pecker"—to be a crude joke. In fact, it is not meant to be an overt sexual reference. In its Victorian context, *pecker* referred to the mouth, not another part of the anatomy. So the line is meant to be Edwin's personal pep-talk mantra, akin to "keep smiling" or "put on a happy face." For a deconstruction of a more complex excerpt from *Trial by Jury*, take this refrain sung by the Counsel:

COUNSEL

Swiftly fled each honeyed hour
Spent with this unmanly male!
Camberwell became a bower,
Peckham an Arcadian Vale,
Breathing concentrated otto!—
An existence *à la* Watteau.

Even a highly educated singer would probably be somewhat stymied by this text at first glance. First, you'd need to know that a bower is a shady arbor, a vale is valley, and that Arcadian means "pastoral." Then you'd need to discern that Camberwell is "a rather undistinguished lower-middle-class suburb of London which grew up in the mid-Victorian period" and that nearby Peckham was "even less distinguished and decidedly working class. Both Camberwell and Peckham, it should be pointed out, are now becoming 'gentrified' and, if not quite Arcadian, then certainly Bohemian."[10] Then, after realizing that *otto* is not referring to a German gentleman or the number eight in Italian, one would have to investigate to learn that it is an infrequent variant of *attar*, an essential oil smelling of rose petals. Finally, you would need to recognize the pastoral paintings of Jean-Antoine Watteau (1684–1721) and their bucolic rococo style. That is a lot of research for one verse, so Bradley's annotation is almost indispensable. Science fiction author Isaac Asimov also published an annotated guide to Gilbert and Sullivan, but Bradley's edition remains the paramount resource.

Another useful guidebook to these references is the lexicon by Henry Benford. Like Bradley and Asimov, he provides detailed definitions and clarifications for the reader along with explanations of characters' names and even a map showing locations in England referenced in Gilbert and Sullivan's operas. All of this information is helpful, but most unique is the insight he provides into Gilbert's habit of strange word pairings. While recognizing Gilbert's wit, he notes that "there are many cases where the humor is in the phonetics rather than in the meaning. In such instances, hanging too heavily on word definitions will simply obscure the thought"; in *Trial by Jury*, we see Gilbert's "penchant for incongruous combinations: 'semi-despondent fury' and 'modified rapture' are two examples."[11] So sometimes Gilbert may have been focused primarily on playing with phonetic sounds in phrases such as "parsonified, conjugally matrimonified" (*The Pirates of Penzance*) or in making up words such as "viviparian" (*Utopia, Limited*). He had to explore foreign terms to come up with *caravanserai* (a Middle Eastern roadside inn) to rhyme with *Chancery* (a court of equity), again in *The Pirates of Penzance*, while he seemed to revel in the easy Italian rhymes he was able to employ in *The Gondoliers* ("Per chi questi fiori, questi fiori bellissimi?").

Unfortunately, there are not yet performance guides or annotated collections of libretti to the operas of Offenbach, Strauss, Lehár, or Kálmán, let alone Herbert, Romberg, or Friml (providing ample projects for many a doctoral dissertation). And Bernstein's *Candide* is in desperate need of an annotated edition comparing its different libretti and musical versions, but at least there are guides to the original Voltaire, which can provide some enlightenment.

STYLE ONSTAGE AND IN FILM

Kitsch. Schmaltz. While these terms might be pejorative in some genres, they are essentially obligatory in light opera. Cheesy romance and nostalgia inhabit the musical style of both Viennese and American operetta with waltzes and love duets, while French and English operetta delight in wit and kitsch.

Keeping kitsch in mind, I directed a production of *Trial by Jury* that included a few inside jokes interpolating musical quotes from other Gilbert and Sullivan shows. The inspiration came from Gilbert's self-referential allusions: *The Pirates of Penzance* mentions "that infernal nonsense *Pinafore*," and *Utopia, Limited* references the characters of both the Mikado and Captain Corcoran, who originally appeared in *Pinafore*. These double entendres amplify the parody and the comedy. Interpolations also inspired director/librettist Heather Nicole Winter to satirize the great satirists in her adaptation *The Pirates of Pinafore* (2014). With a deep knowledge of the musical style, Winter was able to create a pastiche parody piece that is both a caricature and a celebration of Gilbert and Sullivan.

> *The Pirates of Pinafore* is a G&S parody mashing up the (arranged) music of *The Pirates of Penzance*, *HMS Pinafore*, *The Mikado*, *Patience*, *Ruddigore*, *Iolanthe*, *The Yeomen of the Guard*, and *The Gondoliers*. Many of the characters in *The Pirates of Pinafore* originated in Gilbert and Sullivan's other works, and have a new spin in mine along with a complete G&S-esque plot of ridiculous twists and turns poking fun at all things musical and theatrical. Necessity was the mother of this invention. I had several very talented sopranos deserving lead roles and no lead tenor, making finding an existing show nearly impossible. So, naturally, I wrote a show to fit my cast! The students I had to work with combined with my admittedly quirky sense of humor led to the mash-up that has the soprano heroines from many of Gilbert and Sullivan's works all chasing the same "tenor" (a mezzo pants role) who, in good opera/operetta fashion, cannot resist the lure of a soprano voice and therefore falls in love with all of them.[12]

Of course we have no video recordings of productions of the original Offenbach operettas and the premieres of Gilbert and Sullivan's Savoy operas since they predate the technology. But the D'Oyly Carte Company did continue to produce the Gilbert and Sullivan repertoire until its closure in 1982, and then again during its revival from 1988 to 2003. D'Oyly Carte made a number of sound recordings of their shows, beginning with *The Mikado* in 1919 and continuing with video recordings of *The Mikado*, *Patience*, and *HMS Pinafore* from 1965 to 1973. These productions are as close as you can get to the original material, produced in a manner completely faithful to the Gilbert and Sullivan tradition. For a taste of life in the D'Oyly Carte Company, as well as the working relationship between Gilbert and Sullivan, watch the film *Topsy-Turvy* (1999), which portrays the process behind the genesis of *The Mikado*.

With the emphasis on wit and wordplay, Gilbert and Sullivan works require not only clear diction but precise rhythm. College Light Opera Company music director David Weiller observes, "In G&S there's not as much rubato," but he finds American operetta, "Romberg especially, to be much more romantic. The orchestrations are more lush, I think the singing style is maybe more full-bodied perhaps than some of the Victor Herbert."[13] The schmaltziness of cheesy operetta romance demands rubato. While words are still important, the musical line predominates, with the careful shaping of phrases being both a necessity and a luxury for the singer. The nostalgic nature of both Viennese operetta and many American operettas leads to a musical wistfulness not found in Offenbach or Sullivan. For instance, *Pinafore*'s pensive "Sorry Her Lot" cannot compare to the yearning melodies of Lehár's "Lippen schweigen" (*Die lustige Witwe*) or "Lover, Come Back to Me" (Romberg's *The New Moon*).

There are some recordings of Lehár conducting his own works, including *Das Land des Lächelns* (1929), *Giuditta* (1934), *Paganini* (1942), and *Zigeunerliebe* (1942). While not of the best sound quality compared to modern standards, these recordings can provide valuable stylistic guidance from the composer himself. Lehár also lived to see some of his work on film. Richard Tauber starred in the 1930 movie of *Das Land des Lächelns*, which also featured Lehár in a small role as the Kapellmeister.

Hollywood versions of Viennese and American operettas became popular in the 1930s. As one might expect, Hollywood took generous liberties in their film adaptations of light opera, but these classic movies can still provide significant stylistic guidance. Jeanette MacDonald was the undisputed queen of operetta on film. After her screen debut in the musical comedy *The Love Parade*, she made her first foray into operetta with *The Vagabond King* (1930). Only six of Friml's songs are included, and he demanded extra compensation for the inclusion of music by other composers in the film. Friml was more pleased with *The Firefly*

(1937), which used almost all of the music from the original operetta while making changes to the plot. In *The Merry Widow* (1934), MacDonald starred opposite movie star Maurice Chevalier as Danilo, but it was *Naughty Marietta* (1935) that first united her with Nelson Eddy. Their famous pairing continued in *Rose-Marie* (1936), with the song "Indian Love Call" becoming one of their most famous duets. They also acted in *Maytime* (1937), but only one of Romberg's songs appears in the film ("Will You Remember, Sweetheart?"); famous operatic excerpts are interpolated from *Les Huguenots* alongside new songs by Herbert Stothart, who later won an Academy Award for Best Original Score for *The Wizard of Oz* (1939). The first color film MacDonald and Eddy made, *Sweethearts* (1938), also amended Herbert's score with songs by Stothart. Not to be confused with Giacomo Puccini's *verismo* opera *La fanciulla del West* (1910), the MacDonald/Eddy vehicle *The Golden Girl of the West* (1938) used the same plot as the opera, but Romberg wrote new songs for the film. Musical highlights include "Shadows on the Moon" and "Señorita." The first film adaptation of Romberg's *The New Moon* (1930) featured opera stars Grace Moore and Lawrence Tibbett, with MacDonald and Eddy reuniting for the 1940 version. In the remake, Eddy performs the familiar "Softly, as in a Morning Sunrise," but it gets a new up-tempo spin, despite its gloomy lyrics. The song later became a favorite of singers such as Bing Crosby, Bobby Darin, Chet Baker, and Dianne Reeves. Despite the star power of MacDonald and Eddy, the 1940 film of Noël Coward's operetta *Bitter Sweet* was more bitter for him than sweet, since it was less faithful than the 1933 rendering, which featured fellow Brit Anna Neagle. *Bitter Sweet* also marked the final film operetta featuring Jeanette MacDonald and Nelson Eddy, although they did go on to appear in the Rodgers and Hart musical *I Married an Angel* (1942).

These classic films may be available on DVD at your public library, on Turner Classic Movies, or streaming online. Again, while the sound quality and film effects may seem dated or old-fashioned, these versions of operetta on film can help elucidate elements of style in a forthright manner, so spend some time in the realm of MacDonald and Eddy. ♪

After MacDonald, Kathryn Grayson became the new Hollywood operetta queen. She starred in *The Desert Song* (1953) and *The Vagabond King* (1956), not to mention *Show Boat* (1951), which is considered by

Figure 5.2.   Movie poster of Jeanette MacDonald and Nelson Eddy in *May-time* (1937). *Creative Commons (CCBY-SA 3.0)*

some to be an operetta. Grayson also performed in many light operas onstage, playing the title roles in *The Merry Widow* and *Naughty Marietta*. But perhaps the most famous, and ridiculous, rendition of *Naughty Marietta*'s "Ah, Sweet Mystery of Life" is Madeline Kahn's in the Mel Brooks film comedy *Young Frankenstein* (1974).

As a genre, operetta displays "a style which everywhere held sway," in the words of the stylish hat-girl Fifi in Herbert's *Mlle. Modiste*. From Offenbach's premieres at the Théâtre des Bouffes-Parisiens to showings of Hollywood films such as *Rose-Marie*, the characteristic and charismatic style of light opera is evidenced in its French, English, Viennese, and American forms through kitsch, schmaltz, waltz, and romance.

NOTES

1. Kevin Clarke, "Talking with *Schwarzwaldmädel* Star Philip Lüsebrink," Operetta Research Center, accessed February 6, 2017, http://operetta-research-center.org/philip-lusebrink-operette/.

2. James Harding, *Folies de Paris: The Rise and Fall of French Operetta* (London: Chappell, 1979), 27.

3. Audrey Williamson, *Gilbert and Sullivan Opera* (London: Marion Boyars, 1982), 29–30.

4. Camille Crittenden, *Johann Strauss and Vienna: Operetta and the Politics of Popular Culture* (Cambridge: Cambridge University Press, 2000), 126.

5. Ibid., 127.

6. Joe Deer and Rocco Dal Vera, *Acting in Musical Theatre: A Comprehensive Course*, 2nd ed. (London: Routledge, 2015), 250.

7. Ibid., 251.

8. Gerald Bordman, *American Operetta: From H.M.S. Pinafore to Sweeney Todd* (Oxford: Oxford University Press, 1981), 89.

9. Ian Bradley, ed., introduction to *The Complete Annotated Gilbert and Sullivan* (Oxford: Oxford University Press, 1996), vii.

10. Ibid., 26.

11. Henry Benford, *The Gilbert and Sullivan Lexicon in Which Is Gilded the Philosophic Pill*, 2nd ed. (Ann Arbor, MI: Sarah Jennings Press, 1991), 1.

12. Heather Nicole Winter, e-mail interview, February 12, 2017.

13. David Weiller, interview, February 17, 2017.

6

AUDITIONING FOR LIGHT OPERA

Of course, if you want to sing light opera, most likely you must audition. Sometimes even characters in an operetta have to audition, perhaps the most famous occurrence being Adele's audition aria from act III of *Die Fledermaus*: "Spiel ich die Unschuld vom Lande." A similar but lesser known audition aria is sung by Fifi in *Mlle. Modiste*: "If I Were on the Stage (Kiss Me, Again)." Victor Herbert's milliner/ wannabe actress sings, "If I were asked to play the part of simple maiden light of heart . . . I'd sing a merry lilting strain, and gaily dance to this refrain. If they should offer me some day a prima donna role to play . . . I would not act the part amiss, I'd sing a polonaise like this." While your audition aria need not literally enumerate your singing, acting, and dancing talents, it definitely should reveal them, as well as your particular affinity for light opera. ♪

SELECTING AUDITION REPERTOIRE

One of the most important elements of auditioning is selecting the most appropriate repertoire. As with opera auditions, you must have an awareness of your *Fach* or voice type. As mentioned previously

in this book, there are some roles that are sung by a variety of singers and thus seem to defy easy categorization (e.g., Eisenstein in *Die
Fledermaus*, Danilo and Hanna in *Die lustige Witwe*, etc.), but most
parts tend to fall into clear-cut categories. You should know if you are
a leading lady, soubrette, contralto, leading man, character tenor, patter baritone, or buffo bass. And then you should know which roles fit
those paradigms so you can select audition repertoire befitting your
voice and stage personality. (Flip back to chapters 2 and 3 if you want
to review discussions of operetta voice types and character types.)
Within your *Fach*, you should aim to select pieces that showcase different aspects of yourself both vocally and dramatically. Look for contrast
not just in musical tempo and mood but also in vocal elements such as
legato, agility, and articulation. For example, an ingénue or soubrette
soprano might display flashy coloratura in "Glitter and Be Gay" (*Candide*) and then highlight lyrical line in "Romance" (*The Desert Song*).
Unless you are auditioning for a specific show or a company with a
particular specialty (e.g., a Gilbert and Sullivan company or the Lehár
Festival), try to find selections that show a variety of musical styles, be
it light opera from the Viennese, French, British, or American tradition. A lyric tenor could juxtapose Coward with Kálmán by presenting
"If You Could Only Come with Me" (*Bitter Sweet*) and "Wenn man das
Leben durch's Champagnerglas betrachet" (*Die Zirkusprinzessin*). Finally, aim to reveal different dramatic elements to show your range as
an actor. A mezzo-soprano can contrast the Tipsy Waltz (*La Périchole*)
with Mad Margaret's mad scene (*Ruddigore*), revealing the ability to
play both tipsy and crazy.

　　If possible, find out if the company for which you are auditioning likes
to hear excerpts from the show(s) they are casting, as preferences vary
and sometimes they do not want to hear a hundred renditions of "Poor
Wandering One." No one "owns" repertoire, but it is best not offer a
popular audition aria unless you are confident your interpretation will
stand out among the crowded field of Major-Generals. This is especially
the case if you are auditioning for artist representation in Germany;
beware of overdone audition arias such as "Dein ist mein ganzes Herz."
Agents may "find it both hilarious and painful that so many English-
speaking tenors from virtually every tenor *Fach* bring this aria for auditions. The same goes for sopranos and *Viljalied*."[1]

KNOW YOUR VENUE

In selecting repertoire and preparing for your audition, you need to make sure you know your venue. Are you auditioning for an opera company, a light opera company, a theater company, or a competition? There are differing requirements and approaches for each.

Auditioning for Opera Companies and Young Artist Programs

Singers auditioning for opera companies and young artist programs usually prepare an audition package of four to five arias, typically one each in Italian, French, German, and English. If the company requires a fifth aria, sometimes people include an aria in Russian, Czech, or Spanish or an aria that reveals proficiency in baroque or contemporary opera. Or if the company is doing an operetta or musical, the fifth selection may be an English piece that is from operetta or music theater. Check the individual company requirements carefully because they can vary greatly depending on the season the company has planned. For instance, Charlottesville Opera asked applicants for its 2017 young artist program to present an excerpt from the role they hoped to perform/cover and an excerpt from music theater, specifying, "Please, no belting." The website YAP Tracker (www.yaptracker.com) has become the standard means of gathering repertoire requirements and completing applications for most auditions for opera young artist programs.

The four-aria package still seems the standard for many young artist programs. For years, Kim Witman, director of Wolf Trap Opera, has compiled detailed aria-frequency lists that are available on the Wolf Trap blog.[2] Of those auditioning for Wolf Trap's 2016 Filene Young Artist program, here are the light opera arias that singers included in their audition packages:

Sopranos: "Klänge der Heimat" (*Die Fledermaus*): 5 percent of arias
"Glitter and Be Gay" (*Candide*): 3 percent of arias
Adele's Audition Aria (*Die Fledermaus*): 2 percent of arias

	"Mein Herr Marquis" (*Die Fledermaus*): 2 percent of arias
	"Meine Lippen, sie küssen so heiß" (*Giuditta*): 2 percent of arias
Mezzo-sopranos:	"Chacun à son goût" (*Die Fledermaus*): 5 percent of arias
Tenors:	"Dein ist mein ganzes Herz" (*Das Land des Lächelns*): 8 percent of arias
Baritones:	"Fair Moon, to Thee I Sing" (*HMS Pinafore*): 1 percent of arias

Operetta arias obviously aren't dominating these aria lists, but clearly *Die Fledermaus* is dominant when light opera selections are included.

When auditioning for summer opera workshops and music festivals, and other pay-to-sing opera programs, the requirement is more likely to be just two contrasting arias. Among summer festivals, it is noteworthy that the Miami Music Festival includes a unique Zarzuela Program, although a zarzuela aria is not required for the audition.

Auditioning for Light Opera Companies

Teatro de la Zarzuela in Madrid does require two zarzuela arias for their auditions. (For more on zarzuela, see chapter 8.) Most light opera companies ask for singers to bring two to three audition pieces. In their YAP Tracker audition listing, professional company Ohio Light Opera (OLO) asks for two selections "of contrasting styles. These selections should target the applicant's optimum vocal facility, range and character development. At least one selection for the audition must be in English. Musical theatre selections are acceptable." In addition to the vocal selections, OLO applicants must present a one-minute monologue from memory. This is one of the primary differences in auditioning for light opera companies versus traditional opera companies, although occasionally traditional opera companies also have this requirement. The College Light Opera Company audition requires a monologue as well, in addition to two music theater pieces of differing styles (one up-tempo, one ballad) and one opera or operetta aria in English.

When preparing a monologue, try to seek advice and hopefully coaching from a theater professional. Be sure your monologue is age appropriate. Avoid overdone selections; there are numerous websites tallying the offenders, such as Luisa's monologue preceding "Much More" from *The Fantasticks*. It is also a good idea to avoid monologues with obscenities and strong sexual innuendo since those elements are not stylistically appropriate to operetta as a genre. Similarly, a comedic monologue is obviously more fitting than a dramatic one from a Greek tragedy or a Sam Shepard play. *Backstage* magazine has a useful online resource called "The Monologuer," which can help you search monologues by age, gender, and theme. Or you can look for an appropriate monologue that is actually from an operetta. Gilbert and Sullivan has a number of useful excerpts, especially for baritones. Here are some possibilities:

Sopranos:	Princess Ida, *Princess Ida*, act II: "Women of Adamant, fair neophytes."
	Rose, *Ruddigore*, act I: "Hush, dear aunt, for thy words pain me sorely."
Mezzos:	Tessa, *The Gondoliers*, act II: "You see it was like this." [Cut the opening line, "Yes, we thought you'd like it."]
Contraltos:	Hannah, *Ruddigore*, act II: "Well, sir, and what would you with me?"
	Lady Sophy, *Utopia, Limited*, act I: "It is useless. Listen."
Tenors:	Hilarion, *Princess Ida*, act I: "In my mind's eye . . ."
	Fairfax, *The Yeomen of the Guard*, act II: "Two days gone, and no news of poor Fairfax."
Baritones:	John Wells, *The Sorcerer*, act I: "Yes, we practice necromancy . . ."
	Lord Chancellor, *Iolanthe*, act I: "I thank your Lordships." Or act II: "Victory! Victory!"
	Duke of Plaza-Toro, *The Gondoliers*, act II: "I am now about to address myself to the gentleman whom my daughter married."
Bass-Baritones:	Sir Marmaduke, *The Sorcerer*, act I: "Pooh, pooh, sir!"

Sir Despard, *Ruddigore*, act I: "Poor children, how they loathe me."

Alternately, you might put together a monologue by carefully editing dialogue from a scene. Here's an entertaining example from act I of *Iolanthe*.

Original dialogue:

STREPHON. Hush! My bride knows nothing of my fairyhood. I dare not tell her, lest it frighten her. She thinks me mortal, and prefers me so.

LEILA. Your fairyhood doesn't seem to have done you much good.

STREPHON. Much good! My dear aunt! It's the curse of my existence! What's the use of being half a fairy? My body can creep through a key-hole, but what's the good of that when my legs are left kicking behind? I can make myself invisible down to the waist, but that's of no use when my legs remain exposed to view! My brain is a fairy brain, but from the waist downwards I'm a gibbering idiot. My upper half is immortal, but my lower half grows older every day, and some day or other must die of old age. What's to become of my upper half when I've buried my lower half I really don't know!

FAIRIES. Poor fellow!

QUEEN. I see your difficulty, but with a fairy brain you should seek an intellectual sphere of action. Let me see. I've a borough or two at my disposal. Would you like to go into Parliament?

IOLANTHE. A fairy Member! That would be delightful!

STREPHON. I'm afraid I should do no good there—you see, down to the waist, I'm a Tory of the most determined description, but my legs are a couple of confounded Radicals, and, on a division, they'd be sure to take me into the wrong lobby. You see, they're two to one, which is a strong working majority.

Possible monologue:

STREPHON. My bride knows nothing of my fairyhood. I dare not tell her, lest it frighten her. She thinks me mortal, and prefers me so. It's the curse of my existence! What's the use of being half a fairy? My body can creep through a keyhole, but what's the good of that when my legs are left kicking behind? I can make myself invisible down to the waist, but that's of no use when my legs remain exposed to view! My brain is a fairy brain, but from the waist downwards I'm a gibbering idiot. My upper half is immortal, but my lower half grows older every day, and some day or other must die of old age. What's to become of my upper half when I've buried my lower half I really don't know! Down to the waist, I'm a Tory of the most determined description, but my legs are a couple of confounded Radicals, and, on a division, they'd be sure to take me into the wrong lobby. You see, they're two to one, which is a strong working majority.

Auditioning for Theater Companies

The process is very different when auditioning for a theater company, but you shouldn't automatically eliminate the possibility since regional theaters sometimes produce operettas, especially Gilbert and Sullivan. Most likely, you will not sing a song in its entirety. Instead, you will need a sixteen-bar or thirty-two-bar excerpt in the style of the show for which you are auditioning. Most often, theater companies do not permit selections from the actual show being cast. With the information in chapter 3 and appendix C, you should be able to find a comparable piece for your character type to fit the role for which you are vying. For example, if they are casting Nanki-Poo in *The Mikado*, instead of singing "A Wandering Minstrel I" you can sing sixteen bars from the similarly lyrical "Take a Pair of Sparkling Eyes" from *The Gondoliers* instead. In addition, you should have a second, contrasting song ready in case the company requests it. A possible contrast could be found in Edwin's wordy and womanizing "Oh, Gentleman, Listen, I Pray" from *Trial by Jury*. In fact, it's good to have an audition book with some different options too, just in case, but at minimum have an up-tempo and a ballad.

Again, you may be asked to present a monologue. When auditioning for theater companies, I would not recommend doing a monologue from an operetta. Safer bets would be monologues from musicals, although it is best to avoid doing something from a show currently on Broadway. Here are some ideas:

Sopranos:	Eliza Doolittle, *My Fair Lady*: "My aunt died of influenza, so they said."
Contraltos:	Queen Aggravain, *Once Upon a Mattress*: "Well then, how can you say such a thing?"
Tenors:	Sancho Panza, *Man of La Mancha*: "My lady, my master has sent me . . ."
Baritones:	Man in Chair, *The Drowsy Chaperone*: "Okay, now here it comes."

If you choose a monologue from a play, you might consider one written during the age of operetta. Oscar Wilde's plays could have some fruitful possibilities, although you might avoid the highly popular monologues from *The Importance of Being Earnest* in favor of something from *An Ideal Husband*, *Lady Windermere's Fan*, or *A Woman of No Importance*. An intriguing idea might be doing a monologue from a Noël Coward play when auditioning for a Noël Coward operetta. With that in mind, here are some suggestions:

For women:

Myra Arundel, *Hay Fever*: "Well, I'm not going to spare your feelings . . ."
Amanda Prynne, *Private Lives*: "I don't expect you to understand . . ."
Elvira Condomine, *Blithe Spirit*: "I sat there, on the other side, just longing for you . . ."
Judith Bliss, *Hay Fever*: "I'm much more dignified on the stage than in the country . . ."

For men:

Elyot Chase, *Private Lives*: "Let's be superficial and pity the poor philosophers."
Victor Prynne, *Private Lives*: "It's a tremendous relief to me . . ."
Garry Essendine, *Present Laughter*: "I don't give a hoot about posterity." Or: "I was right about you from the first. You're as predatory as hell!"

Hopefully, you will get a callback audition. Then they may ask you to sing something from the show or to do a cold reading of sides from the show. You may even be asked to do a dance audition, so you should dress accordingly and bring character or jazz shoes.

If you are a member of Actors Equity Association, you may do Equity Principal Auditions (EPAs) or Equity Chorus Calls (ECCs). If it is an open audition, then both Equity and non-Equity auditionees may participate equally. (Most opera singers are non-Equity but may be members of AGMA, the American Guild of Musical Artists.) There are also a number of unified auditions where you are seen by multiple theater companies at once. You may pay an audition fee (ranging from $30 to $60), but you save money you would have spent traveling to the fifty to one hundred companies that can hear you at a unified audition. These auditions are often for summer stock and Shakespeare festivals, thus they typically take place in February or March so that they can cast for summer shows or upcoming repertory. Some unifieds are geared to Equity actors or those with a master's degree in theater, such as UPTAs (the United Professional Theatre Auditions) in Memphis. But the StrawHat Auditions held in New York City are non-Equity. You get ninety seconds to present what they call a "song & monologue audition," which should begin with your singing. Other unifieds include SETC (Southeastern Theatre Conference), NETC (New England Theatre Conference) in Boston, and MWTA (Midwest Theatre Auditions) in St. Louis.

Auditioning for Competitions

At the prestigious Metropolitan Opera National Council Auditions, light opera arias are not frequently seen on applicants' repertoire lists. As with the Wolf Trap aria lists, the operetta selections that do tend to appear are the favorites from *Die Fledermaus*. But light opera plays a role in Plácido Domingo's Operalia competition, which has a zarzuela category. Singers in the competition submit a list of four arias, plus two zarzuela arias if they want to be considered for that section of the competition. Operalia typically awards two zarzuela prizes, one to a female singer and one to a male singer. The Pepita Embil Prize and the Don

Plácido Domingo Ferrer Prize are named in honor of Domingo's parents, who founded their own zarzuela company in Mexico.
A true operetta competition is a rarity, but a few do exist. Komárno, Slovakia, hosts the International Operetta Singing Competition of Franz Lehár with the cooperation of the Budapest Operetta Theatre. Aiming to popularize the genre and discover new talent, this operetta competition has three categories: two solo and one duet. The solo categories are for *prima donna* (dramatic and lyric soprano) and *bon vivant* (heroic and lyric tenor), while the duet category is for soubrette and buffo and requires choreography. In the first and second rounds, the soloists offer various arias by classic operetta composers, specified in the guidelines as Johann Strauss II, Emmerich Kálmán, Jacques Offenbach, Franz von Suppé, Jenő Huszka, Albert Szirmai, or a composer from the singer's native country. The preliminary rounds take place throughout Slovakia, Hungary, Poland, Romania, the Czech Republic, and Russia. Competitors sing from a specific list of arias and duets in the finals, which are performed with an orchestra. Here were the selections for the final round of the 2016 competition: ♪

Prima donna arias:

"Liebe, du Himmel auf Erden" (*Paganini*)
"Meine Lippen, sie küssen so heiß" (*Giuditta*)
"Lisa's Entrance" (*Das Land des Lächelns*)
"Hör' ich Zimbalklänge" (*Zigeunerliebe*)

Bon vivant arias:

"Dein ist mein ganzes Herz" (*Das Land des Lächelns*)
"O Mädchen, mein Mädchen" (*Friederike*)
"Ich bin ein Zigeunerkind" (*Zigeunerliebe*)
"Von Apfelblüten einen Kranz" (*Das Land des Lächelns*)

Prima donna/bon vivant duets:

"Lippen schweigen" (*Die lustige Witwe*)
"Wer hat die Liebe uns ins Herz gesenkt" (*Das Land des Lächelns*)
"Bei einem Tee à deux" (*Das Land des Lächelns*)
"Endlich, Józsi, bist du hier" (*Zigeunerliebe*)

Soubrette/buffo duets:

"Bohème-duett" (*Der Graf von Luxemburg*)
"Heute Abend komm ich zu dir" (*Der Zarewitsch*)
"Meine Liebe, deine Liebe" (*Das Land des Lächelns*)

This very extensive and exhaustive competition seems truly dedicated to the art of light opera. A less involved competition is sponsored by the Jackson Symphony Orchestra in Michigan. The Harold Haugh Light Opera Vocal Competition requires entrants to sing two arias, one from light opera and another from opera or oratorio. Unlike most competitions, including the Lehár competition and the Met Auditions, the Harold Haugh Light Opera Competition has no upper age limit, although singers must not have professional representation or full-time performing experience. The 2016 winner triumphed with *Naughty Marietta's* "Italian Street Song," while in 2008 it was Adele's Audition Aria that won the competition.

Figure 6.1. Rebekah Howell sings Adele's Audition Aria at the National Opera Association's 2016 Vocal Competition. *Photo by Richard Poppino*

ADVICE FROM THE CASTING TABLE

Of course, the big question singers long to ask when they audition is, "What are you looking for?" Auditions typically do not include time for feedback or constructive criticism, so singers are left to wonder what the audition panel wants to hear and see from auditionees. For this reason, I surveyed a number of sources (opera directors, theater directors, music directors) to see what they are hoping to see and hear from the casting table. Here are some of their thoughts. Use these insights to help shape your audition preparation and process.

> Just good solid legit singing, with lots of rhythmic life. And a sense of character. Show it through your singing. Make choices. Don't come in as if you're singing a recital program with no sense of who you are. Don't stand in the crook of the piano and be blank. We already know you sing well. That's a given. Show us something that's going to be of interest to us.
>
> —David Weiller, Music Director, College Light Opera Company

> I want to be moved. The voice may be perfect, but if the singer doesn't speak to me (and likely our audience) in a unique way with his/her performance, they're missing the point. Have something to say that only you can say!
>
> —David Holley, Artistic Director,
> Greensboro Light Opera and Song, Greensboro Opera

> In operetta, I'm looking not just for strong vocal ability but also personality, communication, and comedic instincts. It's a difficult combination to find!
>
> —Patrick Harvey, Music Staff, Santa Fe Opera

> In most operettas, I'm looking for triple-threats or, at absolute minimum, double-threats. There are often dance elements, and I want my leads to be part of the action, not off to the side observing the chorus or supers. So, I want to find great singer/actors who can dance as well. They don't have to have all the skills of top-notch musical theatre dancers, but they must at least be somewhat versed in ballroom styles or have the potential to learn quickly. If the dance

skills aren't there, I'll still consider a performer if they have both excellent singing and acting chops.

—Heather Nicole Winter, Director/Librettist,
The Pirates of Pinafore

When casting operetta, I look for three things, although maybe not all in every character, but: dancing, dialogue, and drama; and by that third "d" word I mean comedy. Can the singer move in a stylish way, deliver convincing spoken text, and handle comedy with instinctive timing?

—Paul Houghtaling, Artistic Director, Druid City Opera
Workshop; Director, University of Alabama Opera Theatre

For operetta, I am particularly interested in style. More than anything else, I am interested in performers who have an understanding and comprehension of the musical and dramatic style of the genre. Performers who communicate clearly and artfully while having fun within the style of operetta are of great interest. Seeking the guidance of those who specialize in the area is of the utmost importance.

—James Marvel, Director of Opera, University of Tennessee

I always look for embodiment head to toe of the song. I am always amazed by the idea that someone is so moved that they need to sing, but they often stand stock still. Obviously they should be grounded but they need to be moved literally and figuratively.

—Christopher Edwards, Artistic Director,
Actors' Shakespeare Project

When I'm casting my shows, I'm looking for trained singers who can act! Yes, I want a great voice, but more importantly I want someone who understands what they're singing about! They must be able to convey the emotion and story with interesting and dynamic choices to an audience. If I'm not moved in the audition studio, then I'm sure my audience will not be moved either. And be an individual. Don't be a carbon copy of another performer . . . be yourself! And do your homework. Understand the style and type of show you're going in for and prepare accordingly.

—Kurt Stamm, Artistic Director, Saugatuck Center for the Arts

Musical Theatre singers have an advantage in their ability to put text and story first. If they hang on to that, then lengthen vowels and get consistent vibrato, MT singers sing light opera very successfully. When I'm casting, I am always looking for singers who are connected to the text, and then are singing in the appropriate style.

—Beth Burrier, Musical Director, Penn State School of Theatre;
Principal Conductor, College Light Opera Company

Particularly when we're going to do something in English that has good humor, I'm looking to make sure their English diction is really clear and natural. Then I want to see that they have a personality that's a little whimsical or quirky so that they have something unique and special; because in those kind of shows, even the romantic lead has some quirky, funny moments. So you have to show something that says I have a personality of my own and I have some interesting thoughts of my own, because the more you bring to the director, quite frankly the more they work on other things and tweak what you do and help you along instead of trying to teach you to act essentially, which takes time. I may not want somebody who is scared to try, or scared to look like a fool. Especially when it's operetta, or musical theatre for that matter, you have to be willing to take risks. It needs to feel spontaneous. Even if it's planned, I have to feel they are in the moment.

—Ann Marie Wilcox-Daehn, Director,
Missouri State University Opera Theater

When casting an operetta, I tend to closely examine a singer's ability to deliver spoken text. In the audition room, I often provide singers with a series of sides from the script, and facilitate a cold reading to see how they work with the language. For many classically trained singers, this is, perhaps, the most challenging component. In operetta, like musical theatre, the spoken text is what advances the plot—similar to recitative in the world of opera. A singer's inability to deliver spoken dialogue with ease and clarity is detrimental to the success of any operetta. Second, but certainly of no less importance, is the necessity for flexibility in a singer's physical presentation. Operetta is an incredibly physical art form. Gilbert and Sullivan's canon, for example, is heavily stylized—particularly in those traditional realizations. A singer's ability to remain agile and flexible is imperative for success in this genre. As many operettas incorporate the use of dance (Romberg's *The Student Prince*), stage combat (Gilbert and Sullivan's *The Pirates of Penzance*), and heavily stylized movement (Gilbert and Sullivan's *The Mikado*), it is necessary to assemble a cast of singers who have a strong fluency in physical expression.

> —Justin John Moniz, Associate Executive Director,
> Hawaii Performing Arts Festival

With regard to casting, I will be honest. Not everyone is cut out for comic opera, or operetta. Just like not every singer is appropriate for *Rent* or *Wicked*. And this doesn't just come down to vocal chops. I would say that the mastery of style is the most important quality. An understanding and love for the material is equally important. I have sat in on many casting sessions (both for NY Casting Directors and NYGASP), and I consider myself lucky to have had that insiders' view. You begin to stop thinking about the machine that is the casting process, and really look for what YOU (as the creative staff) need to fill roles and tell the story. NYGASP very specifically seeks singer/actor/dancers with the skills necessary to fit within a preexisting repertory company. In the audition room, we can sense almost immediately if the singer "gets it." I've watched many amazing performers go into the "no" pile because of this lack of understanding. My advice to actors looking to perform operetta is to read and watch as much of it as you can before going into the room. Educate yourself by becoming immersed in the material. Learn about the historical context in which it was written. There aren't many millennials out there who just "get" being a Victorian. I would also advise getting coaching from someone connected to the genre. A good director will coach you on your role once you have the job; why not get ahead of the game? When you walk into the room, be confident and have a good time singing the material. These characters come to life because of honesty. If you enjoy what you're performing, we (and eventually the audience) will enjoy watching you perform it.

> —James Mills, Resident Baritone, New York Gilbert & Sullivan
> Players; Stage Director, College Light Opera Company

NOTES

1. Philip Shepard, *What the Fach?! The Definitive Guide for Singers Auditioning and Working in Germany, Austria and Switzerland*, 2nd ed. (Kansas City, MO: What the Fach?! Press, 2010), 35.

2. Kim Witman, "Aria Frequency Lists," Wolf Trap Opera website, accessed February 26, 2017, http://opera.wolftrap.org/for-artists/audition-resources/.

7

DIRECTING LIGHT OPERA

EMBRACING THE ABSURDITY

As discussed in chapter 5, light opera is about schmaltz and kitsch. It embraces absurdity, for it always seems to demand substantial suspension of disbelief. Numerous operetta plots involve a formula of mistaken identities (*The Gondoliers, The Pirates of Penzance, The Fortune Teller, Arizona Lady, Countess Maritza, Wiener Blut*) and/or implausible disguises (*Die Fledermaus, Die Zirkusprinzessin, La Périchole, Ruddigore, Princess Ida, The Firefly*). F. Paul Driscoll, editor in chief of *Opera News*, appreciates light opera's "atmosphere of absurdity" but notes that "absurdity is relative. It's not Arthur Miller."[1] While some detractors of operetta might malign its formulaic nature, Driscoll defends it, saying it is "formulaic in a glorious sense, but that's because it works."[2] In fact, almost every theatrical art form has some sort of formula or theatrical convention, be it a Shakespearean play, a Rodgers and Hammerstein musical, a television sitcom, or a Michael Jackson music video. Understanding the formula and making it work for the audience is a key part of the director's job. It is no different in operetta, with its abundance of corny shtick, cheesy romance, and dubious denouement. Even the most mainstream operettas are rife with ridiculous situations requiring careful and creative direction to help the audience grasp the complexities and absurdities presented. Director Heather Nicole Winter observes that full and unapologetic commitment is obligatory in mounting an effective light opera production.

> Theatrically, I think that the director and cast must fully and unapologetically embrace the tone of the show. In Gilbert and Sullivan, that is the fun, silly melodrama of "switched-at-birth" and "duty first, even when it doesn't make sense" kinds of plots. In Victor Herbert, it is romanticism that could rival a paperback. In Offenbach, well, just about anything goes. No matter what the tone of the particular show, the creative team must indulge fully in the over-the-top nature because the audience will spot a half-committed performer a mile away.[3]

While most operetta plots are delightfully implausible, there are a few that deserve extra credit for their incredibly inventive (or inane) libretti. Instead of a countess or a princess, Kálmán's *Arizona Lady* (1954) has a racehorse for its title character. In this Viennese operetta set in Tucson, a Hungarian lady named Lona runs a ranch in the American Southwest. When Arizona Lady is stolen, Roy, the Colorado cowboy who tamed her, is arrested for the crime. Despite being jailed, he escapes to a bar that straddles the Mexican-American border but returns to explain his identity to Lona. He is exonerated, Arizona Lady is returned, and Lona gives the horse to Roy. In the climax of the plot, Arizona Lady is entered in the Kentucky Derby, and Lona agrees to marry the Sheriff immediately if the filly wins, which she does. But the Sheriff acknowledges Lona's love for cowboy Roy, who she marries instead. Appropriately, Arizona Opera presented *Arizona Lady* in 2015. Translated by conductor Kathleen Kelly and Arizona poet laureate Alberto Rios into a new English/Spanish/German multilingual adaptation, the production of this rodeo operetta showcased not just singing and dancing but also roping skills.

Another fun but far-fetched Kálmán show is *Die Zirkusprinzessin* (1926) or *The Circus Princess*. As one could imagine, the cast is composed of circus performers, including aerialists and jugglers. The princess of the title, Fedora, is wooed by the mysterious Mister X, a tightrope walker pretending to be a prince who really is Prince Korossow. (Apparently, tightrope walkers in light opera aren't unique to *Die Zirkusprinzessin*, since they also appear in Ganne's *Les saltimbanques* and Offenbach's *La princesse de Trébizonde*.) Mister X is known for his signature move, the "Devil's Leap," in which he plays the violin while on the trapeze before jumping onto the back of a horse. This unlikely maneuver would seem to be painful for both horse and rider/violinist/ tightrope walker! The exciting theatrical possibilities of this circus-themed show make it both challenging and appealing to produce. Not surprisingly, directors are drawn to a big top or even Cirque du Soleil concept, providing an obvious marketing ploy not always available when programming Kálmán. In recent years, *The Circus Princess* has been produced by the Chicago Folks Operetta, Estonian National Opera, Deutsche Oper am Rhein, Komische Oper Berlin, and Volksoper Wien. ♪

Perhaps my favorite absurd operetta, albeit an obscure one, is *Le grand mogol* (1877) by Edmond Audran (1840–1901). Set in eighteenth-century Delhi, this *opéra comique* features a quack Parisian dentist named Joquelet, his snake-charmer sister Irma, and a Grand Vizier or Muslim minister of state. (A grand vizier also appears in Sullivan's *The Rose of Persia* and the zarzuela *El asombro de Damasco* by Pablo Luna.) Joquelet introduces Irma in a scene reminiscent of Tobias's introduction of Pirelli in *Sweeney Todd*, but since it is set in India, Joquelet says to the crowd: "Messieurs les hindous et Mesdames les hindoues" (Hindu gentlemen and Hindu ladies). Irma falls in love with Prince Mingapour, the future Grand Mogol, who must maintain his virginity in order to attain his title. He wears a white pearl collar, formerly worn by Buddha, which will supposedly turn black if his purity is sacrificed. When the pearls turn black in act III, Mingapour is stripped of his title. But in act IV, a scroll floats down the river and reveals that the pearls have no magic powers. In cahoots with the evil Vizier, a corrupt British captain drugs Mingapour with opium and plans to meet Irma for an evening of amours disguised as her prince. But widowed Princess Bengaline meets him instead, disguised as Irma, and after their rendezvous, the captain is forced to marry Bengaline to save her virtue. Irma and Mingapour marry, Mingapour becomes the Grand Mogol, and Joquelet becomes the Grand Vizier.

American light opera star Lillian Russell (1860–1922) headlined the Broadway version, *The Grand Mogul*, in 1881. A revised adaptation of the show, renamed *The Snake Charmer*, retained little of Audran

Figure 7.1. Theatrical poster for Audran's *Le grand mogol* (1886) at the Théâtre Français de Bordeaux. *Creative Commons (CCBY-SA 3.0)*

but showcased Russell as Irma, renamed D'Jemma, posing with fake snakes. A modern director might imagine Irma's snake-charming waltz, "Chanson du Kiri-Kiribi ('Allons, petit serpent')," realized with a live python, as in Britney Spears's famous 2001 MTV Video Music Awards performance. While *Le grand mogol* does not yet appear to be finding its way back into the repertory, the right production could realize its ample design opportunities and reveal the charm in its unique cast of characters. But be it in these lesser-known shows or the familiar staples, the director must accept and embrace the absurdity inherent in light opera as a genre, reveling in ridiculousness and resisting eye-rolling. As College Light Opera Company conductor David Weiller says, the trick is to make sure you are "paying homage to the material and not poking fun at it."[4]

AVOIDING CULTURAL INSULT

Racism

For better or for worse, light opera can reflect the outdated views of a bygone era. Sometimes these views are manifested in racially insensitive portrayals or references. Friml's *Rose-Marie* is a notable example. Set in Saskatchewan, the operetta features a French Canadian heroine and her Royal Canadian Mountie love interest. One of the leading Native American characters, Black Eagle, is portrayed as jealous and hot-blooded, while his lover Wanda, called a "half-blooded Indian," ends up being his murderer. Even the music seems to represent a stereotyped view of Native Americans. ♪

> In the woefully politically incorrect "Totem Tom Tom," not only do Indianist musical clichés such as drone fifths and the incessant repetition of distinctive rhythmic motifs dominate the sound world, but the text promotes an image of Native Canadians as drunkards who only dance and sleep. . . . Possibly the centrality of this musical number has prohibited *Rose-Marie* from enjoying a renewed popularity through revivals.[5]

Sometimes character descriptions can use potentially offensive or outdated language. For instance, Niña Estrella in Manuel Penella's *Don*

Gil de Alcalá is described as a "mulatto orphan," while Kálmán's *Die Herzogin von Chicago* (or *The Duchess of Chicago*) calls for Bobby to be "a black man in the jazz band." But the most overtly offensive reference to African Americans is the song "Jump, Jim Crow!" from *Maytime*. The chorus contains these lyrics: "Jump, jump, oh jump, Jim Crow! Take a little twirl and around you go! Slide, slide and point your toe, you're as naughty as a devil when you jump Jim Crow!" In an odd mixture of styles, the Jim Crow song is preceded by a mazurka and followed by a Spanish dance. Ohio Light Opera wisely omitted "Jump, Jim Crow!" from its 2005 production and CD release.

With the lure of exotic locations, a number of operettas have Middle Eastern settings, even though the librettists probably had little or no firsthand knowledge of the Muslim culture they were portraying. The results can be some potentially insensitive stereotypes in the characterizations, such as the "marauding moor" Mourzouk in Charles Lecocq's *Giroflé-Girofla* and the murderous Melchor in José Serrano's zarzuela *Moros y Cristianos*. For example, Sullivan's *The Rose of Persia* stars a sultan with twenty-five wives, although there are really twenty-six, but he has lost count. His wives have names like Rose in Bloom, Dancing Sunbeam, and Blush of Morning. Accompanied by this harem chorus, the High Priest Abdullah sings his entrance aria, "When Islam First Arose," in which he sings of things that "every Moslem knows," so the Basil Hood lyrics tell us. Act II of Romberg's *The Desert Song* begins with the Spanish-themed chorus "My Little Castagnette," which is followed by a Spanish dance and then the number "Eastern and Western Love." In this piece, Ali Ben Ali sings "Let love come as some rare treasure granted by Allah" before launching into his not-so-subtle polygamous metaphors: "If one flower grows alone in your garden, soft petals blooming must wither someday. Love's bowers should be overflowing with sweet passion flowers of varied perfume. So gather your precious collection, a harem of blossoms, love's fire to consume." Thus, in light opera, there appears to be a somewhat one-dimensional view of Middle Eastern culture and the Muslim religion.

In recent times, the operetta that has faced the most scrutiny for its inherent cultural insult is *The Mikado*. The Seattle Gilbert and Sullivan Society received an outpouring of protest in reaction to their 2014 *Mikado*. In the Pacific Northwest, with its considerable Asian

American population, there was great uproar over the whitewashing of Japanese characters. Of course, the original D'Oyly Carte cast was entirely Caucasian, and W. S. Gilbert was mocking not the Japanese but his fellow Brits. Still, the character names themselves can seem patronizing, along with the caricature characters. *Seattle Times* columnist Sharon Pian Chan described it as "the yellowface of *The Mikado* in your face" that "opens old wounds and resurrects pejorative stereotypes."[6] Similar responses have occurred with recent productions of Puccini's operas *Madama Butterfly* and *Turandot*, John Adams's *Nixon in China*, and the musical *Miss Saigon*, although more effort has been made to cast Asian singers as Asian characters, particularly in the latter's 2017 Broadway revival. Skylight Opera addressed this sensitive issue by collaborating with Asian American company Mu Performing Arts on their 2013 *Mikado*, which was reset in Edwardian England with a predominantly Asian cast and altered character names—for instance, Ko-Ko became Co-Co. The New York Gilbert & Sullivan Players decided to cancel their December 2015 production of *The Mikado* after strong backlash, but they rescheduled for the next year and worked with an advisory panel to find a new context for the show. The final product included a newly written prologue featuring Gilbert and Sullivan as characters in the show, along with Richard D'Oyly Carte, with the three going on to play Pish-Tush, Ko-Ko, and Pooh-Bah in the opera proper. After an outcry from the San Francisco community, the Lamplighters Music Theatre had a different approach for their 2016 *The Mikado*, which eventually took place in Renaissance Milan, Italy. In 2017, the Kentucky Opera avoided controversy with a diverse cast juxtaposing punk and Margaret Thatcher–style conservatism in a setting of 1980s Britain. These examples prove that directing *The Mikado* does not have to be a cultural land mine. It is possible to rethink and reframe the work in a way that is not disrespectful to Japanese Americans. Although it is less familiar in North America, *Das Land des Lächelns* (or *The Land of Smiles*) also presents challenges in respect to its portrayal of Chinese culture, as does Offenbach's *Ba-ta-clan*. Therefore, directors need to be cognizant of twenty-first-century views when producing these nineteenth-century works, and they must ponder new ways to interpret shows like *The Mikado* so they can entertain and satirize without insult. ♪

Sexism

Since light opera originated in the nineteenth century, it typically reflects very traditional gender roles. Women are sweet and obedient—unless they are gypsies—and men are brave soldiers. These paradigms are found in many of these shows, especially the American operettas by Romberg, Friml, and Herbert. There are manly marches, such as "Stout-Hearted Men" (*The New Moon*), "The Mounties" (*Rose-Marie*), and "Tramp! Tramp! Tramp!" (*Naughty Marietta*), which reinforce the strength and masculinity of the male characters in their martial solidity. Meanwhile, women are demure and deferential, as in "Always Do as People Say You Should" (*The Fortune Teller*) and "The Dear Little Girl Who Is Good" (*Mlle. Modiste*). But sometimes there is a slightly new spin, as in *The Desert Song*. Singing "I'll Be a Buoyant Gal," sweet-natured secretary Susan vows to be appealing so she can get a husband, while the female chorus asks "Why did we marry soldiers?" and states that "nights are hell without our men." But then in the "French Military Marching Song," Margot enters with other women dressed as soldiers who sing, "Aren't we fine?" The march is briefly ruled by the ladies until the "gallant fighting men of France" do arrive to reclaim it for the second chorus.

One could argue that there is implied misogyny in songs such as "You Can Never Tell about a Woman" (*The Red Mill*), which describes women as fickle, unfathomable creatures. One could also argue that Gilbert reveals a misogynist and ageist view of his older female characters, such as Ruth (*The Pirates of Penzance*) and Katisha (*The Mikado*), in their roles as desperate spinsters or "cougars." It would seem that *Princess Ida* might be seen as an antidote to sexual stereotypes in other Savoy operas. In her act II monologue/mission statement, Ida proclaims "Woman, in her turn, shall conquer Man" and argues that "though Man professes that he holds our sex in utter scorn, I venture to believe he'd rather pass the day with one of you, than with five hundred of his fellow-men!" *Princess Ida* was written in reaction to the creation of women's colleges such as Girton (founded 1869) and Newnham College (1871) at Cambridge University and Lady Margaret Hall (1878) and Somerville (1879) at Oxford University. Today, *Princess Ida* remains problematic, for in the twenty-first century, "the opera's subject seems even more unfortunate, a heavy-handed, patronizing satire on women's right to be taken seriously, especially in regard to higher education" and "a résumé of situation-comedy clichés about women, their wiles, illogicality and obsession with fashion."[7] As a Newnham alumna and Vassar graduate, I hope someday to stage a version of the operetta that can find the balance between history and humor to both celebrate and spoof. The San Jose Lyric Theatre found a way to bring contemporary relevance to the show by linking its 2017 production with a fund-raiser for the Malala Fund, which was created by Nobel Peace Prize–winner Malala Yousafzai. Malala has been an inspiring advocate for the education of young women, and she reminds us that the subject of *Princess Ida* might not be so outdated after all, since many women across the globe still face discrimination in education. ♪

UPDATING FOR IMPACT

Having sung several seasons with Ohio Light Opera, mezzo-soprano Ann Marie Wilcox-Daehn is well versed in operetta; she acknowledges the challenges of the genre, noting "the clichés and the stereotyping that were completely acceptable at the time and in fact maybe even encouraged. It is very formulaic and that can be problematic, or if you are willing, the nice thing is that so much of this is in the public domain that you can make some small changes."[8] While the company most often has leaned toward traditional realizations, Dr. Daehn recalls performing in Ohio Light Opera's 1994 production of *La belle Hélène,* which was given a 1970s update and an abundance of fluorescent polyester costumes. Now as a director herself, she is planning a version of *Orpheus in the Underworld* that will be presented in an actual cavern in the Missouri Ozarks. This creative concept is in line with current opera trends, which include new and alternative venues and site-specific performing spaces.

Making use of new venues is just one way to breathe new life and bring revitalized interest to these classic operettas. In the 1990s, when I was a proud member of the Cambridge University Gilbert and Sullivan Society (CUGSS), the productions of the Savoy shows were done in traditional theatrical venues such as the Cambridge Arts Theatre. Now CUGSS seems to favor outdoor performing spaces when possible. They have presented *The Gondoliers* at the waterfront of St.

Figure 7.2. University of Alabama Opera Theatre's 2014 production of
Patience. **Photo by Michelle Lepianka Carter**

John's College along the River Cam (which has its own Bridge of
Sighs), and each year they mount a show at the Minack Theatre amid
the cliffs of the Cornwall coast.

Of course, opera directors love to update by changing the time period, especially for timely contemporary political commentary. In 2008,
Opera in the Ozarks set their *Mikado* during the presidential election
and featured a Hillary Clinton Katisha. Similarly, Opera Omaha's 2012
Mikado made reference to the 2012 presidential election. Since Gilbert
and Sullivan's operas are full of political satire, they often work well with
carefully constructed and creative updates. For instance, director Paul
Houghtaling cleverly turned the University of Alabama (UA) Opera
Theatre's 2014 production of *Patience* into an exploration of sorority life
and football culture at UA. In 2016, the Oregon Shakespeare Festival
premiered a country-western adaptation of *The Yeomen of the Guard* in
an "immersive" setting with part of the audience onstage with the actors. The production received several positive reviews, but some Savoy
purists might find it difficult to hear Gilbert and Sullivan accompanied

by banjo and dobro. In a like-minded musical update, the 2011 Guthrie Theater production of *HMS Pinafore* did not change the setting but updated the music with disco-style arrangements à la ABBA. Changing the actual music of an operetta is a risky choice. Changing the setting is an easy way for directors to make something more relatable for modern audiences and more affordable for costume budgets. However, it does not always serve the original work, thus updating concepts need to be contemplated with great care and attention to detail as well as context. Apparently the 2013 Metropolitan Opera production of *Die Fledermaus* was originally going to be updated to modern-day Manhattan. Director Jeremy Sams (b. 1957) eventually decided against this concept.

> Mr. Sams concluded that many of the things that make the plot work would simply not make sense—especially Dr. Falke's desire for revenge for the humiliation he felt years earlier when he was forced to wander the streets dressed as a bat, the *Fledermaus* of the title, after a drunken costume party. "In New York, these things come as standard," Mr. Sams said.[9]

SELECTING THE VERSION

Of course, a major decision is selecting which version of an operetta to direct. For example, if you are doing *The Merry Widow*, will you do the original German version in its entirety? Or will you have the sung portion in German but the dialogue in English? Or if you decide to do it all in English, will it be in the Jeremy Sams or Donald Pippin translation? The answer will depend on your audience and your performers. To make foreign-language operettas more accessible to audiences or to student singers, directors are often choosing to produce them in new English translations. Sams has created translations for operettas such as *The Merry Widow*, *La Périchole*, and *Orpheus in the Underworld*. Publisher Josef Weinberger lists a number of light opera options for licensing on their website; for *The Merry Widow*, they have multiple English versions from which to choose, including translations by Sams, Christopher Hassall, John Wells, Nigel Douglas, and Sheldon Harnick. Donald Pippin (b. 1925), founder of Pocket Opera, has made a number of useful and effective translations, most notably of a dozen Offenbach operettas (among them *The Bandits*, *Bluebeard*, *Carnival in Venice*, and

The Princess of Trebizonde). Despite his considerable contributions, the ever-modest Pippin seems to downplay his translations, saying, "I don't translate, I stay true to the central core of the story, in my own language."[10] Of course, the ultimate way for directors to update an operetta and put their unique spin on it is to create an original translation, but the director must have sufficient time and planning to prepare for such an extensive endeavor. ♪

When programming *Candide*, the director faces a unique conundrum: Which of the five available versions should you produce? Fortunately, the official Leonard Bernstein site clearly elucidates the differences in the five versions available. Composed by the inimitable Leonard Bernstein (1918–1990), *Candide* premiered on Broadway in 1956 but closed after a short two-month run. Director Harold Prince (b. 1928) oversaw the Broadway revival in 1973, which replaced Lillian Hellman's libretto with a new book by Hugh Wheeler. This so-called Chelsea version also incorporated new lyrics by Stephen Sondheim. With its condensed structure and reduced orchestration, the one-act Chelsea version is well suited for smaller theatrical forces and venues. Prince continued his *Candide* collaboration when he directed the 1982 production at the New York City Opera, known as the "opera-house version," which restored many musical numbers and returned to a larger orchestra. Before his death in 1990, Bernstein made his own updates for the "final revised version" or concert version, conducting and recording it in 1989 with the London Symphony Orchestra. In *Candide*'s seemingly continual evolution, the Scottish Opera version (1988) included some new music, while the Royal National Theatre production (1999) featured a revised libretto by director John Caird. Which version of *Candide* you choose determines whether your performance rights are through a theatrical licensing agency or a music publisher: The Chelsea and Royal National Theatre versions are available through Music Theatre International (MTI), while the Scottish Opera, New York City Opera, and concert versions are handled by Bernstein's publisher, Boosey and Hawkes. ♪

Not ready to relinquish his influence on Bernstein's operetta, Prince returned to *Candide* for its 1997 Broadway revival and 2017 New York City Opera performances at Jazz at Lincoln Center's Rose Theater, starring Linda Lavin as the Old Lady. Prince seems to be the definitive director of *Candide*, having guided it through several revisions and updates. Perhaps his unique vision illuminates the work as the rare mid-twentieth-century operetta, still rife with satire but joining the musical traditions of nineteenth-century light opera with the new creativity and rhythmic energy Bernstein brought to his compositions. Biographer Foster Hirsch sees Prince as the ideal interpreter of this work, whether you label it musical or operetta.

> Directed with swaggering theatricality, Prince's opera-house production substantiated his claim that serious musical theatre and opera share common ground and can have a similar impact on audiences. Like Bernstein's score, by turns passionate and sly, Prince's showmanship filled the huge opera stage, demonstrating finally that *Candide* is a total theatre work which dismantles the boundaries between Broadway and Lincoln Center.[11]

SINGERS AS DIRECTORS

In the opera world, the singer turned director is not uncommon. Singers such as Renata Scotto went from careers as international opera stars to international opera stage directors. In light opera, a number of singers turned directors have played prominent parts in the propagation of operetta across the country.

James Stuart (1928–2005) started his performing career with Dorothy Raedler's American Savoyards and the Martyn Green Gilbert and Sullivan Company and went on to found Ohio Light Opera (OLO) in 1979. In his twenty-year tenure as artistic director of the company, Stuart performed in over fifty OLO shows and directed many more of them. For instance, in the opening 1979 season, he directed all nine productions and starred in seven of them (as the Duke of Plaza-Toro in *The Gondoliers*, Sir Joseph Porter in *HMS Pinafore*, the Lord Chancellor in *Iolanthe*, Major-General Stanley in *The Pirates of Penzance*, Ko-Ko in *The Mikado*, Sir Ruthven Murgatroyd in *Ruddigore*, and Jack Point in *The Yeomen of the Guard*). In addition, Stuart created and premiered new English translations for many works, including Kálmán's *Der Zigeunerprimas* and Offenbach's *Monsieur Choufleuri*. In his immense dedication to the genre, Stuart fully realized his goal for OLO: "My objective from the beginning with OLO was to return artistic integrity to operetta. Through coaching on the importance of taking light opera seriously, the company has nurtured an audience that has itself gained a new appreciation for a once seemingly moribund art form."[12]

Lyric tenor David Holley made a name for himself at OLO, playing the title roles in *Fra Diavolo, The Count of Luxembourg, Orpheus in the Underworld,* and *Der Vogelhändler.* After a busy performing career, Holley became director of opera at the University of North Carolina at Greensboro in 1992. In 2012, Holley founded Greensboro Light Opera and Song (GLOS), a young artist summer training program. No doubt inspired in part by OLO, GLOS has shown forward thinking in its efforts to revive operetta and reach new audiences. Their 2016 *Trial by Jury* was produced at the local county courthouse and even featured an actual North Carolina superior court judge playing the part of the Learned Judge.

Another link from OLO to GLOS is Dawn Harris. Harris played more than thirty roles during her time as a resident soprano with OLO, including Fiametta in *Boccaccio,* Kathie in *The Student Prince,* Pepi in *Wiener Blut,* Gabrielle in *La vie parisienne,* and her signature role, Yum-Yum in *The Mikado.* Currently she is codirector of Opera Studio at the University of Illinois at Urbana-Champaign. Harris directed the 2016 GLOS productions of *Trial by Jury* and *Ruddigore,* which featured mezzo-soprano Cheyna Alexander as Mad Margaret. Alexander notes that Harris "did all the choreography herself, and she always showed us physically what she wanted from each character, whether it be the peppiness of the bridesmaids or the crazy mannerisms of Mad Margaret. She would tell us stories about different G&S productions she was in,"[13] thus using her vast experience as a singer to guide the performers in her production.

Following his initial passion for music theater, James Mills discovered Gilbert and Sullivan during his student years performing with the College Light Opera Company (CLOC). His CLOC contacts and impressive patter skills led to a successful audition for the New York Gilbert & Sullivan Players (NYGASP) who asked him to join the company in 2006. Since then, Mills has performed all thirteen Gilbert and Sullivan operas, and over twelve seasons at NYGASP he has risen to the rank of principal comic baritone. In 2016, he returned to CLOC as a stage director and had the chance to direct his favorite Savoy show, *The Yeomen of the Guard*. Mills shares:

> I felt honored to be directing a show I had performed at CLOC, and to be sharing my passion for G&S with the young artists. The schedule was nerve-wracking. Putting on a show in a week is no easy feat for anyone. Coaching the principals and shaping the ensemble was priority number one. We worked very hard to add focus, nuance and tension to this, the most serious and realistic of Gilbert's libretti. What I discovered was that it isn't hard to make magic on stage when your actors are so receptive and believe in the story they are telling. It's a two-way street. I was lucky and had a great cast, but I do credit much of my success on the production to my love for the material and my unwavering desire to get beautiful, honest performances from my cast.[14]

James Mills, Dawn Harris, David Holley, James Stuart—the lineage, from Ohio Light Opera to Greensboro Light Opera and Song and from College Light Opera Company to New York Gilbert & Sullivan Players shows the strength of the singer turned director as a powerful proponent of operetta in America.

CHOREOGRAPHERS AS DIRECTORS

Another trend in light opera is the choreographer as director. Dance can comprise a significant portion of characterization in operetta, so it is not surprising that a director grounded in movement could be helpful in this genre. Choreographers are usually former dancers, therefore their extensive training in style and line, be it from ballet or ballroom dance, is a perfect fit for the stylized waltzes and specialized can-cans that inhabit the repertory. Furthermore, choreographers often think in beautiful "stage pictures" befitting the nineteenth-century origin and ethos of so many light operas. I had the pleasure of being directed by Dorothy Danner in the Piedmont Opera Theatre's 1999 production of *The Merry Widow*. I watched intently as she moved seamlessly from directing dialogue to choreographing dance numbers. The unified gestalt brought a streamlined quality to the show. Dorothy, a.k.a.

Figure 7.3.   College Light Opera Company's 2015 production of *The Merry Widow*. Photo by Juliana MacLachlan

Dottie, danced on Broadway in nine shows, including Michael Bennett's *Ballroom*. In a 2012 radio interview about her *Mikado* production for Opera Omaha, Danner spoke of the impact of her dance background on her directing: "I was a Broadway gypsy for years, had a wonderful time, and that gives you a certain rhythm in your work and a certain physicality which I think is very right for comedy."[15] It is also very right for light opera, which no doubt is why Danner has had a long career directing *Candide, The Student Prince, HMS Pinafore, The Pirates of Penzance, Iolanthe, Die Fledermaus, La Périchole*, and *The Grand Duchess of Gerolstein* for the Chautauqua Opera, Cleveland Opera, Dayton Opera, Glimmerglass Opera, Houston Grand Opera, Orlando Opera, Virginia Opera, and other companies.

Before Danner, another Dorothy paved the way for the operetta director/choreographer. Dorothy Raedler (1917–1993) founded the Masque and Lyre Light Opera Company in 1939, later renaming the troupe the American Savoyards in 1952. Raedler went on to direct productions for the City Center Gilbert and Sullivan Company, Baltimore Civic Opera, and New York City Opera, as well as off-Broadway at the

Sullivan Street Playhouse. Known for her "painstakingly precise direction," Raedler had done exhaustive research in England on Gilbert and Sullivan, consulting "their original promptbooks, paying careful attention to staging, with the intent of blocking her operettas in a manner similar to the originals."[16] Although she adhered strictly to the D'Oyly Carte ideals, Raedler was known for doing all of her own choreography.

More recently, an example of the director/choreographer is Susan Stroman. In an interview with Lyn Cramer, Stroman described her unified and stylistic theatrical vision, which is ideal for operetta:

> I just loved the whole idea of singing and dancing. Ever since I was a little girl, I have had this passion, this obsession. When I hear music, I see visions of people dancing. It's always been that way, so I can't listen to music if I want to relax. I dream of people moving, dancing, and acting. . . . I think when you are a choreographer or director in the theatre, you do immerse yourself in a specific geographical area, decade, and societal norms of that particular time period.[17]

As the Metropolitan Opera started to hire more Broadway stage directors, Stroman was a natural fit when they were looking for someone to helm a dance-heavy show like *The Merry Widow*. Stroman's *Merry Widow* was produced by the Lyric Opera of Chicago in 2015 and returns to the Met for the 2017–2018 season, starring Susan Graham. With their work, Raedler, Danner, and Stroman have paved the way for the next generation of directors/choreographers in light opera and female directors/choreographers in particular.

NOTES

1. F. Paul Driscoll, phone interview, February 23, 2017.
2. Ibid.
3. Heather Nicole Winter, e-mail interview, February 12, 2017.
4. David Weiller, interview, February 17, 2017.
5. William A. Everett, "Romance, Nostalgia and Nevermore: American and British Operetta in the 1920s," *The Cambridge Companion to the Musical*, ed. William A. Everett and Paul R. Laird (Cambridge: Cambridge University Press, 2002), 50.

6. Sharon Pian Chan, "The Yellowface of *The Mikado* in Your Face," *Seattle Times*, July 13, 2014, accessed April 11, 2017, http://old.seattletimes.com/html/opinion/2024050056_mikadosharonpianchancolumn14xml.html.

7. Geoffrey Smith, *The Savoy Operas: A New Guide to Gilbert and Sullivan* (New York: Universe Books, 1985), 115, 123.

8. Ann Marie Wilcox-Daehn, interview, April 9, 2017.

9. Michael Cooper, "Mirth amid Strauss Waltzes: Jeremy Sams Directs *Die Fledermaus* at the Met," *New York Times*, December 26, 2013, accessed April 21, 2017, www.nytimes.com/2013/12/29/arts/music/jeremy-sams-directs-die-fledermaus-at-the-met.html.

10. Donald Pippin, interview with Janos Gereben, "Pippin of the Pocket," *San Francisco Classical Voice*, April 13, 2010, accessed April 21, 2017, https://www.sfcv.org/article/pippin-of-the-pocket.

11. Foster Hirsch, *Harold Prince and the American Musical Theatre*, expanded ed. (New York: Applause Theatre & Cinema Books, 2005), 156.

12. James F. Stuart, "Taking Light Opera Seriously! The Legacy of OLO Founder James F. Stuart," *The Ohio Light Opera 2016 Program*, June 14, 2015, accessed April 12, 2017, https://issuu.com/lpcpub/docs/olo_program15_final-4issuu.

13. Cheyna Alexander, e-mail interview, April 12, 2017.

14. James Mills, e-mail interview, April 12, 2017.

15. Dorothy Danner, radio interview with Dave Ringert, Opera Omaha, YouTube, April 10, 2012, accessed April 10, 2017, www.youtube.com/watch?v=FEbI2byGc0s.

16. Anne Fliotsos and Wendy Vierow, *American Women Stage Directors of the Twentieth Century* (Urbana: University of Illinois Press, 2008), 365, 360.

17. Susan Stroman, interview with Lyn Cramer, *Creating Musical Theatre: Conversations with Broadway Directors and Choreographers* (London: Bloomsbury, 2013), 203, 211.

8

ZARZUELA

Christopher Webber

Given the genre's long history and wide stylistic variety, you may be surprised to find Spanish zarzuela[1] popping up in a book devoted to singing light opera. It is quite true that many classic zarzuelas center on those sunny, amorous plots associated with the lighter operatic repertoire. The difference is that the fun is almost always tied to the social, political, or aesthetic concerns central to Spanish *comedia*, which encompasses rich and poor alike, tragedy as well as comedy. All human life is here: the nineteenth- and twentieth-century zarzuela repertoire boasts everything from swashbuckling historical epic to *verismo* melodrama and sexy, satirical revue. Zarzuelas come in all shapes and sizes. The eminent composer Ruperto Chapí (1851–1909), for example, turned out everything from Wagnerian-length, three-act tragedies such as *Curro Vargas* (1898) to half-hour vaudeville squibs, taking in shapely French-style romantic operettas and brilliant one-act farces along the way such as *La revoltosa* (1897). Zarzuela's range is dazzling and extends far beyond the "escapism" usually thought—fairly or unfairly—to define light opera.

On the other hand, if we look at the question from the practical performer's point of view, a different perspective emerges. There are of course exceptions, but zarzuela may be described broadly as a popular,

Figure 8.1. Palau de les Arts Reina Sofia's 2007 production of Chapí's *La bruja*. Photo by *Tato Baeza*

Spanish-language operatic form with spoken dialogue—lots of it. So if you want to sing zarzuela, whether as a soloist or a chorus singer, you are going to have to master the same range of sung and spoken techniques that you would need to perform Offenbach, Sullivan, Victor Herbert, or Lehár, with their widely differing styles. And that's just for starters. You will need to study operatic singing intensively. Training in classical acting and farce would also be advisable, along with dance classes plus a general grounding in Spain's literary heritage and her *costumbrista* (everyday folk culture). Not surprisingly, a lyric genre that has its roots in the Renaissance demands a Renaissance woman or man to do it justice.

For those reasons, I believe that zarzuela's place in this book is justified. My aim is to provide a brief historical outline for readers new to the genre together with information on the vocal types of singers and actors employed, plus a little about training and the preparation needed to perform zarzuela nowadays. Especially in the United States, with its growing Hispanic population, the genre is likely to present many more opportunities than it has in the past, whether in Spanish or English; and quite aside from the satisfaction it gives both sides of the footlights when performed well, zarzuela training is unquestionably an advantage for any

singer who wishes to spend time onstage or in the concert hall, whether
as an amateur or professional. No less a singer than Plácido Domingo—
whose parents ran a large company touring Spain and Mexico—regards
zarzuela as the foundation of his whole vocal and dramatic art.[2]

HISTORICAL OVERVIEW

Baroque Zarzuela

Zarzuela owes its existence to the Spanish royal family's desire to put
their country on the operatic map. For political reasons, King Philip
IV needed to devise an alternative to the opera fashionable in early to
mid-seventeenth-century France and Italy. There was plenty of music at
his royal courts, but the difficulty was that Spain boasted a flourishing,
high-powered theatrical tradition all her own, which had to be accom-
modated. As with Shakespeare in England, Spain's great "Golden Age"
playwrights could call on impressive acting and scenic resources far superior to anything previously seen in theater history. Music already had
an important place in this scheme of things, and royal patrons had no ap-
petite for the through-sung recitative operas coming to the fore in Italy
and (later) at the French court in Versailles. So although Spain needed
to show that she was abreast of the fashion, fully fledged opera was to
remain an exotic rarity in Spanish theater, just as it did in England.

The answer lay in compromise. At the royal hunting lodge of La Zarzuela outside Madrid, the "creative team" could muster a motley bunch
of female actor-singers, rustic clowns, and dancers, plus a handful of instrumentalists led by the court harpist Juan Hidalgo (1614–1685). It was
the celebrated playwright Pedro Calderón de la Barca (1600 1681) who
skillfully mixed these elements together in mythological plots combining
verse drama for the gods and heroes, pastoral prose comedy for the rustic clowns, and songs and dances. The birth of these so-called zarzuela
entertainments is symbolically celebrated in *El laurel de Apolo* (music
lost but probably by Hidalgo, 1658), although in reality they originated
at least a decade earlier. The new form proved popular in Spain's public
theaters as well as at court, and eventually zarzuela came to represent
native Spanish-speaking musical drama, very much in opposition to
foreign-language opera from France and Italy.

Tonadilla escénica

By the mid-eighteenth century, zarzuela was losing the game. Just as in George Frideric Handel's London, Italian opera seria was now the Madrid fashion, and the native product descended into coarse comedies with simple, popular music. By the 1770s, the only flourishing Spanish-language lyric theater was the *tonadilla escénica*, twenty-minute vignettes of popular life and character often placed as *intermedios* (intermezzos) between the acts of long Italian operas. The literary master of the form was Ramón de la Cruz (1731–1794), who kept the idea of native music theater alive—he also provided the libretto for one of the very few "quality" zarzuelas of the time, the two-act comedy *Clementina* (1786), which has excellent music by Luigi Boccherini (1743–1805) in a classical, Mozartian vein. Although the *tonadilla escénica* died out after the Napoleonic era, its ethos of scathing antiestablishment social commentary embedded in fast-moving amorous intrigue was to hint at zarzuela's future.

Romantic Zarzuela

The rebirth of zarzuela during the time of Queen Isabella II (who reigned on and off from 1833 to 1868) was largely down to the influence of one hugely influential composer and musicologist—Francisco Asenjo Barbieri (1823–1894)—and his talented circle of writers, musicians, and singers. For Barbieri, modern zarzuela could embody a national artistic expression, mirroring Spain's contemporary struggle for political and social liberalization. Soon it came to represent that struggle, enshrined as *the* national art form in such seminal zarzuelas as Barbieri's *Pan y toros* (1864, a historical epic set in French-dominated Napoleonic Madrid) and the exuberant political comedy *El barberillo de Lavapiés* (1874). These works are cornerstones of the modern repertoire. ♪

In the hundred years between 1850 and 1950, something like 10,000 zarzuelas were written, most of course ephemeral but surprisingly many—about 120 or so—still widely loved and performed throughout Spain and the Spanish-speaking world. During that century, romantic zarzuela developed many forms, and at its apogee during the 1890s it completely dominated Spanish theatrical life. Although modern musicology has shown that the conventionally accepted time line of these subgenres is far too simplistic, it is still helpful to describe the six most important.

Zarzuela grande   "Large zarzuela." The three-act zarzuela was developed in the 1850s by Barbieri and his friends, initially using librettos adapted from Parisian opéra comique and Italianate music in bel canto style, but using Spanish song and dance rhythms in some solo numbers and ensembles. Madrid's elegant Teatro de la Zarzuela was built in 1856 as a permanent home for the reborn genre. Like its French parent, *zarzuela grande* covers a huge range of subject matter—comic, fantastic, and tragic—and it employs the full orchestral and choral resources of the nineteenth-century opera house, with a large roster of vocal soloists and actors. There are impressive examples throughout romantic zarzuela's history, from Barbieri's longer works until the turbulent years before the Spanish Civil War. Amadeo Vives's (1871–1932) three-act masterpiece *Doña Francisquita* (1923), a glowingly nostalgic portrait of mid-nineteenth-century Madrid based on a "Golden Age" play by Lope de Vega (1562–1635), in a way sums up this entire zarzuela tradition. ♪

Género chico   "Short genre." Madrid's many popular theaters in the late nineteenth and early twentieth century employed a system of *teatro por horas* (i.e., "theater by the hour"). Three or more works would be performed during the course of an evening, and patrons could attend as many or as few as they liked.[3] This system engendered a staggering number of *sainetes* (short plays) with more or less music performed in rotation by permanent companies of actors and singers. These plays were farcical and satirical and were almost always set in the poor quarters of the capital itself, peopled by working-class and "low-life" characters. Many of the very greatest zarzuelas—one-act classics such as *La verbena de la Paloma* (1894) by Tomás Bretón (1850–1923) and Chapí's *La revoltosa*—were written for Madrid's *teatro por horas* companies, performing at legendary venues such as Teatro Apolo. The music for these works is lighter in style than *zarzuela grande*. It is based on urban Spanish dance and song styles, needs a mixture of operatic and popular-style voices, and still features a very important role for the chorus. For many aficionados, *género chico* zarzuela is the unique flower of Spanish lyric theater, with the best examples able to stand proudly beside the greatest operas and operettas of their time for dramatic and musical interest.

Zarzuela chica   "Short zarzuela." Throughout the history of romantic zarzuela, another one-act comedic form thrived, similar to French equivalents such as Chabrier's *Une éducation manquée* (1879), and dealing (like that work) with middle-class domestic or theatrical life. *Zarzuela chica* is similar in scale to the dominant *género chico* form but more polite in aesthetic and more cosmopolitan in musical style. Like the three-act *zarzuelas grandes*, these shorter works require bel canto operatic singers. Well-known examples would be *La viejecita* (1897) by Manuel Fernández Caballero (1835–1906), which is based on the contemporary English farce *Charley's Aunt*, and the same composer's *El dúo de "La africana"* (1893), which hilariously details amorous intrigues between cast members of a touring Italian opera company trying unsuccessfully to perform Meyerbeer's *L'Africaine*. It's rather like the Marx Brothers' *A Night at the Opera* and just as funny.

Zarzuela ínfima   "Insignificant zarzuela" was the name proudly adopted by a later, populist style of *género chico* work, more sexually liberated, atheistic, and socially committed than the 1890s classics—and consequently castigated by respectable critics and middle-class audiences for its immorality. These works are outward looking and feature popular songs and dances, many in foreign modes imported from Paris, such as the ubiquitous *cuplé* (saucy or satirical strophic song). The chorus tended to be female only, and costumes were often skimpy. Several *ínfimo* works survived in the repertoire until they were banned by General Francisco Franco's repressive regime, but they are starting to make a comeback. The most famous of them, and one of the most frequently performed of all zarzuelas, is the irrepressible *La corte de Faraón* (1910) by Vicente Lleó (1870–1922), a wickedly salacious retelling of the biblical story of Joseph and Potiphar's wife, with clever parodies of Verdi's *Aida* thrown in for good measure. So although many of the songs need light delivery, *zarzuela ínfima* still needs at least a sprinkling of operatically trained voices.

Opereta-zarzuela   The "operetta-zarzuela" flourished briefly for more than a decade after 1910, adapting the modern modes of continental operetta and the English musical play to Spanish tastes. These large-scale, often full-length, romantic works were less satirical and more sentimental than most zarzuelas and received luxurious productions—usually featuring exotic, foreign settings—in custom-built theaters as technically advanced as any in the world. Yet though they may feature classic and modern Spanish and Latin American dance forms, their music is vocally and orchestrally demanding, deploying the sophisticated harmonies and vocal power of Puccini and Italian *verismo*. Amadeo Vives and Pablo Luna (1879–1942) were major stage composers whose works in this style are still performed; a more populist example would be *La montería* (1923), a featherlight comedy by Jacinto Guerrero (1895–1951) set in rural England, featuring the "hunting and shooting" aristocracy and contemporary London "flappers."

Revista española "Spanish revue" covers a wide field of lightly plotted stage pieces (in one or more acts) written between the 1880s and 1950s, certain of which have been accepted into the zarzuela canon due to their substantial musical scores. Of these, the most famous is *La gran vía* by Federico Chueca (1846–1908), an unlikely 1886 satire on

Figure 8.2. Self-portrait of composer Federico Chueca. *Creative Commons (CCBY-SA 3.0)*

urban planning in which many of the solo singers represent streets or buildings. It proved to be Spain's most popular and internationally well-traveled stage musical.[4] Two other revues still much performed are the same composer's *El año pasado por agua* (1889) and Francisco Alonso's (1887–1948) deliciously naughty Madrid farce *Las Leandras* (1931). *Revista* needs a mixture of operatically trained voices and *cupletistas* (popular *cuplé* singers).

Critics have come up with several other variants such as the Offenbach-like *zarzuela bufa*; *operone* (opera-scale) *zarzuela*; and the nationalistic *zarzuela regional* from the 1920s, set in a specific Spanish province such as Asturias or Murcia and flavored with local folk music. There were also strongly creative twentieth-century zarzuela traditions in other Spanish-speaking countries, notably Cuba and the Philippines, but I think I had better stop there, as further discussion of all these alleged generic divisions and subdivisions might give the reader (as well as the writer) a severe headache.

Zarzuela in Decline

By the mid-1930s, it was obvious that the popularity and artistic vitality of zarzuela was faltering. One composer who managed to buck the trend was Pablo Sorozábal (1897–1988), whose *La del manojo de rosas* (1934) and *La tabernera del puerto* (1936) are nowadays the two most frequently performed works in the entire repertoire[5] and whose sweet-and-sour music is highly distinctive. Federico Moreno Torroba's (1891–1982) more conservative three-act political drama *Luisa Fernanda* (1932) has proved equally resilient—it recently toured opera theaters worldwide in a production mounted by the Washington Opera and featuring Plácido Domingo. The catastrophic Spanish Civil War (1936–1939) and the censorship that followed effectively dealt a death blow to creation of new zarzuelas; and only a handful of works written after the war by Sorozábal, such as his daringly satirical homage to Viennese operetta *Black, el payaso* (1942), have gained a firm place on the Spanish stage alongside the earlier romantic classics. ♪

USEFUL WORDS

Alborada: Dawn serenade, intended to gently awaken the beloved.
Canción: Song, generally strophic in form and simpler in content than a *romanza*.
Cantables: Sung texts.
Comedia: Spanish drama that often includes tragic elements.
Coplas: Couplets, rhyming verses. Broadly applied in zarzuela to strophic songs with comic, satirical, or risqué texts, the singular *copla* later identifies a distinct song form, especially popular in Madrid.
Dúo: Duet.
Hablados: Spoken dialogues.
Madrileña(-o): Woman (man) of Madrid.
Romanza: Romantic aria or song.
Rondalla: Traditional band of mandolin and/or bandurria players associated with weddings, fiestas, and other celebrations. Often onstage in zarzuela, adding instrumental color.
Salida: Entry song.
Terceto: Trio.
Tiple: Soprano, often specifically a light soprano or soubrette.
Zarzuelero: Composer, writer, or performer of zarzuela.

THE SINGER IN ZARZUELA: VOCAL TYPES AND STYLES

As will be apparent, the range of vocal types and styles across the history of zarzuela is as wide as we find in opera, operetta, and musical theater put together. There is no "one way" to sing zarzuela—many celebrated works from the romantic era mix characters using operatic and "popular" vocal production, even within a single musical number. It may therefore be helpful to describe the requirements of specific historical periods rather than simply order things in the "soprano, mezzo-soprano, tenor, baritone, bass" list conventional in most operatic forms.

When I put together four volumes of zarzuela songs for Music Sales Inc. some years ago, it was of course inevitable for marketing purposes to group them under the customary four voice types, but I was continually faced with questions along the lines of "Should this go in the soprano or mezzo book?" "Is this a tenor or a baritone number?" or even with one notorious hit taken from *La viejecita* (the zarzuela based on the cross-dressing farce *Charley's Aunt*), "Does this belong in the soprano or the tenor repertoire?" In other words, it should be firmly borne in mind that most of these works were written for a particular singer in a particular time and place. You may well find that a song that suits one lyric soprano perfectly may sit uneasily with another; that a mezzo-soprano chanteuse shines brilliantly in a number originally intended for light soprano; or even that a tenor may be more at ease in a baritone part than many lower voices would be. It is all a matter of what's right for you and your voice.

Singing Baroque and Classical Zarzuela

Although the surviving theater works of seventeenth- and eighteenth-century composers such as Juan Hidalgo, Sebastián Durón (1660–1716), and José de Nebra (1702–1768) sometimes speak with a Spanish accent, they share a common musical language with their contemporaries across Europe. This is first and foremost aristocratic music of the royal courts, even if on occasion the fine ladies appear before us in peasant-girl fancy dress. I specify "ladies" because nearly all of the gods, goddesses, and male heroes in these early zarzuelas were written with the monarch's resident sopranos in mind. On occasion, a bass actor might take the part of a clown in the rustic subplots, and—as in the contemporary operas of Cavalli and Rameau—a tenor might find himself *en travesti* as a lubricious, elderly female servant.

Production onstage and in concert of seventeenth- and eighteenth-century zarzuela is very much the domain of professional, historically informed baroque specialists. Yet I have seen two extremely good Hidalgo productions performed by university undergraduates in Sheffield, England, both under the direction of the leading baroque harpist Andrew Lawrence-King—most appropriately, as Hidalgo himself would certainly have led the instrumentalists in his capacity as court harpist. What is more, the original soprano soloists (who would have combined with the handful of males to sing the short choruses) would have been extremely young by modern standards, perhaps in their early or mid-teens.

The vocal production needed for these works is very similar to requirements for other operatic works of the time. The vibrato-limited, light "head voice," which allows its natural character to emerge without much if any chest resonance, is what's required for Hidalgo and Durón—just as it would be for late Monteverdi and Cavalli. The soprano range is limited, rarely straying outside the treble stave; and the same limitation holds good for the handful of male roles. Some pioneering productions outside Spain have made the mistake of saucing the instrumentation with the "Spanishry" of castanets and strumming guitars while asking the singers to produce throaty, guttural sounds and vocal flourishes more suitable to a tourist flamenco café than the gentle, rhythmic lilt and subtle wit such music calls for. This "Spanishry" is as wrong as it is vulgar, and any young soprano approaching baroque zarzuela needs to remember that it was written for sophisticated court singers, not village entertainers or Carmen wannabes.

Moving on, the vocal technique needed to sing Nebra's mid-eighteenth-century zarzuelas is very close to that of his contemporary Handel. The voice must remain light on vibrato, but given the flexibility needed to master opera seria coloratura passage work, as well as the legato line of long phrases, the student must pay closer attention to breathing and diaphragm support. Rules for improvised ornamentation of Nebra's da capo repeats apply as in Handel, with the voice working almost exclusively within the written vocal compass of the aria (quite *how* exclusively is a matter of passionate debate!). In Spanish stage works of this or any period, textual meaning must never be eclipsed by "instrumental" oversinging.

Speaking of those texts, much ink has been spilled over the alleged difficulty of singing Spanish with the purity of vowel sounds and clarity of consonants so easily obtained in Italian. In practice, this is a very natural language for vocalists, well forward in the mouth and easy to project, while the subtleties of its regular strong and weak *diptongos* (diphthongs) allows for those shades of coloring that give Spanish art song its special character. Pronunciation—different in Spain than Hispanic New World countries—has not changed radically over the last three and a half centuries, though vocabulary has; so a grounding in modern Castilian is sufficient to perform this music without much help from specialist language coaches.

Because baroque zarzuela has only recently exploded into the modern musical world, individual works—at least those from the earlier period—are being realized by historically informed performers such as Emilio Moreno working from archived manuscript scores, which consist simply of vocal parts and texts underwritten by instrumental bass lines. Printed libretti are easier to obtain (at least from academic libraries) than the music, very little of which has been commercially published. This is a pity, because many of the early Spanish *tonadas* (songs) would be as healthful "medicine for the voice" as the famous Italian *arie antiche* from the same period. Aside from listening to recordings by leading practitioners such as Raquel Andueza, singers must rely on taking part in live performances and recordings rather than private study if they are to enjoy the challenges of this corner of the zarzuela repertoire.

Singing Romantic Zarzuela

When it comes to "medicine for the voice," we find that the best-known twentieth- and twenty-first-century Spanish-speaking opera singers often point to zarzuela's role in honing their vocal muscles and shaping their artistic personality. Plácido Domingo's lifelong involvement with the genre has already been mentioned, and much the same could be said for Teresa Berganza, Montserrat Caballé, Alfredo Kraus, José Carreras, and the Mexican Rolando Villazón, all of whom have performed and recorded zarzuela—Kraus even set up his own commercial record label (Carillon) for that sole purpose. ♪

Why is this? Simply because zarzuela is much more commonly performed in Hispanic countries than opera and operetta, it provides great opportunities for inexperienced singers to learn their craft, whether at amateur or professional level. Another part of its appeal is that zarzuela music is not on the "junior slopes" of technical difficulty. Just as Mabel's "Poor Wandering One" in *The Pirates of Penzance* requires a really adept coloratura to surmount its difficulties, so a piece as demanding as "Sierras de Granada" in *La tempranica* (1900) by Gerónimo Giménez (1854–1923) calls on the full resources of the operatically trained female voice—even more than that, as this particular *romanza* also demands knowledge of flamenco *cante jondo* style if it is to communicate the emotions beneath the vocal pyrotechnics.

Theatrical Context

Here we come to a crucial point. I often hear solo songs and *romanzas* from the zarzuela repertoire nicely sung in concert. I less often hear them performed with a sense of theater, and program notes cannot always fill the gap. That's why many listeners—and even, judging from my inbox, some practitioners—wrongly understand "a zarzuela" to refer to a song (rather than a stage) genre. I'm more encouraged to hear from singers who, having discovered a lovely *romanza* in some forgotten, nineteenth-century *zarzuela grande*, ask me if I can help them find out something about the role and why the character is singing this number at that point of the story. If a singer does not do some homework on theatrical context, the result—no matter how technically impressive or beautiful on the ear—will not engage an audience deeply. That's why a zarzuela song performed by Victoria de los Ángeles or Alfredo Kraus remains fresh and memorable: These master-singers always convey a sense of situation and personality along with the musical qualities proper to each individual number.

Vocal Types

With the proviso that romantic zarzuela was often tailored to an individual talent, it is worth exploring the vocal types and divisions common to the nineteenth- and twentieth-century Spanish repertoire. Although most are familiar from opera, there are differences.

The medium-weight lyric soprano is as central to *zarzuela grande* as to French opéra comique, often in rather passive central roles. She may be required to display some dexterity, but true coloratura is a rarity in zarzuela. Lighter voices are reserved for the comedy characters, often as part of a "second couple" singing perhaps just a duet or two but bearing the main weight of the dialogue. You may come across the word *tiple* in old scores: this can mean any female singer, but it usually applies to the lighter comedian—very similar to the soubrette in Gilbert and Sullivan or operetta—rather than the romantic lead. Both lighter and heavier sopranos need classic opera training, making use of the resources of vibrato and chest voice to project over substantial pit orchestras.

Figure 8.3.   Cover of score for Moreno Torroba's *Luisa Fernanda*. *Creative Commons (CCBY-SA 3.0)*

Although mezzo-soprano is not often seen as a descriptor in Spanish vocal scores (or composer's manuscripts), many significant roles were written for women who could call upon darker timbres and ample reserves of tone both above and beneath the stave. As in nineteenth-century opera and operetta, a fair number of these were "trouser roles"—as late as 1936, Sorozábal wrote the part of the cabin boy in *La tabernera del puerto* for mezzo-soprano in homage to those earlier singers. In reality, a great operatic mezzo-soprano such as Teresa Berganza with an extension up to high B can pretty much encompass nearly any major female role in the repertoire, as her impressive list of complete zarzuela recordings shows.

The most famous operatic mezzo-soprano role of all proved a more controversial model. Though Georges Bizet took pains to provide his Carmen with at least one irrefutably Spanish song—her *Habanera* is a revision of *El arreglito* by Sebastián Iradier (1809–1865)—Madrid's critics and audiences were loath to acknowledge this freewheeling gypsy as representative of decent Spanish womanhood. Composers and librettists were more pragmatic, and Carmen's "Andalusian" vocal type, with its strong chest voice, guttural throat colorings, and audible breaks between the low, middle, and high registers, became an exotic cliché in late nineteenth- and early twentieth-century *género chico* and *zarzuela ínfima*. Typical examples of these early liberated women would be Lota (Mrs. Potiphar) in *La corte de Faraón*, who tries to seduce Joseph with some sexually provocative Egyptian gypsy flamenco turns and appoggiaturas; and the feisty actress Aurora, love-rival to the sweet heroine of *Doña Francisquita*.

Beyond this, there is an important place for nonoperatic singers in the *género chico* repertoire. I've already mentioned the role of the *cupletista* in *zarzuela ínfima* and revue, where communication of textual nuance counts for everything. The term "singing actress" has I think been overused lately to mean a good singer who can act a bit. Zarzuela conversely requires good actresses who can sing a bit. Beauty and depth of sung tone is unimportant for such roles as the vengeful wife Gargantua in *La revoltosa* or bawdy Aunty Antonia in *La verbena de la Paloma* with her terrifying pack of dogs—most of what they do is in spoken dialogue, and provided they can cut loudly through the operatic-style ensembles, it doesn't much matter how they sound. "Belt," Anglo-American commercial pop training (or none at all) is fine here. Character is everything.

The tenor is as important to romantic zarzuela as to opera and operetta, though the high, agile *tenore di grazia* familiar from Rossini is absent; after all, Barbieri and his contemporaries were striving to liberate Spanish lyric theater by eliminating such "showy" singing. Lyric tenor roles abound for lovers and libertines, some taking on the weightier and darker *spinto* qualities of Verdi, Puccini, and Wagner—it is no coincidence that one of the most-recorded zarzuela tenors was Miguel Fleta, who created the heavy role of Calaf in *Turandot* (1926). There are rich opportunities here for singers who can produce an even, attractive, and vibrant weight of tone in the two octaves around middle C, but the ability to fine the voice down to an effortless pianissimo above the stave (with or without falsetto) in such gentle *romanzas* as "Flor roja" from Guerrero's 1923 *Los gavilanes* is what divides the great from the good.

Just as indispensable is the *tenor cómico*, a light vocal type equivalent to the buffo tenor of French or Italian opera. The key qualities for the successful singer are the ability to "act through the voice" (differentiating character through varied timbre and weight of tone) and perfect diction. In Spain, many comic tenor roles are played by singers at the start of their careers to give young voices stage experience without putting undue pressure on their still-developing vocal apparatus. At the other end of the spectrum, lyric tenors often extend their careers in character work once their voices no longer have the amplitude to command the romantic heights. In zarzuela, the *tenor cómico* can sometimes find himself in a starry leading role: a famous example is Casto José ("Chaste Joseph") in *La corte de Faraón*, where Lleó brilliantly writes a very one-sided, extended love duet for the thin-voiced, evasive hero and his voluptuous admirer, Lota.

A type unique to *opereta-zarzuela* and late romantic zarzuela is the *tenor-barítono*, closer kin to the French *baryton-martin* than to the light baritone of Anglo-American operetta and musical theater. The timbre of this rare voice is essentially baritonal, darker if less weighty and cutting than a *Heldentenor* but with an extension well into the tenor range (up to high A). The tenor-baritone excels in cultivating a beautiful, rich falsetto above the stave. The two most notable exponents were the Cordovan-born, Italian-trained Marcos Redondo and his younger, honey-voiced rival Luis Sagi-Vela. Their distinctive style pervades the many lyrical-heroic lead roles written specially for them from the late 1920s until well after the Spanish Civil War; and in the 1930s, their mere appearance in a new zarzuela anywhere in Spain practically ensured commercial success. That was certainly an era of singer power!

An unusual feature of romantic zarzuela is that the leading baritone will often be cast as the hero rather than (as in so many operas and light operas) the villain of the piece. In the twentieth century, this almost became the rule rather than the exception, particularly after the advent of Emilio Sagi Barba, father of Luis Sagi-Vela and the first great male *divo* of zarzuela. The *Fach* of the zarzuela baritone is Verdian, with the emphasis on legato and lyric power rather than agility. As with the soprano, lack of an obvious break between registers is something the zarzuela-trained baritone should aim at, plus a *Lieder* singer's attention to verbal nuance. Juan Pons is among the finest recent exemplars. Although there are character roles for baritones, except in *opereta-zarzuela* these are rarely as prominent in the Spanish repertoire as those for tenor.

From its bel canto beginnings through the whole century of romantic zarzuela, the bass usually finds himself in familiar operatic territory as a father, priest, or authoritative elder. Also as in opera, this diet may be varied by some comedic and villainous opportunities (the popular bass Francisco Salas was a prominent member of the group around Barbieri and made sure he had many such parts written for him). The lowest male voice almost disappeared in the *género chico* era but made a strong comeback in *opereta-zarzuela* and the sunset years before the Spanish Civil War, when Sorozábal in particular wrote some excellent roles for cavernous basses, including the haunting tango for the drunken English sailor Simpson in *La tabernera del puerto*.

The Zarzuela Chorus

That tango features (unforgettably) a humming chorus of sleeping African American sailors, and in general terms romantic zarzuela offers good opportunities for chorus singers of both sexes. As in French opéra comique, Donizetti, and Verdi, the three-act *zarzuela grande* and later *opereta-zarzuela* usually feature one or more set-piece choruses, some of them, such as the Smoking Chorus from Caballero's *Los sobrinos del capitán Grant* (1877) and the Lovers' Chorus from *Doña Francisquita*, are as famous as any solo number or duet. There are also plenty of substantial (and technically demanding) choral scenes in *género chico* zarzuela; sometimes the chorus is at the very heart of the action, as in Chueca's *Agua, azucarillos y aguardiente* (1897). *Zarzuela ínfima* and revue almost invariably dispense with the masculine chorus but spotlight the feminine one.

Zarzuela traditionally avoids vocal ensembles for more than three solo voices, and in all but the grandest *zarzuelas grandes*, finales tend to be short and functional rather than musically elaborate. Having said that, many zarzuelas, large and small, require a host of small-part players, and more often than not, these are shared out among the chorus. Modern zarzuela production needs a substantial SATB body that can act, individuate character, and sing well too. Choral demands, as with any stage work, are less to do with projection and individuality of voice and more to do with the ability to blend well and to pay close attention to what one's colleagues (and the conductor) are doing. As to style, whereas solo singing in romantic zarzuela—especially the more Puccinian works toward the end of the era—involves subtle operatic use of rubato, portamento, and tonal inflexion, choral singing relies on dynamic control, precision, and an unfailing lack of egotism. Choruses in Spain are excellent proving grounds for young singers getting to know the repertoire, especially as contracts generally include some understudy work.

TRAINING AND OPPORTUNITIES

At all levels, there is a vast difference between the training available in Spain and Hispanic-speaking countries and elsewhere—even, perhaps surprisingly, in the United States. This is simply a matter of supply and demand, for while in Spain the classic repertoire thrives, especially with amateurs, in the United States there isn't as yet a high-enough level of activity to justify academic institutions resourcing zarzuela on a regular basis. The situation is healthiest in Florida, with its lively community of Cuban émigrés, New Mexico (where the Santa Fe Opera has toured small-scale zarzuela adaptations), and cosmopolitan New York. The Jarvis Conservatory in Napa, California, was an exception to the rule, offering courses for students and amateurs devoted exclusively to the genre, culminating in high-quality public stagings. Alas, Jarvis is no more; and though I often hear of music schools and colleges mounting the occasional zarzuela, that is generally due to the enthusiasm of a particular teacher or, even more encouragingly, the students themselves.

It is a chicken-and-egg problem, part of which relates to the broader "Hispanic Question." When a zarzuela gets professionally staged in Germany, it will be translated without question into the vernacular. Given the large quantity of spoken dialogue, to leave it in Castilian would make no sense unless you imported Spanish-speaking principals and didn't mind the audience following a lot of fast-moving surtitles rather than the stage action. Such a simple solution is not possible in the United States, where to translate Spanish-language cultural assets may give offense. Jarvis's answer was to perform the songs in Spanish (with surtitles) and the dialogue in English (without them), a perfectly sensible compromise that unfortunately didn't enhance the holistic integrity of the works themselves. Ohio Light Opera has included zarzuela just once in its long and distinguished history (1999), though I know from talking with the company that the artistic team loves the genre and would be well up to the stylistic challenge. But practical difficulties—poor availability of orchestral material outside Spain, the paucity of English translations—make it very hard to proceed on a tight professional budget.

So the main route would-be zarzuela singers can pursue is to attend a school or college specializing in the preparation of opera, light opera, and concert singing and to do everything they can to work with their teachers on individual songs and *romanzas* from the repertoire. Some American postgraduates are able to continue their studies abroad at one of the major Spanish institutions, such as Madrid Conservatoire, where revered singers[6] share their secrets with young professionals. Last but not least, Plácido Domingo's glamorous opera competition Operalia encourages students from around the world to compete for an important zarzuela prize, which brings many benefits, including the opportunity to sing and work within the genre in Spain. ♪

A Question of Dialogue

I have emphasized that zarzuela singers must be proficient in acting and dialogue, perhaps even more so than in light opera (or *Fidelio*, come to that!). A major headache for performers mixing song with spoken drama is that the two disciplines require different vocal techniques to project from stage to auditorium. In my practical experience, this chopping and changing worries some singers more than others. At worst, it can result in sing-song delivery of the dialogue in an attempt to square the technical circle. Alas, this comic opera *Sprechgesang* can too easily produce the wrong kind of amusement for audiences. Acting fashions change with the generations, and unfortunately the nineteenth- and early twentieth-century declamatory stage style is no longer viable for performers and audiences born in the televisual and Internet age. Zarzuela *hablados* widen this gap. Whether written in poetic meters or prose, they are often of good literary quality and demand an emotional and dynamic range, which makes even the sing-song solution impossible. Subtle amplification of dialogue scenes can alleviate the difficulty; and though it is true that microphones in the opera house encourage some bad technical habits, if it leaves singers and audiences free to concentrate on the drama, my response is "why not?"

I can't leave this subject without flagging up to potential singers another "solution" that is gaining ground around the operatic world in general and in Spain in particular. Recent productions at Teatro de la Zarzuela have taken to cutting dialogue to the bone, rewriting it, or on occasion removing it entirely. This unfortunately reduces zarzuelas to "concerts in costume" that make no theatrical sense. Convenient though the shortcut may be to managements keen to reduce the challenge (and expense) of mixed-form lyric theater, it is lazy. Singers don't like it either as it removes their opportunity to learn about their craft by performing these stage works in their integral form. One hopes that this particular fashion, at least, will soon run its course.

RESOURCES

Listening to recordings is one of the best ways a singer can develop a feeling for zarzuela and learn how to communicate in Spanish. If you're drawn to the baroque, Raquel Andueza's disc of zarzuela *tonadas* by Sebastián Durón on Naxos is the perfect introduction. Victoria de los Ángeles's classic EMI/Angel album *Zarzuela Arias* remains an incomparable introduction to romantic zarzuela, and there is a very satisfying Brilliant Classics box (3-CD set) of Teresa Berganza and José Carreras's recordings, simply titled *Zarzuela!* Tenors should check out Plácido Domingo's solo zarzuela discs (EMI) and Rolando Villazón's *Gitano* album on Virgin Classics. Baritones—do listen to those old records of Luis Sagi-Vela and Marcos Redondo online if you can. Recordings of complete scores are harder to source, even online; Deutsche Grammophon's recent, excellent series was not distributed outside Spain, though if you can find the one featuring María Bayo in *La tempranica*, she offers a model of modern zarzuela vocal technique. There is plenty of zarzuela to be found on YouTube, mainly of amateur productions, most of it with less-than-optimal picture and sound quality. Still, with live zarzuela productions in American theaters still a rarity, that is better than nothing.

Further Reading

If you need a handy guide to the genre, I must first recommend my own book *The Zarzuela Companion* (Scarecrow Press, 2002). I would blush deeper, if it were not currently the *only* such guide in English! It has synopses and analyses of many major zarzuelas; biographies of the leading composers, writers, and singers; and much else. Despite its dry title, Clinton D. Young's *Music Theater and Popular Nationalism in Spain, 1880–1930* (Louisiana State University Press, 2016) is a very readable and illuminating historical guide to romantic zarzuela's richest period. If you read Spanish, the *Diccionario de la zarzuela* (ICCMU, 2 vols., ed. Emilio Casares Rodicio, 2006) is your bible, full of excellent entries on Cuban as well as Iberian zarzuela.

As to song books, Music Sales America published two sets of zarzuela compilations that are readily available. The first set is titled *Zarzuela!* (2001), the second *Siempre zarzuela* (2012). Both consist of four books (soprano, mezzo-soprano, tenor, and baritone) containing twelve songs each in a variety of styles; and both provide full English translations and contextual notes, giving singers a clear idea about who is singing, where, and why. These are currently the best primary sources available to singers keen to study this rich repertoire.

FINAL THOUGHTS

Given its musical and theatrical attractions—not to mention champion-
ing from such prominent singers as Domingo and Villazón—zarzuela's
low profile in non-Hispanic countries remains baffling. For when audiences (even in China and Japan) *do* get the chance to see and hear the
género chico and three-act classics, their enthusiasm is great. The old
excuses for ignoring the genre—lack of orchestral materials, the difficulty of obtaining performing rights, competition from opera and operetta—hold little water these days when well-edited critical editions are
digitally available from Madrid and where YouTube and Spotify enable
us to get acquainted with the music in a couple of clicks. It is probably
a question of time. Zarzuela's star in the United States is rising, and it
is not only young Hispanic singers who are exploring its potential. Zarzuela is truly for anyone and everyone interested in singing and acting
beyond the boundaries of the traditional operatic repertoire.

NOTES

1. *Zarzuela* can be pronounced either [θar'θwela] (Spanish Castilian style)
or [zar'zwela] (Spanish New World and American English style), according to
personal preference.

2. See Domingo's introduction to Christopher Webber, *The Zarzuela Companion* (Lanham, MD: Scarecrow Press, 2002).

3. Hervé and Offenbach had instituted similar systems in the 1850s in Paris
for the promotion of their own short works.

4. Curiously, *La gran vía* was much praised by the philosopher Friedrich
Nietzsche, who viewed its witty, cabaret-style songs as a trenchant counterblast
to overblown Wagnerian music drama. He saw an Italian production in Turin
during 1889.

5. According to the records of SGAE (Sociedad General de Autores y Edi-
tores) in Madrid, which is responsible for licensing performance of in-copyright
works and collecting royalties for member composers and writers.

6. Not least is Ana-María Iriarte, who recorded many complete works on the
Alhambra label way back in the 1950s! Her foundation also sponsors zarzuela
productions in Madrid.

9

SINGING AND VOICE SCIENCE

Scott McCoy

This chapter presents a concise overview of how the voice functions as a biomechanical, acoustic instrument. We will be dealing with elements of anatomy, physiology, acoustics, and resonance. But don't panic: the things you need to know are easily accessible, even if it has been many years since you last set foot in a science or math class!

All musical instruments, including the human voice, have at least four things in common, consisting of a power source, sound source (vibrator), resonator, and a system for articulation. In most cases, the person who plays the instrument provides power by pressing a key, plucking a string, or blowing into a horn. This power is used to set the sound source in motion, which creates vibrations in the air that we perceive as sound. Musical vibrators come in many forms, including strings, reeds, and human lips. The sound produced by the vibrator, however, needs a lot of help before it becomes beautiful music—we might think of it as raw material, like a lump of clay that a potter turns into a vase. Musical instruments use resonance to enhance and strengthen the sound of the vibrator, transforming it into sounds we identify as a piano, trumpet, or guitar. Finally, instruments must have a means of articulation to create the nuanced sounds of music. Let's see how these four elements are used to create the sounds of singing.

PULMONARY SYSTEM: THE POWER SOURCE OF YOUR VOICE

The human voice has a lot in common with a trumpet: both use flaps of tissue as a sound source, both use hollow tubes as resonators, and both rely on the respiratory (pulmonary) system for power. If you stop to think about it, you quickly realize why breathing is so important for singing. First and foremost, it keeps us alive through the exchange of blood gases—oxygen in, carbon dioxide out. But it also serves as the storage depot for the air we use to produce sound. Most singers rarely encounter situations in which these two functions are in conflict, but if you are required to sustain an extremely long phrase, you could find yourself in need of fresh oxygen before your lungs are totally empty.

Misconceptions about breathing for singing are rampant. Fortunately, most are easily dispelled. We must start with a brief foray into the world of physics in the guise of Boyle's Law. Some of you no doubt remember this principle: the pressure of a gas within a container changes inversely with changes of volume. If the quantity of a gas is constant and its container is made smaller, pressure rises. But if we make the container get bigger, pressure goes down. Boyle's law explains everything that happens when we breathe, especially when we combine it with another physical law: nature abhors a vacuum. If one location has reduced pressure, air flows from an area of higher pressure to equalize the two, and vice versa. So if we can create a zone of reduced air pressure by expanding our lungs, air automatically flows in to restore balance. When air pressure in the lungs is increased, it has no choice but to flow outward.

As we all know, the air we breathe goes in and out of our lungs. Each lung contains millions and millions of tiny air sacs called alveoli, where gases are exchanged. The alveoli also function like ultra-miniature versions of the bladder for a bag pipe, storing the air that will be used to set the vocal folds into vibration. To get the air in and out of them, all we need to do is make the lungs larger for inhalation and smaller for exhalation. Always remember this relationship between cause and effect during breathing: we inhale because we make ourselves large; we exhale because we make ourselves smaller. Unfortunately, the lungs are organs, not muscles, and have no ability on their own to accomplish this feat. For this reason, your bodies came from the factory with special muscles designed to enlarge and compress your entire thorax (rib cage), while simultaneously moving your lungs. We can classify these muscles in two main categories: any muscle that has the ability to increase the volume capacity of the thorax serves an inspiratory function; any muscle that has the ability to decrease the volume capacity of the thorax serves an expiratory function.

Your largest muscle of inspiration is called the diaphragm (figure 9.1). This dome-shaped muscle originates from the bottom of your sternum (breastbone) and completely fills the area from that point around your ribs to your spine. It's the second-largest muscle in your body, but you probably have no conscious awareness of it or ability to directly control it. When we take a deep breath, the diaphragm contracts and the central

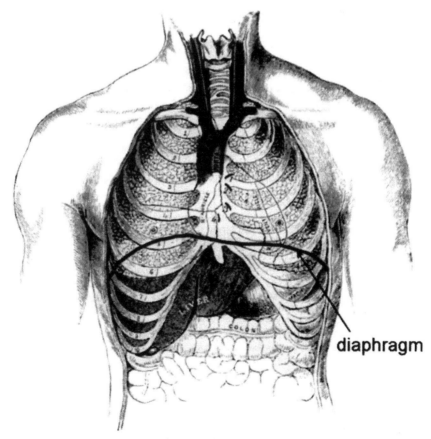

diaphragm

Figure 9.1. Location of diaphragm. *Courtesy of Scott McCoy*

portion flattens out and drops downward a couple inches into your abdomen, pressing against all of your internal organs. If you release tension from your abdominal muscles as you inhale, you will feel a gentle bulge in your upper or lower belly, or perhaps in your back, resulting from the displacement of your innards by the diaphragm. This is a good thing and can be used to let you know you have taken a good inhalation.

The diaphragm is important, but we must remember that it cannot function in isolation. After you inhale, it relaxes and gently returns to its resting position through an action called elastic recoil. This movement, however, is entirely passive and makes no significant contribution to generating the pressure required to sustain phonation. Therefore, it makes no sense at all to try to "sing from your diaphragm"—unless you intend to sing while you inhale, not exhale!

Eleven pairs of muscles assist the diaphragm in its inhalatory efforts, which are called the external intercostal muscles (figure 9.2). These muscles start from ribs one through eleven and connect at a slight angle downward to ribs two through twelve. When they contract, the entire thorax moves up and out, somewhat like moving a bucket handle. With the diaphragm and intercostals working together, you are able to increase the capacity of your lungs by about three to six liters, depending on your gender and overall physical stature; thus, we have quite a lot of air available to power our voices.

Eleven additional pairs of muscles are located directly under the external intercostals, which, not surprisingly, are called the internal intercostals (figure 9.2). These muscles start from ribs two through twelve and connect upward to ribs one through eleven. When they contract, they induce the opposite action of their external partners: the thorax is made smaller, inducing exhalation. Four additional pairs of expiratory muscles are located in the abdomen, beginning with the rectus (figure 9.2). The two rectus abdominis muscles run from your pubic bone to your sternum and are divided into four separate portions, called bellies of the muscle (lots of muscles have multiple bellies; it is coincidental that the bellies of the rectus are found in the location we colloquially refer to as our belly). Definition of these bellies results in the so-called ripped abdomen or six-pack of body builders and others who are especially fit.

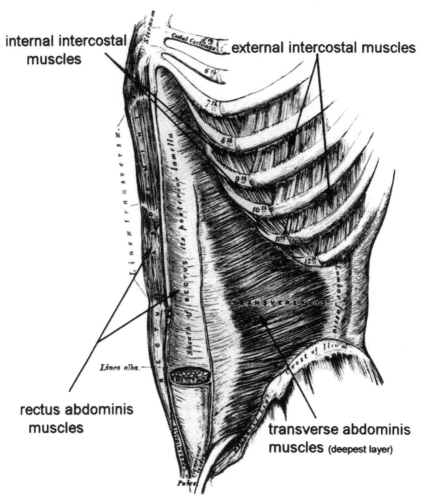

internal intercostal muscles

external intercostal muscles

rectus abdominis muscles

transverse abdominis muscles (deepest layer)

Figure 9.2. Intercostal and abdominal muscles. *Courtesy of Scott McCoy*

The largest muscles of the abdomen are called the external obliques (figure 9.3), which run at a downward angle from the sides of the rectus, covering the lower portion of the thorax, and extend all the way to the spine. The internal obliques lie immediately below, oriented at an angle that crisscrosses the external muscles. They are slightly smaller, beginning at the bottom of the thorax, rather than extending over it. The deepest muscle layer is the transverse abdominis (figure 9.2), which is oriented with fibers that run horizontally. These four muscle pairs com-

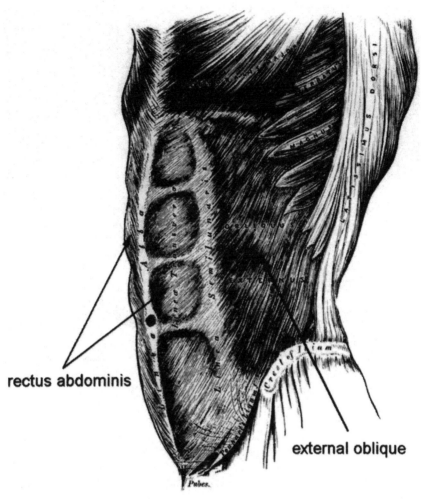

rectus abdominis

external oblique

Figure 9.3. External oblique and rectus abdominis muscles. *Courtesy of Scott McCoy*

pletely encase the abdominal region, holding your organs and digestive system in place while simultaneously helping you breathe.

Your expiratory muscles are quite large and can produce a great deal of pulmonary or air pressure. In fact, they easily can overpower the larynx. Healthy adults generally can generate more than twice the pressure that is required to produce even the loudest sounds; therefore, singers must develop a system for moderating and controlling airflow and breath pressure. This practice goes by many names, including breath support, breath control, and breath management, all of which rely on the principle of muscular antagonism. Muscles are said to have an antagonistic relationship when they work in opposing directions, usually pulling on a common point of attachment, for the sake of increasing stability or motor control. You can see a clear example of muscular antagonism in the relationship between your biceps (flexors) and triceps (extensors) when you hold out your arm. In breathing for singing, we activate inspiratory muscles (e.g., diaphragm and external intercostals) during exhalation to help control respiratory pressure and the rate at which air is expelled from the lungs.

One of the things you will notice when watching a variety of singers is that they tend to breathe in many different ways. You might think that voice teachers and scientists, who have been teaching and studying singing for hundreds, if not thousands of years, would have come to agreement on the best possible breathing technique. But for many reasons, this is not the case. For one, different musical and vocal styles place varying demands on breathing. For another, humans have a huge variety of body types, sizes, and morphologies. A breathing strategy that is successful for a tall, slender woman might be completely ineffective in a short, robust man. Our bodies actually contain a large number of muscles beyond those we've already discussed that are capable of assisting with respiration. For an example, consider your latissimi dorsi muscles. These large muscles of the arm enable us to do pull-ups (or pull-downs, depending on which exercise you perform) at the fitness center. But because they wrap around a large portion of the thorax, they also exert an expiratory force. We have at least two dozen such muscles that have secondary respiratory functions, some for exhalation and some for inhalation. When we consider all these possibilities, it is no surprise at all that there are many ways to breathe that can produce beautiful singing. Just remember to practice some muscular antagonism—maintaining a degree of inhalation posture during exhalation—and you should do well.

LARYNX: THE VIBRATOR OF YOUR VOICE

The larynx, sometimes known as the voice box or Adam's apple, is a complex physiologic structure made of cartilage, muscle, and tissue.

Biologically, it serves as a sphincter valve, closing off the airway to prevent foreign objects from entering the lungs. When firmly closed, it also is used to increase abdominal pressure to assist with lifting heavy objects, childbirth, and defecation. But if we gently close this valve while we exhale, tissue in the larynx begins to vibrate and produce the sounds that become speech and singing.

The human larynx is a remarkably small instrument, typically ranging from the size of a pecan to a walnut for women and men, respectively. Sound is produced at a location called the glottis, which is formed by two flaps of tissue called the vocal folds (aka vocal cords). In women, the glottis is about the size of a dime; in men, it can approach the diameter of a quarter. The two folds are always attached together at their front point but open in the shape of the letter V during normal breathing, an action called abduction. To phonate, we must close the V while we exhale, an action called adduction (just like the machines you use at the fitness center to exercise your thigh and chest muscles).

Phonation only is possible because of the unique multilayer struc-ture of the vocal folds (figure 9.4). The core of each fold is formed by muscle, which is surrounded by a layer of gelatinous material called the lamina propria. The vocal ligament also runs through the lamina

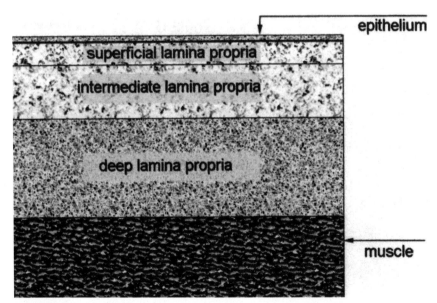

Figure 9.4.   Layered structure of the vocal fold. *Courtesy of Scott McCoy*

propria, which helps to prevent injury by limiting how far the folds can be stretched for high pitches. A thin, hairless epithelial layer that is constantly kept moist with mucus secreted by the throat, larynx, and trachea surrounds all of this. During phonation, the outer layer of the fold glides independently over the inner layer in a wavelike motion, without which phonation is impossible.

We can use a simple demonstration to better understand the independence of the inner and outer portions of the folds. Explore the palm of your hand with your other index finger. Note that the skin is attached quite firmly to the flesh beneath it. If you poke at your palm, that flesh acts as padding, protecting the underlying bone. Now explore the back of your hand. You will observe that the skin is attached quite loosely—you easily can move it around with your finger. And if you poke at the back of your hand, it is likely to hurt; there is very little padding between the skin and your bones. Your vocal folds combine the best attributes of both sides of your hand. They provide sufficient padding to help reduce impact stress, while permitting the outer layer to slip like the skin on the back of your hand, enabling phonation to occur. When you are sick with laryngitis and lose your voice (a condition called aphonia), inflammation in the vocal folds couples the layers of the folds tightly together. The outer layer no longer can move independently over the inner, and phonation becomes difficult or impossible.

The vocal folds are located within the five cartilaginous structures of the larynx (figure 9.5). The largest is called the thyroid cartilage, which is shaped like a small shield. The thyroid connects to the cricoid cartilage below it, which is shaped like a signet ring—broad in the back and narrow in the front. Two cartilages that are shaped like squashed pyramids sit atop the cricoid, called the arytenoids. Each vocal fold runs from the thyroid cartilage in front to one of the arytenoids at the back. Finally, the epiglottis is located at the top of the larynx, flipping backward each time we swallow to prevent food and liquid from entering our lungs. Muscles connect between the various cartilages to open and close the glottis and to lengthen and shorten the vocal folds for ascending and descending pitch, respectively. Because they sometimes are used to identify vocal function, it is a good idea to know the names of the muscles that control the length of the folds. We've already mentioned that a muscle forms the core of each fold. Because it runs between the

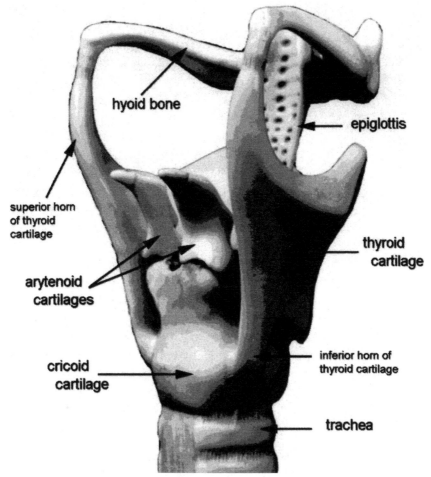

Figure 9.5. Cartilages of the larynx, viewed at an angle from the back.
Courtesy of Scott McCoy

thyroid cartilage and an arytenoid, it is named the thyroarytenoid muscle (formerly known as the vocalis muscle). When the thyroarytenoid,
or TA muscle, contracts, the fold is shortened and pitch goes down.
The folds are elongated through the action of the cricothyroid, or CT
muscles, which run from the thyroid to cricoid cartilage.

   Vocal color (timbre) is created by the combined effects of the sound
produced by the vocal folds and the resonance provided by the vocal
tract. While these elements can never be completely separated, it is
useful to consider the two primary modes of vocal fold vibration and

their resulting sound qualities. The main differences are related to the relative thickness of the folds and their cross-sectional shape (figure 9.6). The first option depends on short, thick folds that come together with nearly square-shaped edges. Vibration in this configuration is given a variety of names, including Mode 1, thyroarytenoid (TA) dominant, chest mode, or modal voice. The alternate configuration uses longer, thinner folds that only make contact at their upper margins. Common names include Mode 2, cricothyroid (CT) dominant, falsetto mode, or loft voice. Singers vary the vibrational mode of the folds according to the quality of sound they wish to produce.

Before we move on to a discussion of resonance, we must consider the quality of the sound that is produced by the larynx. At the level of the glottis, we create a sound not unlike the annoying buzz of a duck call. That buzz, however, contains all the raw material we need to create speech and singing. Vocal or glottal sound is considered to be complex, meaning it consists of many simultaneously sounding frequencies (pitches). The lowest frequency within any tone is called the fundamental, which corresponds to its named pitch in the musical scale. Orchestras tune to a pitch called A-440, which means it has a frequency of 440 vibrations per second, or 440 Hertz (abbreviated Hz). Additional frequencies are included above the fundamental, which are called overtones. Overtones in the glottal sound are quieter than the fundamental. In voices, the overtones usually are whole number multiples of the fundamental, creating a pattern called the harmonic series (e.g., 100 Hz, 200 Hz, 300 Hz, 400 Hz, 500 Hz, etc. or G2, G3, D4, G4, B4—note that pitches are named by the international system in which the lowest C of the piano keyboard is C1; middle-C therefore becomes C4, the fourth C of the keyboard; figure 9.7).

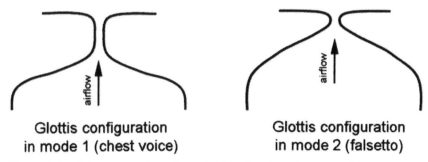

Glottis configuration in mode 1 (chest voice)   Glottis configuration in mode 2 (falsetto)

Figure 9.6. Primary modes of vocal fold vibration. *Courtesy of Scott McCoy*

Singers who choose to make coarse or rough sounds as might be appropriate for rock or blues often add overtones that are inharmonic, or not part of the standard numerical sequence. Inharmonic overtones also are common in singers with damaged or pathological voices.

Under most circumstances, we are completely unaware of the presence of overtones—they simply contribute to the overall timbre of a voice. In some vocal styles, however, harmonics become a dominant feature. This is especially true in throat singing or overtone singing, as is found in places like Tuva. Throat singers tune their vocal tracts so precisely that single harmonics are highlighted within the harmonic spectrum as a separate, whistle-like tone. These singers sustain a low-pitched drone and then create a melody by moving from tone to tone within the natural harmonic series. You can learn to do this too. Sustain a comfortable pitch in your range and slowly morph between the vowels [i] and [u]. If you listen carefully, you will hear individual harmonics pop out of your sound.

The mode of vocal fold vibration has a strong impact on the overtones that are produced. In mode 1, high-frequency harmonics are relatively strong; in mode 2, they are much weaker. As a result, mode 1 tends to yield a much brighter, brassier sound.

VOCAL TRACT: YOUR SOURCE OF RESONANCE

Resonance typically is defined as the amplification and enhancement (or enrichment) of musical sound through supplemental vibration. What does this really mean? In layman's terms, we could say that resonance makes instruments louder and more beautiful by reinforcing the original vibrations of the sound source. This enhancement occurs in two primary ways, which are known as forced and free resonance (there is nothing pejorative in these terms: free resonance is not superior to forced resonance). Any object that is physically connected to a vibrator can serve as a forced resonator. For a piano, the resonator is the soundboard (on the underside of a grand or on the back of an upright); the vibrations of the strings are transmitted directly to the soundboard through a structure known as the bridge, which also is found on violins and guitars. Forced resonance also plays a role in voice production. Place your hand on your

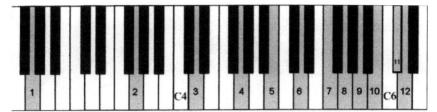

Figure 9.7. Natural harmonic series, beginning at G2. *Courtesy of Scott McCoy*

chest and say [a] at a low pitch. You almost certainly felt the vibrations of forced resonance. In singing, this might best be considered your private resonance; you can feel it and it might impact your self-perception of sound, but nobody else can hear it. To understand why this is true, imagine what a violin would sound like if it were encased in a thick layer of foam rubber. The vibrations of the string would be damped out, muting the instrument. Your skin, muscles, and other tissues do the same thing to the vibrations of your vocal folds.

By contrast, free resonance occurs when sound travels through a hollow space, such as the inside of a trumpet, an organ pipe, or your vocal tract, which consists of the pharynx (throat), oral cavity (mouth), and nasal cavity (nose). As sound travels through these regions, a complex pattern of echoes is created; every time sound encounters a change in the shape of the vocal tract, some of its energy is reflected backward, much like an echo in a canyon. If these echoes arrive back at the glottis at the precise moment a new pulse of sound is created, the two elements synchronize, resulting in a significant increase in intensity. All of this happens very quickly—remember that sound is traveling through your vocal tract at more than seven hundred miles per hour.

Whenever this synchronization of the vocal tract and sound source occurs, we say that the system is in resonance. The phenomenon occurs at specific frequencies (pitches), which can be varied by changing the position of the tongue, lips, jaw, palate, and larynx. These resonant frequencies, or areas in which strong amplification occurs, are called formants. Formants provide the specific amplification that changes the raw, buzzing sound produced by your vocal folds into speech and singing. The vocal tract is capable of producing many formants, which are labeled sequentially by ascending pitch. The first two, F1 and F2, are used to create vowels; higher formants contribute to the overall timbre and individual characteristics of a voice. In some singers, especially those who train to sing in opera, formants three through five are clustered together to form a super formant, eponymously called the singer's formant, which creates a ringing sound and enables a voice to be heard in a large theater without electronic amplification.

Formants are vitally important in singing, but they can be a bit intimidating to understand. An analogy that works really well for me is to think of formants like the wind. You cannot see the wind, but you know it is present when you see leaves rustling in a tree or feel a breeze on your face. Formants work in the same manner. They are completely invisible and directly inaudible. But just as we see the rustling leaf, we can hear, and perhaps even feel, the action of formants through how they change our sound. Try a little experiment. Sing an ascending scale beginning at B♭3, sustaining the vowel [i]. As you approach the D♯ or E♭ of the scale, you likely will feel (and hear) that your sound becomes a bit stronger and easier to produce. This occurs because the scale tone and formant are on the same pitch, providing additional amplification. If you change to an [u] vowel, you will feel the same thing at about the same place in the scale. If you sing to an [o] or [e] and continue up the scale, you'll feel a bloom in the sound somewhere around C5 (an octave above middle C); [a] is likely to come into its best focus at about G5.

To remember the approximate pitches of the first formants for the main vowels, [i]-[e]-[a]-[o]-[u], just think of a C-major triad in first inversion, open position, starting at E4: [i] = E4, [e] = C5, [a] = G5, [o] = C5, and [u] = E4 (figure 9.8). If your music theory isn't strong, you

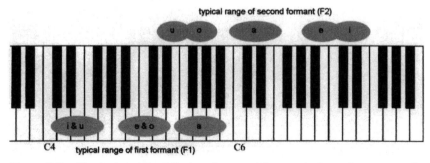

Figure 9.8.   Typical range of first and second formants for primary vowels.
Courtesy of Scott McCoy

could use the mnemonic "every child gets candy eagerly." These pitches might vary by as much as a minor third higher and lower but no farther: once a formant changes by more than that interval, the vowel that is produced must change.

Formants have absolutely no preference for what they amplify—they are indiscriminate lovers, just as happy to bond with the first harmonic as the fifth. When men or women sing low pitches, there almost always will be at least one harmonic that comes close enough to a formant to produce a clear vowel sound. The same is not true for women with high voices, especially sopranos, who routinely must sing pitches that have a fundamental frequency higher than the first formant of many vowels. Imagine what happens if she must sing the phrase "and I'll leave you forever," with the word "leave" set on a very high, climactic note. The audience won't be able to tell if she is singing leave or love; the two will sound identical. This happens because the formant that is required to identify the vowel [i] is too far below the pitch being sung. Even if she tries to sing leave, the sound that comes out of her mouth will be heard as some variation of [a].

Fortunately, this kind of mismatch between formants and musical pitches rarely causes problems for anyone but opera singers, choir so-pranos, and perhaps ingénues in classic music theater shows. Almost everyone else generally sings low enough in their respective voice ranges to produce easily identifiable vowels.

Second formants also can be important, but more so for opera singers than everyone else. They are much higher in pitch, tracking the pattern [u] = E5, [o] = G5, [a] = D6, [e] = B6, [i] = D7 (you can use the mnemonic "every good dad buys diapers" to remember these pitches) (figure 9.8). Because they can extend so high, into the top octave of the piano keyboard for [i], they interact primarily with higher tones in the natural harmonic series. Unless you are striving to produce the loudest unamplified sound possible, you probably never need to worry about the second formant; it will steadfastly do its job of helping to produce vowel sounds without any conscious thought or manipulation on your part.

If you are interested in discovering more about resonance and how it impacts your voice, you might want to install a spectrum analyzer on your computer. Free (or inexpensive) programs are readily available for download over the Internet that will work with either a PC or Mac computer. You don't need any specialized hardware—if you can use Skype or FaceTime, you already have everything you need. Once you've installed something, simply start playing with it. Experiment with your voice to see exactly how the analysis signal changes when you change the way your voice sounds. You'll be able to see how harmonics change in intensity as they interact with your formants. If you sing with vibrato, you'll see how consistently you produce your variations in pitch and amplitude. You'll even be able to see if your tone is excessively nasal for the kind of singing you want to do. Other programs are available that will help you improve your intonation (how well you sing in tune) or enhance your basic musicianship skills. Technology truly has advanced sufficiently to help us sing more beautifully.

MOUTH, LIPS, AND TONGUE: YOUR ARTICULATORS

The articulatory life of a singer is not easy, especially when compared to the demands placed on other musicians. Like a pianist or brass player, we must be able to produce the entire spectrum of musical articulation, including dynamic levels from hushed pianissimos to thunderous fortes, short notes, long notes, accents, crescendos, diminuendos, and so on. We produce most of these articulations the same way instrumentalists do, which is by varying our power supply. But singers have another layer of articulation that makes everything much more complicated; we must produce these musical gestures while simultaneously singing words.

As we learned in our brief examination of formants, altering the resonance characteristics of the vocal tract creates the vowel sounds of language. We do this by changing the position of our tongue, jaw, lips, and sometimes palate. Slowly say the vowel pattern [i]-[e]-[a]-[o]-[u]. Can you feel how your tongue moves in your mouth? For [i], it is high in the front and low in the back, but it takes the opposite position for [u]. Now slowly say the word Tuesday, noting all the places your tongue comes into contact with your teeth and palate and how it changes shape as you produce the vowels and diphthongs. There is a lot going on in there—no wonder it takes so long for babies to learn to speak!

Our articulatory anatomy is extraordinarily complex, in large part because our bodies use the same passageway for food, water, air, and sound. As a result, our tongue, larynx, throat, jaw, and palate are all interconnected with common physical and neurologic points of attachment. Our anatomical Union Station in this regard is a small structure called the hyoid bone. The hyoid is one of only three bones in your entire body that do not connect to other bones via a joint (the other two are your patellae, or kneecaps). This little bone is suspended below your jaw, freely floating up and down every time your swallow. It is a busy place, serving as the upper suspension point for the larynx, the connection for the root of the tongue, and the primary location of the muscles that open your mouth by dropping your jaw.

Good singing—in any genre—requires a high degree of independence in all these articulatory structures. Unfortunately, nature conspires against us to make this difficult to accomplish. From the time we were born, our bodies have relied on a reflex reaction to elevate the palate and raise the larynx each time we swallow. This action becomes habitual: palate goes up, larynx also lifts. But depending on the style of music we are singing, we might need to keep the larynx down while the palate goes up (opera and classical) or palate down with the larynx up (country and bluegrass). As we all know, habits can be very hard to change, which is one of the reasons that it can take a lot of study and practice to become an excellent singer. Understanding your body's natural reflexive habits can make some of this work a bit easier.

There is one more significant pitfall to the close proximity of all these articulators: tension in one area is easily passed along to another. If your jaw muscles are too tight while you sing, that hyperactivity will likely be transferred to the larynx and tongue—remember, they all are interconnected through the hyoid bone. It can be tricky to determine the primary offender in this kind of chain reaction of tension. A tight tongue could just as easily be making your jaw stiff, or an elevated, rigid larynx could make both tongue and jaw suffer.

Neurology complicates matters even further. You have sixteen muscles in your tongue, fourteen in your larynx, twenty-two in your throat and palate, and another sixteen that control your jaw. Many of these are very small and lie directly adjacent to each other, and you often are required to contract one quite strongly while its next-door neighbor must remain totally relaxed. Our brains need to develop laser-like control, sending signals at the right moment with the right intensity to the precise spot where they are needed. When we first start singing, these brain signals come more like a blast from a shotgun, spreading the neurologic impulse over a broad area to multiple muscles, not all of which are the intended target. Again, with practice and training, we learn to refine our control, enabling us to use only those muscles that will help, while disengaging those that would get in the way of our best singing.

FINAL THOUGHTS

This brief chapter has only scratched the surface of the huge field of voice science. To learn more, you might visit the websites of the National Association of Teachers of Singing (NATS), the Voice Foundation (TVF), or the National Center for Voice and Speech (NCVS). You can easily locate the appropriate addresses through any Internet search engine. Remember: knowledge is power. Occasionally, people are afraid that if they know more about the science of how they sing, they will become so analytical that all spontaneity will be lost or they will become paralyzed by too much information and thought. In my forty-plus years as a singer and teacher, I've never encountered somebody who actually suffered this fate. To the contrary, the more we know, the easier—and more joyful—singing becomes.

10

VOCAL HEALTH FOR THE LIGHT OPERA SINGER

Wendy LeBorgne

GENERAL PHYSICAL WELL-BEING

All singers, regardless of genre, should consider themselves as "vocal athletes." The physical, emotional, and performance demands necessary for optimal output require that the artist consider training and maintaining their instrument as an athlete trains for an event. With increased vocal and performance demands, it is unlikely that a vocal athlete will have an entire performing career completely injury free. This may not be the fault of the singer, as many injuries occur due to circumstances beyond the singer's control such as singing through an illness or being on a new medication seemingly unrelated to the voice.

Vocal injury has often been considered taboo to talk about in the performing world as it has been considered to be the result of faulty technique or poor vocal habits. In actuality, the majority of vocal injuries presenting in the elite performing population tend to be overuse and/or acute injury. From a clinical perspective over the past seventeen years, younger, less experienced singers with fewer years of training (who tend to be quite talented) generally are the ones who present with issues related to technique or phonotrauma (nodules, edema, contact ulcers), while more mature singers with professional performing careers tend to present with acute injuries (hemorrhage) or overuse and misuse injuries (muscle tension dysphonia, edema, GERD) or injuries following an illness. There are no current studies documenting use and training in correlation to laryngeal pathologies. However, there are studies that document that somewhere between 35 percent and 100 percent of professional vocal athletes have abnormal vocal fold findings on stroboscopic evaluation. Many times these "abnormalities" are in singers who have no vocal complaints or symptoms of vocal problems. From a performance perspective, uniqueness in vocal quality often gets hired and perhaps a slight aberration in the way a given larynx functions may become quite marketable. Regardless of what the vocal folds may look like, the most integral part of performance is that the singer must maintain agility, flexibility, stamina, power, and inherent beauty (genre appropriate) for their current level of performance taking into account physical, vocal, and emotional demands.

Unlike sports medicine and the exercise physiology literature where much is known about the types and nature of given sports injuries, there is no common parallel for the vocal athlete model. However, because the vocal athlete utilizes the body systems of alignment, respiration, phonation, and resonance with some similarities to physical athletes, a parallel protocol for vocal wellness may be implemented/considered for vocal athletes to maximize injury prevention knowledge for both the singer and teacher. This chapter aims to provide information on vocal wellness and injury prevention for the vocal athlete.

CONSIDERATIONS FOR WHOLE BODY WELLNESS

Nutrition

You have no doubt heard the saying "You are what you eat." Eating is a social and psychological event. For many people, food associations and eating have an emotional basis resulting in either overeating or being malnourished. Eating disorders in performers and body image issues may have major implications and consequences for the performer on both ends of the spectrum (obesity and anorexia). Singers should be encouraged to reprogram the brain and body to consider food as fuel. You want to use high-octane gas in your engine, as pouring water in your car's gas tank won't get you very far. Eating a poor diet or a diet that lacks appropriate nutritional value will have negative physical and vocal effects on the singer. Effects of poor dietary choices for the vocal athlete may result in physical and vocal effects ranging from fatigue to life-threatening disease over the course of a lifetime. Encouraging and engaging in healthy eating habits from a young age will potentially prevent long-term negative effects from poor nutritional choices. It is beyond the scope of this chapter to provide a complete overview of all the dietary guidelines for pediatrics, adolescents, adults, and the mature adult; however, a listing of additional references to help guide your food and beverage choices for making good nutritional choices can be found online at websites such as Dietary Guidelines for Americans, Nutrition.gov Guidelines for Tweens and Teens, and Fruits and Veggies Matter. See the online companion web page on the National Association of Teachers of Singing (NATS) website for links to these and other resources.

Hydration

"Sing wet, pee pale." This phrase was echoed in the studio of Van Lawrence regarding how his students would know if they were well hydrated. Generally, this rule of pale urine during your waking hours is a good indicator that you are well hydrated. Medications, vitamins, and certain foods may alter urine color despite adequate hydration. Due to the varying levels of physical and vocal activity of many performers, in order to maintain adequate oral hydration, the use of a hydration calculator based on activity level may be a better choice. These hydration calculators are easily accessible online and take into account the amount and level of activity the performer engages in on a daily basis. In a recent study of the vocal habits of musical theater performers, one of the findings indicated a significantly underhydrated group of performers.[1]

Laryngeal and pharyngeal dryness as well as "thick, sticky, mucus" are often complaints of singers. Combating these concerns and maintaining an adequate viscosity of mucus for performance has resulted in some research. As a reminder of laryngeal and swallowing anatomy, nothing that is swallowed (or gargled) goes over or touches the vocal folds directly (or one would choke). Therefore, nothing that a singer eats or drinks ever touches the vocal folds, and in order to adequately hydrate the mucous membranes of the vocal folds, one must consume enough fluids for the body to produce a thin mucus. Therefore, any "vocal" effects from swallowed products are limited to potential pharyngeal and oral changes, not the vocal folds themselves.

The effects of systemic hydration are well documented in the literature. There is evidence to suggest that adequate hydration will provide some protection of the laryngeal mucosal membranes when they are placed under increased collision forces as well as reducing the amount of effort (phonation threshold pressure) to produce voice. This is important for the singer because it means that with adequate hydration and consistency of mucus, the effort to produce voice is less and your vocal folds are better protected from injury. Imagine the friction and heat produced when two dry hands rub together and then what happens if you put lotion on your hands. The mechanisms in the larynx to provide appropriate mucus production are not fully understood, but there is enough evidence at this time to support oral hydration as a vital component of every singer's vocal health regime to maintain appropriate mucosal viscosity.

Although very rare, overhydration (hyperhidrosis) can result in dehydration and even illness or death. An overindulgence of fluids essentially makes the kidneys work "overtime" and flushes too much water out of the body. This excessive fluid loss in a rapid manner can be detrimental to the body.

In addition to drinking water to systemically monitor hydration, there are many nonregulated products on the market for performers that lay claim to improving the laryngeal environment (e.g., Entertainer's Secret, Throat Coat Tea, Greathers Pastilles, Slippery Elm, etc.). Although there may be little detriment in using these products, quantitative research documenting change in laryngeal mucosa is sparse. One study suggests that the use of Throat Coat when compared to a placebo treatment for pharyngitis did show a significant difference in decreasing the perception of sore throat.[2] Another study compared the use of Entertainer's Secret to two other nebulized agents and its effect on phonation threshold pressure (PTP).[3] There was no positive benefit in decreasing PTP with Entertainer's Secret.

Many singers use personal steam inhalers and/or room humidification to supplement oral hydration and aid in combating laryngeal dryness. There are several considerations for singers who choose to use external means of adding moisture to the air they breathe. Personal steam inhalers are portable and can often be used backstage or in the hotel room for the traveling performer. Typically, water is placed in the steamer and the face is placed over the steam for inhalation. Because the mucus membranes of the larynx are composed of a saltwater solution, one study looked at the use of nebulized saline in comparison to plain water and its potential effects on effort or ease to sound production in classically trained sopranos.[4] Data suggested that perceived effort to produce voice was less in the saline group than the plain water group. This indicated that the singers who used the saltwater solution reported less effort to sing after breathing in the saltwater than singers who used plain water. The researchers hypothesized that because the body's mucus is not plain water (rather it is a saltwater—think about your tears), when you use plain water for steam inhalation, it may actually draw the salt from your own saliva, resulting in a dehydrating effect.

In addition to personal steamers, other options for air humidification come in varying sizes of humidifiers from room size to whole house humidifiers. When choosing between a warm air or cool mist humidifier, considerations include both personal preference and needs. One of the primary reasons warm mist humidifiers are not recommended for young children is due to the risk of burns from the heating element. Both the warm mist and cool air humidifiers act similarly in adding moisture to the environmental air. External air humidification may be beneficial and provide a level of comfort for many singers. Regular cleaning of the humidifier is vital to prevent bacteria and mold buildup. Also, depending on the hardness of the water, it is important to avoid mineral buildup on the device and distilled water may be recommended for some humidifiers.

For traveling performers who often stay in hotels, fly on airplanes, or are generally exposed to other dry-air environments, there are products on the market designed to help minimize drying effects. One such device is called a Humidflyer, which is a face mask designed with a filter to recycle the moisture of a person's own breath and replenish moisture on each breath cycle.

For dry nasal passages or to clear sinuses, many singers use Neti pots. Many singers use this homeopathic flushing of the nasal passages regularly. Research supports the use of a Neti pot as a part of allergy relief and chronic rhinosinusitis control when utilized properly, sometimes in combination with medical management.[5] Conversely, long-term use of nasal irrigation (without taking intermittent breaks from daily use) may result in washing out the "good" mucus of the nasal passages, which naturally helps to rid the nose of infections. A study presented at the 2009 American College of Allergy, Asthma, and Immunology (ACAAI) annual scientific meeting reported that when a group of individuals who were using twice-daily nasal irrigation for one year discontinued using it, they had an increase in acute rhinosinusitis.[6]

Tea, Honey, and Gargle to Keep the Throat Healthy

Regarding the use of general teas (which many singers combine with honey or lemon), there is likely no harm in the use of decaffeinated tea (caffeine may cause systemic dryness). The warmth of the tea may provide a soothing sensation to the pharynx and the act of swallowing can be relaxing for the muscles of the throat. Honey has shown promising results as an effective cough suppressant in the pediatric population.[7] The dose of honey given to the children in the study was two teaspoons. Gargling with salt or apple cider vinegar and water are also popular home remedies for many singers with the uses being from soothing the throat to curing reflux. Gargling plain water has been shown to be efficacious in reducing the risk of contracting upper respiratory infections. I suggest that when gargling, the singer only "bubble" the water with air and avoid engaging the vocal folds in sound production. Saltwater as a gargle has long been touted as a sore throat remedy and can be traced back to 2700 BCE in China for treating gum disease. The science behind a saltwater rinse for everything from oral hygiene to sore throat is that salt (sodium chloride) may act as a natural analgesic (pain killer) and may also kill bacteria. Similar to the effects that not enough salt in the water may have on drawing the salt out of the tissue in the steam inhalation, if you oversaturate the water solution with excess salt and gargle it, it may act to draw water out of the oral mucosa, thus reducing inflammation.

Another popular home remedy reported by singers is the use of apple cider vinegar to help with everything from acid reflux to sore throats. Dating back to 3300 BCE, apple cider vinegar was reported as a medicinal remedy, and it became popular in the 1970s as a weight loss diet cocktail. Popular media reports apple cider vinegar can improve conditions from acne and arthritis to nosebleeds and varicose veins. Specific efficacy data regarding the beneficial nature of apple cider vinegar for the purpose of sore throat, pharyngeal inflammation, and/or reflux has not been reported in the literature at this time. Of the peer-reviewed studies found in the literature, one discussed possible esophageal erosion and inconsistency of actual product in tablet form.[8] Therefore, at this time, strong evidence supporting the use of apple cider vinegar is not published.

Medications and the Voice

Medications (over the counter, prescription, and herbal) may have resultant drying effects on the body and often the laryngeal mucosa. General classes of drugs with potential drying effects include: antidepressants, antihypertensives, diuretics, ADD/ADHD medications, some oral acne medications, hormones, allergy drugs, and vitamin C in high doses. The National Center for Voice and Speech (NCVS) provides a listing of some common medications with potential voice side effects including laryngeal dryness. This listing does not take into account all medications, so singers should always ask their pharmacist of the potential side effects of a given medication. Due to the significant number of drugs on the market, it is safe to say that most pharmacists will not be acutely aware of "vocal side effects," but if dryness is listed as a potential side effect of the drug, you may assume that all body systems could be affected. Under no circumstances should you stop taking a prescribed medication without consulting your physician first. As every person has a different body chemistry and reaction to medication, just because a medication lists dryness as a potential side effect it does not necessarily mean you will experience that side effect. Conversely, if you begin a new medication and notice physical or vocal changes that are unexpected, you should consult with your physician. Ultimately, the goal of medical management for any condition is to achieve the most benefits with the least side effects. Please see the companion page on the NATS website for a list of possible resources for the singer regarding prescription drugs and herbs.

In contrast to medications that tend to dry, there are medications formulated to increase saliva production or alter the viscosity of mucus. Medically, these drugs are often used to treat patients who have had a loss of saliva production due to surgery or radiation. Mucolytic agents are used to thin secretions as needed. As a singer, if you feel that you need to use a mucolytic agent on a consistent basis, it may be worth considering getting to the root of the laryngeal dryness symptom and seeking a professional opinion from an otolaryngologist.

Reflux and the Voice

Gastroesophageal reflux (GERD) and/or laryngopharyngeal reflux (LPR) can have a devastating impact on the singer if not recognized and treated appropriately. Although GERD and LPR are related, they are considered as slightly different diseases. GERD (Latin root meaning "flowing back") is the reflux of digestive enzymes, acids, and other stomach contents into the esophagus (food pipe). If this backflow is propelled through the upper esophagus and into the throat (larynx and pharynx), it is referred to as LPR. It is not uncommon to have both GERD and LPR, but they can occur independently.

More frequently, people with GERD have decreased esophageal clearing. Esophagitis, or inflammation of the esophagus, is also associated with GERD. People with GERD often feel heartburn. LPR symptoms are often "silent" and do not include heartburn. Specific symptoms of LPR may include some or all of the following: lump in the throat sensation, feeling of constant need to clear the throat/postnasal drip, longer vocal warm-up time, quicker vocal fatigue, loss of high frequency range, worse voice in the morning, sore throat, and bitter/raw/brackish taste in the mouth. If you experience these symptoms on a regular basis, it is advised that you consider a medical consultation for your symptoms. Prolonged, untreated GERD or LPR can lead to permanent changes in both the esophagus and/or larynx. Untreated LPR also provides a laryngeal environment that is conducive for vocal fold lesions to occur as it inhibits normal healing mechanisms.

Treatments of LPR and GERD generally include both dietary and lifestyle modifications in addition to medical management. Some of the dietary recommendations include elimination of caffeinated and carbonated beverages, smoking cessation, no alcohol use, and limiting tomatoes, acidic foods and drinks, and raw onions or peppers, to name a few. Also, avoidance of high-fat foods is recommended. From a lifestyle perspective, suggested changes include not eating within three hours of lying down, eating small meals frequently (instead of large meals), elevating the head of your bed, avoiding tight clothing around the belly, and not bending over or exercising too soon after you eat.

Reflux medications fall in three general categories: antacids, H2 blockers, and proton pump inhibitors (PPI). There are now combination drugs that include both an H2 blocker and proton pump inhibitor. Every medication has both associated risks and benefits, and singers should be aware of the possible benefits and side effects of the medications they take. In general terms, antacids (e.g., Tums, Mylanta, Gaviscon) neutralize stomach acid. H2 (histamine) blockers, such as Axid (nizatidine), Tagamet (cimetidine), Pepcid (famotidine), and Zantac (ranitidine), work to decrease acid production in the stomach by preventing histamine from triggering the H2 receptors to produce more acid. Then there are the PPIs: Nexium (esomeprazole), Prevacid (lansoprazole), Protonix (pantoprazole), AcipHex (rabeprazole), Prilosec (omeprazole), and Dexilant (dexlansoprazole). PPIs act as a last line of defense to decrease acid production by blocking the last step in gastric juice secretion. Some of the most recent drugs to combat GERD/LPR are combination drugs (e.g., Zegrid [sodium bicarbonate plus omeprazole]), which provide a short-acting response (sodium bicarbonate) and a long release (omeprazole). Because some singers prefer a holistic approach to reflux management, strict dietary and lifestyle compliance is recommended and consultation with both your primary care physician and naturopath are warranted in that situation. Efficacy data on nonregulated herbs, vitamins, and supplements is limited, but some data does exist.

Physical Exercise

Vocal athletes, like other physical athletes, should consider how and what they do to maintain both cardiovascular fitness and muscular strength. In today's performance culture, it is rare that a performer stands still and sings, unless in a recital or choral setting. The range of physical activity can vary from light movement to high-intensity choreography with acrobatics. As performers are being required to increase their on-stage physical activity level from the operatic stage to the pop-star arena, overall physical fitness is imperative to avoid compromise in the vocal system. Breathlessness will result in compensation by the larynx, which is now attempting to regulate the air. Compensatory vocal behaviors over time may result in a change in vocal performance. The health benefits of both cardiovascular training and strength training are well documented for physical athletes but relatively rare in the literature for vocal performers.

Mental Wellness

Vocal performers must maintain a mental focus during performance and a mental toughness during auditioning and training. Rarely during vocal performance training programs is this important aspect of performance addressed, and it is often left to the individual performer to develop their own strategy or coping mechanism. Yet, many performers are on antianxiety or antidepressant drugs (which may be the direct result of performance-related issues). If the sports world is again used as a parallel for mental toughness, there are no elite-level athletes (and few junior-level athletes) who don't utilize the services of a performance/sports psychologist to maximize focus and performance. I recommend that performers consider the potential benefits of a performance psychologist to help maximize vocal performance. Several references that may be of interest to the singer include Joanna Cazden's *Visualization for Singers* (Joanna Cazden, 1992) and Shirlee Emmons and Alma Thomas's *Power Performance for Singers: Transcending the Barriers* (Oxford, 1998).

Unlike instrumentalists, whose performance is dependent on accurate playing of an external musical instrument, the singer's instrument is uniquely intact and subject to the emotional confines of the brain and body in which it is housed. Musical performance anxiety (MPA) can be career threatening for all musicians, but perhaps the vocal athlete is more severely impacted. The majority of literature on MPA is dedicated to instrumentalists, but the basis of definition, performance effects, and treatment options can be considered for vocal athletes. Fear is a natural reaction to a stressful situation, and there is a fine line between emotional excitation and perceived threat (real or imagined). The job of a performer is to convey to an audience through vocal production, physical gestures, and facial expression a most heightened state of emotion. Otherwise, why would audience members pay top dollar to sit for two or three hours for a mundane experience? Not only is there the emotional conveyance of the performance but also the internal turmoil often experienced by the singers themselves in preparation for elite performance. It is well documented in the literature that even the most elite performers have experienced debilitating performance anxiety. MPA is defined on a continuum with anxiety levels ranging from low to high and has been reported to comprise four distinct components: affect, cognition, behavior, and physiology. Affect comprises feelings (e.g., doom, panic, anxiety). Affected cognition will result in altered levels of concentration, while the behavior component results in postural shifts, quivering, and trembling. Finally, physiologically the body's autonomic nervous system (ANS) will activate, resulting in the "fight or flight" response.

In recent years, researchers have been able to define two distinct neurological pathways for MPA. The first pathway happens quickly and without conscious input (ANS), resulting in the same fear stimulus as if a person were put into an emergent, life-threatening situation. In those situations, the brain releases adrenaline, resulting in physical changes of increased heart rate, increased respiration, shaking, pale skin, dilated pupils, slowed digestion, bladder relaxation, dry mouth, and dry eyes, all of which severely affect vocal performance. The second pathway that has been identified results in a conscious identification of the fear/threat and a much slower physiologic response. With the second neuromotor response, the performer has a chance to recognize the fear, process how to deal with the fear, and respond accordingly.

Treatment modalities to address MPA include psycho-behavioral therapy (including biofeedback) and drug therapies. Elite physical performance athletes have been shown to benefit from visualization techniques and psychological readiness training, yet within the performing arts community, stage fright may be considered a weakness or character flaw precluding readiness for professional performance. On the contrary, vocal athletes, like physical athletes, should mentally prepare themselves for optimal competition (auditions) and performance. Learning to convey emotion without eliciting an internal emotional response by the vocal athlete may take the skill of an experienced psychologist to help change ingrained neural pathways. Ultimately, control and understanding of MPA will enhance performance and prepare the vocal athlete for the most intense performance demands without vocal compromise.

VOCAL WELLNESS: INJURY PREVENTION

In order to prevent vocal injury and understand vocal wellness in the singer, general knowledge of common causes of voice disorders is imperative. One common cause of voice disorders is vocally abusive behaviors or misuse of the voice to include phonotraumatic behaviors such as yelling, screaming, loud talking, talking over noise, throat clearing, coughing, harsh sneezing, and boisterous laughing. Chronic or less than optimal vocal properties such as poor breathing techniques, inappropriate phonatory habits during conversational speech (glottal fry, hard glottal attacks), inapt pitch, loudness, rate of speech, and/or hyperfunctional laryngeal-area muscle tone may also negatively impact vocal function. Medically related etiologies, which also have the potential to impact vocal function, range from untreated chronic allergies and sinusitis to endocrine dysfunction and hormonal imbalance. Direct trauma, such as a blow to the neck or the risk of vocal fold damage during intubation, can impact optimal performance in vocal athletes depending on the nature and extent of the trauma. Finally, external irritants ranging from cigarette smoke to reflux directly impact the laryngeal mucosa and ultimately can lead to laryngeal pathology.

Vocal hygiene education and compliance may be one of the primary essential components for maintaining the voice throughout a career. This section will provide the singer with information on prevention of vocal injury. However, just like a professional sports athlete, it is unlikely that a professional vocal athlete will go through an entire career without some compromise in vocal function. This may be a common upper respiratory infection that creates vocal fold swelling for a short time, or it may be a "vocal accident" that is career threatening. Regardless, the knowledge of how to take care of your voice is essential for any vocal athlete.

Train Like an Athlete for Vocal Longevity

Performers seek instant gratification in performance sometimes at the cost of gradual vocal building for a lifetime of healthy singing. Historically, voice pedagogues required their students to perform vocalises exclusively for up to two years before beginning any song literature. Singers gradually built their voices by ingraining appropriate muscle memory and neuromotor patterns through development of aesthetically pleasing tones, onsets, breath management, and support. There was an intensive master-apprentice relationship and rigorous vocal guidelines to maintain a place within a given studio. Time off was taken if a vocal injury ensued or careers potentially were ended, and students were asked to leave a given singing studio if their voices were unable to withstand the rigors of training. Training vocal athletes today has evolved and appears driven to create a "product" quickly, perhaps at the expense of the longevity of the singer. Pop stars emerging well before puberty are doing international concert tours, yet many young artist programs in the classical arena do not consider singers for their programs until they are in their mid- to late twenties.

Each vocal genre presents with different standards and vocal demands. Therefore, the amount and degree of vocal training are varied. Some would argue that performing extensively without adequate vocal training and development is ill-advised, yet singers today are thrust onto the stage at very young ages. Dancers, instrumentalists, and physical athletes all spend many hours per day developing muscle strength, memory, and proper technique for their craft. The more advanced the artist or athlete, generally the more specific the training protocol becomes. Consideration of training vocal athletes in this same fashion is recommended. One would generally not begin a young, inexperienced singer on a Wagner aria without previous vocal training. Similarly, in nonclassical vocal music, there are easy, moderate, and difficult pieces to consider pending level of vocal development and training.

Basic pedagogical training of alignment, breathing, voice production, and resonance are essential building blocks for development of good voice production. Muscle memory and development of appropriate muscle patterns happen slowly over time with appropriate repetitive practice. Doing too much, too soon for any athlete (physical or vocal) will result in an increased risk for injury. When the singer is being asked to do "vocal gymnastics," they must be sure to have a solid basis of strength and stamina in the appropriate muscle groups to perform consistently with minimal risk of injury.

Vocal Fitness Program

One generally does not get out of bed first thing in the morning and try to do a split. Yet many singers go directly into a practice session or audition without proper warm-up. Think of your larynx like your knee, made up of cartilages, ligaments, and muscles. Vocal health is dependent upon appropriate warm-ups (to get things moving), drills for technique, and then cool-downs (at the end of your day). Consider vocal warm-ups a "gentle stretch." Depending on the needs of the singer, warm-ups should include physical stretching; postural alignment self-checks; breathing exercises to promote rib cage, abdominal, and back expansion; vocal stretches (glides up to stretch the vocal folds and glides down to contract the vocal folds); articulatory stretches (yawning, facial stretches); and mental warm-ups (to provide focus for the task at hand). Vocalises, in my opinion, are designed as exercises to go beyond warm-ups and prepare the body and voice for the technical and vocal challenges of the music they sing. They are varied and address the technical level and genre of the singer to maximize performance and vocal growth. Cool-downs are a part of most athletes' workouts. However, singers often do not use cool-downs (physical, mental, and vocal) at the end of a performance. A recent study looked specifically at the benefits of vocal cool-downs in singers and found that singers who used a vocal cool-down had decreased effort to produce voice the next day.[9]

Systemic hydration as a means to keep the vocal folds adequately lubricated for the amount of impact and friction that they will undergo has been previously discussed in this chapter. Compliance with adequate oral hydration recommendations is important and subsequently so is the minimization of agents that could potentially dry the membranes (e.g., caffeine, medications, dry air). The body produces approximately two quarts of mucus per day. If not adequately hydrated, the mucus tends to be thick and sticky. Poor hydration is similar to not putting enough oil in the car engine. Frankly, if the gears do not work as well, there is increased friction and heat, and the engine is not efficient.

Speak Well, Sing Well

Optimize the speaking voice utilizing ideal frequency range, breath, intensity, rate, and resonance. Singers generally are vocally enthusiastic individuals who talk a lot and often talk loudly. During typical conversation, the average fundamental speaking frequency (times per second the vocal folds are impacting) for a male varies from 100 to 150 Hz and 180 to 230 Hz for women. Because of the delicate structure of the vocal folds and the importance of the layered microstructure vibrating efficiently and effectively to produce voice, vocal behaviors or outside factors that compromise the integrity of the vibration patterns of the vocal folds may be considered phonotrauma.

Phonotraumatic behaviors can include yelling, screaming, loud talking, harsh sneezing, and harsh laughing. Elimination of phonotraumatic behaviors is essential for good vocal health. The louder one speaks, the farther apart the vocal folds move from midline, the harder they impact, and the longer they stay closed. A tangible example would be to take your hands, move them only six inches apart, and clap as hard and as loudly as you can for ten seconds. Now, move your hands two feet apart and clap as hard, loudly, and quickly as possible for ten seconds. The farther apart your hands are, the more air you move and the louder the clap, and the skin on the hands becomes red and ultimately swollen (if you do it long enough and hard enough). This is what happens to the vocal folds with repeated impact at increased vocal intensities. The vocal folds are approximately 17 mm in length and vibrate at 220 times per second on A3, 440 on A4, 880 on A5, and more than 1,000 per second when singing a high C. That is a lot of impact for little muscles. Consider this fact when singing loudly or in a high tessitura for prolonged periods of time. It becomes easy to see why women are more prone than men to laryngeal impact injuries due to the frequency range of the voice alone.

In addition to the amount of cycles per second (cps) the vocal folds are impacting, singers need to be aware of their vocal intensity (volume). One should be aware of the volume of the speaking and singing voice and consider using a distance of three to five feet (about an arms-length distance) as a gauge for how loud to be in general conversation. Using cell phones and speaking on a Bluetooth device in a car generally results in greater vocal intensity than normal, and singers are advised to minimize unnecessary use of these devices.

Singers should be encouraged to take "vocal naps" during their day. A vocal nap would be a short period of time (five minutes to an hour) of complete silence. Although the vocal folds are rarely completely still (because they move when you swallow and breathe), a vocal nap minimizes impact and vibration for a short window of time. A physical nap can also be refreshing for the singer mentally and physically.

Avoid Environmental Irritants: Alcohol, Smoking, Drugs

Arming singers with information on the actual effects of environmental irritants so that they can make informed choices on engaging in exposure to these potential toxins is essential. The glamour that continues to be associated with smoking, drinking, and drugs can be tempered with the deaths of popular stars such as Amy Winehouse and Cory Monteith who engaged in life-ending choices. There is extensive documentation about the long-term effects of toxic and carcinogenic substances, but here are a few key facts to consider when choosing whether to partake.

Alcohol, although it does not go over the vocal folds directly, does have a systemic drying effect. Due to the acidity in alcohol, it may increase the likelihood of reflux, resulting in hoarseness and other laryngeal pathologies. Consuming alcohol generally decreases one's inhibitions, and therefore you are more likely to sing and do things that you would not typically do under the influence of alcohol.

Beyond the carcinogens in nicotine and tobacco, the heat at which a cigarette burns is well above the boiling temperature of water (water boils at 212°F; cigarettes burn at over 1400°F). No one would consider pouring a pot of boiling water on their hand, and yet the burning temperature for a cigarette results in significant heat over the oral mucosa and vocal folds. The heat alone can create a deterioration in the lining, resulting in polypoid degeneration. Obviously, cigarette smoking has been well documented as a cause for laryngeal cancer.

Marijuana and other street drugs are not only addictive but can cause permanent mucosal lining changes depending on the drug used and the method of delivery. If you or one of your singer colleagues is experiencing a drug or alcohol problem, research or provide information and support on getting appropriate counseling and help.

SMART PRACTICE STRATEGIES FOR SKILL DEVELOPMENT AND VOICE CONSERVATION

Daily practice and drills for skill acquisition are an important part of any singer's training. However, overpracticing or inefficient practicing may be detrimental to the voice. Consider practice sessions of athletes: they may practice four to eight hours per day broken into one- to two-hour training sessions with a period of rest and recovery in between sessions. Although we cannot parallel the sports model without adequate evidence in the vocal athlete, the premise of short, intense, focused practice sessions is logical for the singer. Similar to physical exercise, it is suggested that practice sessions do not have to be all "singing." Rather, structuring sessions so that one-third of the session is spent on warm-up; one-third on vocalises, text work, rhythms, character development, and so on; and one-third on repertoire will allow the singer to function in a more efficient vocal manner. Building the amount of time per practice session—increasing duration by five minutes per week, building to sixty to ninety minutes—may be effective (e.g., Week 1: twenty minutes three times per day; Week 2: twenty-five minutes three times per day, etc.).

Vary the "vocal workout" during your week. For example, if you do the same physical exercise in the same way day after day with the same intensity and pattern, you will likely experience repetitive strain–type injuries. However, cross-training or varying the type and level of exercise aids in injury prevention. So when planning your practice sessions for a given week (or rehearsal process for a given role), consider varying your vocal intensity, tessitura, and exercises to maximize your training sessions, building stamina, muscle memory, and skill acquisition. For example, one day you may spend more time on learning rhythms and translation and the next day you spend thirty minutes performing coloratura exercises to prepare for a specific role. Take one day a week off from vocal training and give your voice a break. This does not mean complete vocal rest (although some singers find this beneficial), but rather a day without singing and limited talking.

Practice Your Mental Focus

Mental wellness and stress management are equally as important as vocal training for vocal athletes. Addressing any mental health issues is paramount to developing the vocal artist. This may include anything from daily mental exercises/meditation/focus to overcoming performance anxiety to more serious mental health issues/illness. Every person can benefit from improved focus and mental acuity.

VOCAL WELLNESS TIPS FOR LIGHT OPERA SINGERS

General vocal wellness guidelines for all singers hold true for the light opera singer. Because light opera singing is similar in vocal skill set to traditional opera singers', training, daily practice, and demands, strict vocal health and wellness guidelines prevail. The light opera literature may be lighter in content/theme and decreased in length than a traditional opera, but the vocal load is not significantly reduced from the traditional opera singer.

Strict compliance with vocal health, hygiene, and hydration recommendations are advised for the light opera singer. Rehearsals and personal practice may require several hours per day of concentrated voice use. The content of light operas is often comedic and fun. These singers are required to connect with the audience from a vocal and emotional standpoint. There is movement and often physical comedy, which is heightened from traditional opera singing. Therefore, both physical and vocal fitness should be foremost in the minds of anyone desiring to perform light opera today. Light opera singers should be physically and vocally in shape to meet the necessary performance, costuming, and endurance demands of a given show.

Performance of light opera requires that the singer has a flexible, agile, dynamic instrument with appropriate stamina. The singer must have a good command of his or her instrument, as well as exceptional underlying intention to what he or she is singing as it is about relaying a message and connecting with the audience. The voices that convey the songs must reflect the mood and intent of the composer, requiring dynamic control, vocal control/power, and an emotional connection to the text.

Due to the versatility often required of the light opera singer, the concept of "vocal cross-training" (which can mean singing in both high and low registers with varying intensities and resonance options) before and after practice sessions and performances is likely a vital component to minimizing vocal injury.

FINAL THOUGHTS

Ultimately, the singer must learn to provide the most output with the least "cost" to the system. Taking care of the physical instrument through daily physical exercise, adequate nutrition and hydration, and focused attention on performance will provide a necessary basis for vocal health during performance. Small doses of high-intensity singing (or speaking) will limit impact stress on the vocal folds. Finally, attention to the mind, body, and voice will provide the singer with an awareness when something is wrong. This awareness and knowledge of when to rest or seek help will promote vocal well-being for the singer throughout his or her career.

NOTES

1. W. LeBorgne et al., "Prevalence of Vocal Pathology in Incoming Freshman Musical Theatre Majors: A 10-Year Retrospective Study," Fall Voice Conference, New York, 2012.

2. J. Brinckmann et al., "Safety and Efficacy of a Traditional Herbal Medicine (Throat Coat) in Symptomatic Temporary Relief of Pain in Patients with Acute Pharyngitis: A Multicenter, Prospective, Randomized, Double-Blinded,

Placebo-Controlled Study," *Journal of Alternative and Complementary Medicine* 9, no. 2 (2003): 285–298.

3. N. Roy et al., "An Evaluation of the Effects of Three Laryngeal Lubricants on Phonation Threshold Pressure (PTP)," *Journal of Voice* 17, no. 3 (2003): 331–342.

4. K. Tanner et al., "Nebulized Isotonic Saline versus Water Following a Laryngeal Desiccation Challenge in Classically Trained Sopranos," *Journal of Speech Language and Hearing Research* 53, no. 6 (2010): 1555–1566.

5. C. Brown and S. Graham, "Nasal Irrigations: Good or Bad?" *Current Opinion in Otolaryngology, Head and Neck Surgery* 12, no. 1 (2004): 9–13.

6. T. Nsouli, "Long-Term Use of Nasal Saline Irrigation: Harmful or Helpful?" American College of Allergy, Asthma and Immunology Annual Scientific Meeting, Abstract 32, 2009.

7. M. Shadkam et al., "A Comparison of the Effect of Honey, Dextromethorphan, and Diphenhydramine on Nightly Cough and Sleep Quality in Children and Their Parents," *Journal of Alternative and Complementary Medicine* 16, no. 7 (2010): 787–793.

8. L. Hill et al., "Esophageal Injury by Apple Cider Vinegar Tablets and Subsequent Evaluation of Products," *Journal of the American Dietetic Association* 105, no. 7 (2005): 1141–1144.

9. R. O. Gottliebson, "The Efficacy of Cool-Down Exercises in the Practice Regimen of Elite Singers," PhD diss., University of Cincinnati, 2011.

APPENDIX A

Light Opera Repertoire Lists

GERMAN *SINGSPIEL*

Carl Ditters von Dittersdorf (1739–1799)

Doktor und Apotheker	1786
Betrug durch Aberglauben	1786
Die Liebe im Narrenhaus	1787
Das rothe Käppchen	1788
Die Hochzeit des Figaro	1789
Hieronymus Knicker, aus als Hokus Pokus	1789
Der Schiffspatron	1789
Das Gespenst mit der Trommel	1794
Don Quixote der Zweyte	1795
Gott Mars und der Hauptmann von Bärenzahn	1795
Der Schach von Schiras	1795
Ugolino	1796
Die lustigen Weiber von Windsor	1796
Der Ternengewinnst	1797
Der Mädchenmarkt	1797
Der Seefahrer	1798

Johann Adam Hiller (1728–1804)

Der verwandelten Weiber	1766
Die lustige Schuster	1766
Lisuart und Dariolette	1766
Lottchen am Hofe	1767
Die Muse	1767
Die Liebe auf dem Lande	1768
Die Jagd	1770
Der Dorfbarbier	1771
Der Aerndtkranz	1771
Der Krieg	1772
Der Jubelhochzeit	1773
Poltis, oder Das gerettete Troja	1777
Das Grab des Mufti	1779

Albert Lortzing (1801–1851)

Ali Pascha von Janina	1824
Zar und Zimmermann	1837
Caramo, oder Das Fischerstechen	1839
Hans Sachs	1840
Casanova	1841
Der Wildschütz	1842
Der Waffenschmied	1846

Wolfgang Amadeus Mozart (1756–1791)

Bastien und Bastienne	1768
Zaide	1781
Die Entführung aus dem Serail	1782
Der Schauspieldirektor	1786
Die Zauberflöte	1791

Antonio Salieri (1750–1825)

Der Rauchfangkehrer	1781
Die Neger	1802/revised 1804

Franz Schubert (1797–1828)

Des Teufels Lustschloß	1813
Claudine von Villa Bella	1815
Der vierjährige Posten	1815
Die Zwillingsbrüder	1821
Die Verschworenen	1823

Carl Maria von Weber (1786–1826)

Abu Hassan	1811
Der Freischütz	1821

FRENCH *OPÉRA BOUFFE*

Edmond Audran (1840–1901)

L'ours et le pacha	1862
La chercheuse d'esprit	1864
Le grand mogol	1877/revised 1884
Les noces d'Olivette	1879
La mascotte	1880
Gillette de Narbonne	1882
Les pommes d'or	1883
La dormeuse éveillée	1883
Serment d'amour	1886
La cigale et la fourmi	1886
La fiancée des verts poteaux	1887
Le puits qui parle	1888
La petite fronde	1888
La fille à Cacolet	1889
L'oeuf rouge	1890
Miss Helyett	1890
L'oncle Célestin	1891
Article de Paris	1892
La sainte Freya	1892
Madame Suzette	1893

Mon prince	1893
L'enlèvement de la Toledad	1894
La duchesse de Ferrare	1895
La poupée	1896
Monsieur Lohengrin	1896
Les petites femmes	1897
Les soeurs Gaudichard	1898

Reynaldo Hahn (1874–1947)

Nausicaa	1919
Ciboulette	1923
Brummel	1931
Malvina	1935

Hervé (1825–1892)

L'ours et le pacha	1842
Don Quichotte et Sancho Pança	1848
Les gardes françaises	1849
Passiflor et Cactus	1851
L'enseignement mutual	1852
Roméo et Mariette	1852
Les folies dramatiques	1853
Prologue d'ouverture	1854
La perle de l'Alsace	1854
Un mari trompette	1854
Le compositeur toque	1854
Amour, Poésie et Turlupinade	1854
Les folies nouvelles	1854
La caravane de l'amour	1854
La fine-fleur de l'Andalousie	1854
La belle créature	1855
Vadé au cabaret!	1855
L'intrigue espagnole	1855
Le sergent Laramée	1855

Fanfare	1855
Un drame en 1779	1855
Latrouillat et Truffaldini	1855
Un ténor très léger	1855
Le testament de Polichinelle	1855
Le trio d'enfoncés	1855
Fifi et Nini	1856
Agamemnon	1856
Toinette et son carabinier	1856
Femme à vendre	1856
Le pommier ensorcelé	1857
Brin d'amour	1857
Phosphorus	1857
La belle espagnole	1858
La voiturier	1858
La dent de sagesse	1858
L'alchimiste	1858
Simple histoire	1858
La belle Nini	1860
Le hussard persecute	1862
La fanfare de Saint-Cloud	1862
Le retour d'Ulyssse	1862
Les toréadors de Grenade	1863
Les Troyens en Champagne	1863
Moldave et Circassienne	1864
Le joueur de flûte	1864
La liberté des théâtres	1864
La revue pour tire, ou Roland à Ronceveaux	1864
La biche au bois	1865
Une fantasia	1865
Les deux chanteurs sans place	1866
Le compositeur toqué	1867
Les chevaliers de la table ronde	1867
Le pédicure	1867
Les métamorphoses de Tartempion	1867
L'oeil crevé	1867

L'enfant de la troupe	1867
Clodoche et Normande	1867
Le gardien de sérail	1868
Trombolino	1868
Chilpéric	1868
Le roi Amatibou	1868
Entre deux vins	1868
Nini c'est fini	1868
Juliette et Dupiton	1868
Le petit Faust	1869
Une giboulée d'amoureux	1869
Les turcs	1869
Aladdin the Second	1870
Le trône d'Écosse	1871
La veuve du Malabar	1873
La France et la chanson	1874
La noce à Briochet	1874
Alice de Nevers	1875
La belle poule	1875
Estelle et Némorin	1876
Up the River	1877
La marquise des rues	1879
Panurge	1879
La femme à papa	1879
Le voyage en Amérique	1880
La mére des compagnons	1880
Les deux roses	1881
La roussotte (begun by Lecocq)	1881
Lili	1882
Mam'zelle Nitouche	1883
Le vertigo	1883
Le cosaque	1884
La nuit aux soufflets	1884
Mam'zelle Gavroche	1885
Frivoli	1886
Fla-Fla	1886

La noce à Nini	1889
Les bagatelles de la porte	1890
Bacchanale	1892
Le cabinet Piperlin	1897

Charles Lecocq (1832–1918)

Le docteur Miracle	1857
Huis-clos	1859
Le baiser à la porte	1864
Liline et Valentin	1864
Le myosotis	1866
Ondines au champagne	1866
Le cabaret de Ramponneau	1867
L'amour et son carquois	1868
Fleur-de-thé	1868
Les jumeaux de Bergame	1868
Le carneval d'un merle blanc	1868
Gandolfo	1869
Deux portières pour un cordon	1869
Le rajah de Mysore	1869
Le beau dunois	1870
Le testament de M. de Crac	1871
Le barbier de Trouville	1871
Sauvons la caisse	1871
Les cent vierges	1872
La fille de Madame Angot	1872
Giroflé-Girofla	1874
Les prés Saint-Gervais	1874
Le pompon	1875
La petite mariée	1875
Kosiki	1876
La marjolaine	1877
Le petit duc	1878
La camargo	1878
Le grand Casimir	1879

La petite mademoiselle	1879
La jolie persane	1879
Janot	1881
La roussotte (completed by Hervé)	1881
Le jour et la nuit	1881
Le coeur et la main	1882
La princesse des Canaries	1883
L'oiseau bleu	1884
La vie mondaine	1885
Plutus	1886
Les grenadiers de Mont-Cornette	1887
Ali-Baba	1887
La volière	1888
L'égyptienne	1890
Nos bons chasseurs	1894
Ninette	1896
Ruse d'amour	1897
Barbe-Bleue	1898
La belle au bois dormant	1900
Yetta	1903
Rose-Mousse	1904
La salutiste	1905
Le trahison de Pan	1911

André Messager (1853–1929)

François les bas-bleus	1883
La fauvette du temple	1885
La béarnaise	1885
Le bourgeois de Calais	1887
Les premières armes de Louis XV	1888
Le mari de la reine	1889
La basoche	1890
Miss Dollar	1893
Madame Chrysanthème	1893
Mirette	1894

La fiancée en lotérie	1896
Le chevalier d'Harmental	1896
Les p'tites Michu	1897
Véronique	1898
Les dragons de l'impératrice	1905
Fortunio	1907
Béatrice	1914
Cyprien, ôte ta main de là!	1916
Monsieur Beaucaire	1919
La petite fonctionnaire	1921
L'amour masqué	1923
Passionnément	1926
Coups de roulis	1928
Sacha	1930

Jacques Offenbach (1819–1880)

L'alcôve	1847
Le trésor à Mathurin	1853
Pépito	1853
Luc et Lucette	1853
Une nuit blanche	1855
Les deux aveugles	1855
Le rêve d'une nuit d'été	1855
Madame Papillon	1855
Les violoneux	1855
Ba-ta-clan	1855
Oyayaie, ou La reine des îles	1855
Paimpol et Périnette	1855
Béranger à l'académie	1855
Élodie, ou Le forfait nocturne	1855
Un postillon en gage	1855
Tromb-al-ca-zar	1856
La rose de Saint-Flour	1856
Les dragées du baptême	1856
Le 66	1856

Le financier et le savetier	1856
La bonne d'enfant	1856
Les baisers du diable	1857
Croquefer, ou Le dernier des paladins	1857
Dragonette	1857
Vent du soir, ou L'horrible Festin	1857
Une demoiselle en lotterie	1857
Les deux pêcheurs, ou Le lever du soleil	1857
Mesdames de la Halle	1858
La chatte métamorphosée en femme	1858
Orphée aux enfers	1858
Un mari à la porte	1859
Les vivandières de la grande-armée	1859
Geneviève de Brabant	1859/revised 1867 and 1875
Daphnis et Chloé	1859
Barkouf	1860
La chanson du Fortunio	1860
Le pont des soupirs	1861/revised 1868
M. Choufleuri restera chez lui le . . .	1861
Apothicaire et perruquier	1861
Le roman comique	1861
Monsieur et Madame Denis	1862
Les bavards	1862/revised 1863
Le voyage de MM. Dunanan père et fils	1862
Jacqueline	1862
Il signor Fagotto	1863
L'amour chanteur	1864
Les Géorgiennes	1864
Le fifre enchanté, ou Le soldat magician	1864
Jeanne qui pleure et Jean qui rit	1864
La belle Hélène	1864
Coscoletto, ou Le lazzarone	1865
Les bergers	1865
Barbe-Bleue	1866
La vie parisienne	1866/revised 1873

La Grande-Duchesse de Gérolstein	1867
La permission de dix heures	1867/revised 1873
La leçon de chant électromagnétique	1867
Robinson Crusoé	1868
Le château à Toto	1868
L'île de Tulipatan	1868
La Périchole	1868/revised 1874
Vert-vert	1869
La diva	1869
La princesse de Trébizonde	1869
Les brigands	1869
La romance de la rose	1869
Boule de neige	1871
Le roi carotte	1871
Fantasio	1872
Fleurette, oder Trompeter und Näherin	1872
Le corsair noir	1872
Les braconniers	1873
Pomme d'Api	1873
La jolie parfumeuse	1873
Bagatelle	1874
Madame l'archiduc	1874
Whittington	1874
La boulangère a des écus	1875
La voyage dans la lune	1875
La créole	1875
Pierrette et Jacquot	1876
La boîte au lait	1876
Le docteur Ox	1877
La foire Saint-Laurent	1877
Maître Péronilla	1878
Madame Favart	1878
La marocaine	1879
La fille du Tambour-Major	1879
Belle Lurette	1880
Mam'zelle Moucheron	1881

VIENNESE OPERETTA

Ralph Benatzky (1884–1957)

Ein Komet kommt	1910
Der Nachtwächter	1910
Der Record	1910
Die Walzerkomtesse	1910
Der Walzer von heute Nacht	1910
Laridon	1911
Cherchez la femme	1911
Pomponette	1911
Kokettchens Mission	1911
Das blonde Abenteuer	1911
Der lachende Dreibund	1913
Prinzchens Frühlingserwachen	1914
Anno 1914	1914
Das Scheckbuch des Teufels	1914
General Wutsikoff	1914
Fräulein Don Juan	1915
Du goldige Frau	1916
Liebe im Schnee	1916
Die tanzende Maske	1918
Die Verliebten	1919
Graf Cheveraux	1920
Yuschi tanzt	1920
Bluffodont	1920
Apachen!	1920
Ein Märchen aus Florenz	1923
Adieu Mimi	1926
Die Nacht von San Sebastian	1926
Casanova	1928
Die drei Musketiere	1929
Mit dir allein auf einer einsamen Insel	1929
Meine Schwester und ich	1930
Im weißen Rößl (with Stolz)	1930
Cocktail	1930

Zur gold'nen Liebe	1931
Circus Aimee	1932
Bezauberndes Fräulein	1933
Deux sous de fleurs	1933
Das kleine Café	1934
Büxl	1935
Der König mit dem Regenschirm	1935
Axel an der Himmelstür	1936
Herzen im Schnee	1936
Egy lany, aki mindenkie	1936
Pariserinnen	1937
Majestät privat	1937
Landrinette, oder Der Silberhof	1939
Angielina	1940
Kleinstadtzauber	1947
Liebesschule, oder Don Juans Wiederkehr	1950

Leo Fall (1873–1925)

Paroli oder Frau Denise	1902
Einen Jux will er sich machen	1904
Irrlicht	1905
Der Rebell	1905
Der Fuß	1906
Der fidele Bauer	1907
Die Dollarprinzessin	1907
Die geschiedene Frau	1908
Der Schrei nach der Ohrfeige	1909
Brüderlein fein	1909
Das Puppenmädel	1910
Die schöne Risette	1910
Die Sirene	1911
The Eternal Waltz	1911
Der liebe Augustin	1912
Die Studentengräfin, oder Die stille Stadt	1913
Der Nachtschnellzug	1913

Jung-England	1914
Der künstliche Mensch	1915
Die Kaiserin	1915
Fürstenliebe	1916
Seemannsliebchen	1916
Die Rose von Stambul	1916
Tantalus im Dachstüberl	1916
Der goldene Vogel	1920
Die spanische Nachtigall	1920
Frau Ministerpräsident	1920
Die Straßensängerin	1921
Der heilige Ambrosius	1921
Madame Pompadour	1922
Der süße Kavalier	1923
Jugend im Mai	1926
Rosen aus Florida (finished by Korngold)	1929
Der junge Herr Rene	1951

Emmerich Kálmán (1882–1953)

Tatárjárás	1908
Ein Herbstmanöver	1909
Der Zigeunerprimas	1912
The Blue House	1912
Der kleine König	1912
Gold gab ich für Eisen	1914
Die Csárdásfürstin	1915
Zsuzsi kisasszony	1915
Miss Springtime	1916
Die Faschingsfee	1917
Das Hollandweibchen	1920
Die Bajadere	1921
Gräfin Mariza	1924
Die Zirkusprinzessin	1926
Golden Dawn	1927
Die Herzogin von Chicago	1928

Das Veilchen vom Montmartre	1930
Der Teufelsreiter	1932
Kaiserin Josephine	1936
Marinka	1945
Arizona Lady (finished by Charles Kálmán)	1954

Franz Lehár (1870–1948)

Kukuška/Tatjana	1896/revised 1905
Wiener Frauen	1902
Der Rastelbinder	1902
Der Göttergatte	1904
Die Juxheirat	1904
Die lustige Witwe	1905
Der Schlüssel zum Paradies	1906
Peter und Paul reisen ins Schlaraffenland	1906
Mitislaw, der Moderne	1907
Der Mann mit den drei Frauen	1908
Das Fürstenkind	1908
Der Fürst der Berge	1909
Der Graf von Luxemburg	1909/revised 1937
Zigeunerliebe	1910/revised 1943
Eva, oder Das Fabriksmädel	1911
Rosenstock und Edelweiss	1912
Dir ideale Gattin	1913
Endlich allein	1914
Der Sterngucker	1916
Wo die Lerche singt	1918
Die blaue Mazur	1920
Die Tangokönigin	1921
Frühling	1922
La danze delle libellule	1922
Frasquita	1922
Die gelbe Jacke	1923
Libellentanz	1923
Cloclo/Clo-Clo	1924

Paganini	1925
Gigolette	1926
Der Zarewitsch	1927
Frühlingsmädel	1928
Friederike	1928
Das Land des Lächelns	1929
Schön ist die Welt	1930
Der Fürst der Berge	1932
Giuditta	1934
Garabonciás Diák	1943

Robert Stolz (1880–1975)

Studentenulke	1901
Schön Lorchen	1903
Manöverliebe	1906
Die lustigen Weiber von Wien	1908
Die Commandeuse	1909
Grand Hotel Excelsior	1910
Das Glücksmädel	1910
Der Minenkönig	1911
Die eiserne Jungfrau	1911
Du liebes Wien	1913
Das Lumperl	1914
Der Favorit	1916
Der Tanz ins Glück	1920
Die Rosen der Madonna	1920
Das Sperrsechserl	1920
Kikeriki	1921
Die Tanzgräfin	1921
Mädi	1923
Märchen im Schnee	1925
Eine einzige Nacht	1927
Prinzessin Ti-Ti-Pa	1927
Peppina	1930

Der verlorene Walzer	1930
Im weißen Rößl (with Benatzky)	1930
Venus in Seide	1932
Wenn die kleinen Veilchen blühen	1932
Zwei Herzen im Dreivierteltakt	1933
Himmelblaue Träume	1934
Rise and Shine	1936
Die Reise um die Erde in 80 Minuten	1937
Der süßeste Schwindel der Welt	1937
Balaika	1938
Night of Love	1941
Mr. Strauss Goes to Boston	1945
Schicksal mit Musik	1946
Drei von der Donau	1947
Ein Lied aus der Vorstadt	1948
Fest in Casablanca	1949
Frühling im Prater	1949
Karneval in Wien	1950
Das Glücksrezept	1951
Rainbow Square	1951
Ballade vom lieben Augustin	1953
Kleiner Schwindel in Paris	1956
Trauminsel	1962
Ein schöner Herbst	1963
Frühjahrsparade	1964
Hochzeit am Bodensee	1969

Oscar Straus (1870–1954)

Die lustigen Nibelungen	1904
Zur indischen Witwe	1905
Hugdietrichs Braufahrt	1906
Ein Walzertraum	1907
Der tapfere Soldat	1908
Didi	1908

Das Tal der Liebe	1909
Mein junger Herr	1910
Die kleine Freundin	1911
Der tapfere Cassian	1912
The Dancing Viennese	1912
Love and Laughter	1913
Rund um die Liebe	1914
Liebeszauber	1916
Der letzte Walzer	1920
Die Perlen der Cleopatra	1923
Die Teresina	1925
Die Königin	1926
Marietta	1927/revised 1928
Die Musik kommt	1928/revised 1950
Eine Frau, die weiss, was sie will	1932
Drei Walzer	1935
Bozena	1952

Johann Strauss II (1825–1899)

Indigo und die vierzig Räuber	1871
Der Karneval in Rom	1873
Die Fledermaus	1874
Cagliostro in Wien	1875
Prinz Methusalem	1877
Blindekuh	1878
Das Spitzentuch der Königin	1880
Der lustige Krieg	1881
Eine Nacht in Venedig	1883
Der Zigeunerbaron	1885
Simplicius	1887
Ritter Pázmán	1892
Fürstin Ninetta	1893
Jabuka	1894
Waldmeister	1895
Die Göttin der Vernunft	1897
Wiener Blut	1899

Josef Strauss (1827–1870)*

*While he did not write in the genre during his lifetime, his music was repurposed into operettas posthumously.

Frühlingsluft	1903
Frauenherz	1905
Das Schwalberl aus dem Wienerwald	1906
Das Teufelsmädel	1908
Die weisse Fahne	1911
Freut euch des Lebens	1932
Walzerträume	1942
Die Straussbuben	1946

Franz von Suppé (1819–1895)

Virginia	1837
Gertrude della valle	1841
Dichter und Bauer	1846
Das Mädchen vom Lande	1847
Dame Valentine	1851
Paragraph 3	1858
Das Pensionat	1860
Die Kartenaufschlägerin, oder Pique Dame	1862
Zehn Mädchen und kein Mann	1862
Die flotten Burschen	1863
Das Corps der Rache	1864
Franz Schubert	1864
Dinorah	1865
Die schöne Galathée	1865
Die Freigeister	1866
Leichte Kavallerie	1866
Banditenstreiche	1867
Die Frau Meisterin	1868
Tantalusqualen	1868
Isabella	1869
Lohengelb	1870
Cannebas	1872

Fünfundzwanzig Mädchen und kein Mann	1873
Fatinitza	1876
Der Teufel auf Erden	1878
Boccaccio	1879
Donna Juanita	1880
Der Gascogner	1881
Das Herzblättchen	1882
Die Afrikareise	1883
Des Matrosen Heimkehr	1885
Bellmann	1887
Die Jagd nach dem Glück	1888
Das Modell	1895
Die Pariserin	1898
Der große Unbekannte	1925

Carl Zeller (1842–1898)

Joconde	1876
Die Fornarina	1879
Die Carbonari	1880
Capitän Nicoll	1880
Der Vagabund	1886
Der Vogelhändler	1891
The Mine Foreman	1894
Der Obersteiger	1894
Der Kellermeister (finished by Johannes Brandl)	1901

ENGLISH OPERETTA

Noël Coward (1899–1973)

Bitter Sweet	1929

Arthur Sullivan (1842–1900)
*with W. S. Gilbert

Cox and Box	1866
The Contrabandista	1867

Thespis°	1871
Trial by Jury°	1875
The Zoo	1875
The Sorcerer°	1877/revised 1884
HMS Pinafore°	1878
The Pirates of Penzance°	1879
Patience°	1881
Iolanthe°	1882
Princess Ida°	1884
The Mikado°	1885
Ruddigore°	1887
The Yeomen of the Guard°	1888
The Gondoliers°	1889
Haddon Hall	1892
Utopia, Limited°	1893
The Chieftain	1894
The Grand Duke°	1896
The Rose of Persia	1899
The Emerald Isle (with Edward German)	1901

AMERICAN OPERETTA

Leonard Bernstein (1918–1990)

Candide	1956

Rudolf Friml (1879–1972)

The Firefly	1912
High Jinks	1913
Katinka	1915
You're in Love	1917
Kitty Darlin'	1917
Sometime	1918
Gloriana	1918

Tumble In	1919
The Little Whopper	1919
June Love	1920
The Blue Kitten	1922
Cinders	1923
Rose-Marie	1924
The Vagabond King	1925
The Wild Rose	1926
White Eagle	1927
The Three Musketeers	1928
Luana	1930
Music Hath Charms	1934

Victor Herbert (1859–1924)

Prince Ananis	1894
The Wizard of the Nile	1895
The Gold Bug	1896
The Serenade	1897
The Idol's Eye	1897
The Fortune Teller	1898
The Ameer	1899
Cyrano de Bergerac	1899
The Singing Girl	1899
The Viceroy	1900
Babes in Toyland	1903
Babette	1903
Mlle. Modiste	1905
The Red Mill	1906
The Magic Knight	1906
Dream City	1906
The Tattooed Man	1907
The Songbirds	1907
The Prima Donna	1908
Naughty Marietta	1910

The Duchess	1911
The Enchantress	1911
The Lady of the Slipper	1912
Sweethearts	1913
The Madcap Duchess	1913
The Princess Pat	1915
Eileen	1917
Her Regiment	1917
The Girl in the Spotlight	1920

Sigmund Romberg (1887–1951)

The Blue Paradise	1915
Follow Me	1916
Maytime	1917
Blossom Time	1921
The Rose of Stamboul	1922
The Student Prince	1924
The Desert Song	1926
The New Moon	1928
May Wine	1935
The Girl in Pink Tights	1954

John Philip Sousa (1854–1932)

Katherine	1879
The Smugglers	1882
The Queen of Hearts	1885
The Wolf	1888
Désirée	1893
El Capitan	1896
The Bride Elect	1898
The Charlatan	1898
The Free Lance	1906
The Amsterdam Maid	1913

SPANISH ZARZUELA

Francisco Asenjo Barbieri (1823–1894)
*with Gaztambide and Hernando

Gloria y peluca	1850
Tramoya	1850
*Escenas en Chamberí**	1850
La picaresca (with Gaztambide)	1850
Jugar con fuego	1851/revised 1857
*Por seguir a una mujer viaje**	1851
El Manzanares	1852
Gracias a Dios que está puesta la mesa	1852
El marqués de Caravaca	1853
*Don Simplicio Bodadilla**	1853
Galanteos en Venecia	1853
Aventura de un cantante	1854
Los diamantes de la corona	1854
Mis dos mujeres	1855
Los dos ciegos	1855
El Sargento Federico (with Gaztambide)	1855/revised 1857
El vizconde	1855
El diablo en el poder	1856
El relámpago	1857
Amar sin conocer (with Gaztambide)	1858
Un caballero particular	1858
Por conquista	1858
El robo de las sabinas	1859
Entre mi mujer yel negro	1859
El niño	1859
Un tesoro escondido	1861/revised 1867
El secreto de una dama	1862
Dos pichones del Turia	1863
Pan y toros	1864
Gibraltar en 1890	1866
El pan de la boda	1868
Le trésor caché	1869

Robinsón	1870
Los holgazanes	1871
Don Pacifico	1871
El hombres es débil	1871
Sueños de oro	1872
Los comediantes de antaño	1873
El matrimonio interrumpido	1873
El barberillo de Lavapiés	1874
El domador de fieras	1874
La vuelta al mundo	1875
Chorizos y polacos	1876
La confitera	1876
Juan de Urbina	1876
Artistas para la Habana	1877
Los caboneros	1877
El triste Chactas	1878
Los chicones	1879
¡A Sevilla por todo!	1880
Anda, valiente	1881
Sobre el canto de Ultreja	1883
Hoy sale, hoy . . . ! (with Chueca)	1884
Los fusileros	1884
Novillos en Polvoranca	1885
El señor Luis el Tumbón	1891

Tomás Bretón (1850–1923)

El alma en un hilo	1874
Los dos caminos	1874
Los dos leones (with Nieto)	1874
El bautizo de Pepín	1874
Por un cantar jugete	1875
El noventa y tres	1875
Un chaparrón de maridos	1875
El inválido	1875
María	1875

Por un cantar	1876
El capitán Mendoza	1876
Contar con la huéspeda (with Chueca/Valverde)	1877
¡Cuidado con los estudiantes!	1877
Novio, padre y suegro	1877
Estudiantes y alguaciles	1877
¡Bonito país! (with Chueca/Valverde)	1877
El campanero de Begoña	1878
Corona contra corona	1879
Las señoritas de Conil	1880
Los amores de un príncipe	1881
Vista y sentencia (with González)	1886
El caballo del señorito	1890
La verbena de la Paloma	1894
El domingo de Ramos	1894
Al fin se casa la Nieves	1895
Botín de guerra	1896
El guardia de corps	1897
El puente del diablo	1898
El reloj de cuco	1898
La cariñosa	1899
El clavel rojo	1899
Covadonga	1901
La bien plantá	1902
El certamen de Cremona	1906
¡Ya se van los quintos, madre!	1908
Piel de oso	1909
Las percheleras	1911
Los husares del Zar	1914

Manuel Fernández Caballero (1835–1906)

La marsellesa	1876
Los sobrinos del capitán Grant	1877
El salto del pasiego	1878
Chateau Margaux	1887

El dúo de "La africana"	1893
El cabo primero	1896
La viejecita	1897
El señor Joaquín	1898
Gigantes y cabezudos	1898

Ruperto Chapí (1851–1909)

Música clasica	1880
La tempestad	1882
El milagro de la Virgen	1884
La bruja	1887
El rey que rabió	1891
El tambor de granaderos	1894
Las bravías	1896
La revoltosa	1897
La chavala	1898
Curro Vargas	1898
El barquillero	1900
El puñao de rosas	1902
La venta de Don Quijote	1902
La patria chica	1907

Gerónimo Giménez (1854–1923)

Las niñas desenvueltas	1878
El esclavo	1887
Escuela modelo	1888
La tiple	1889
Tannhauser el estanquero	1890
La república de Chamba	1890
Tannhauser cesante	1890
Trafalgar	1890
¡Pero cómo está Madrid!	1891
La cencerrada	1892
El hijo de su excelencia	1892

La madre del cordero	1892
El ventorrillo del Chato	1892
Candidita	1893
La mujer del molinero	1893
Los voluntaries	1893
Viento en popa	1894
La sobrina del sacristan	1895
De vuelta del vivero	1895
Las mujeres	1896
El mundo comedia es	1896
Aquí va a haber algo gordo	1897
La boda de Luis Alonso	1897
La guardia amarilla	1897
Amor engendra	1899
Los borrachos	1899
La familia de Sicur	1899
Joshé Martín, el tamborilero	1900
La tempranica	1900
El barbero de Sevilla (with Nieto)	1901
Correo interior (with Nieto and Cereceda)	1901
Enseñanza libre	1901
Los timplaos	1901
Maria del Pilar	1902
El morrongo	1902
La torre del oro	1902
La camarona	1903
El general	1903
La morenita	1903
La visión de Fray Martín	1903
Cuadros al fresco	1904
El húsar de la guardia (with Vives)	1904
Los pícaros celas	1904
La sequía	1904
El amigo del alma	1905
El arte de ser bonita (with Vives)	1905
Cascabel	1905

Las granadinas (with Vives)	1905
Los guapos	1905
¡Libertad! (with Vives)	1905
El diablo verde (with Vives)	1906
La gatita blanca (with Vives)	1906
El golpe de estado (with Vives)	1906
El guante amarillo (with Vives)	1906
La Machaquito (with Vives)	1906
La marcha real (with Vives)	1906
La venta de la alegría	1906
La antorcha del himeneo	1907
Cinematógrafo nacional	1907
El príncipe real	1907
A.B.C.	1908
La dos rivales	1908
La eterna revista (with Chapí)	1908
El grito de independencia	1908
La leyenda mora	1908
El trust de las mujeres	1908
Las mil y pico de noches	1909
El patinillo	1909
Pepe el liberal	1909
Los juglares	1911
Lirio entre espinas	1911
La suerte de Isabelita (with Calleja)	1911
Los viajes de Gulliver (with Vives)	1911
Los ángeles Mandan	1912
El coche del diablo	1912
El cuento del dragon	1912
Las hijas de Venus	1912
Los hombres que son hombres	1912
Ovación y oreja	1913
El príncipe Pío	1913
El gran simulacro	1914
Malagueñas	1914
El ojo de gallo	1914

Las castañuelas	1915
Cine fantomas	1915
La pandereta	1915
La última operetta	1915
Ysidrin, o Las cuarenta y nueve provincias	1915
La embajadora	1916
La Eva ideal	1916
La guitarra del amor (with Bretón)	1916
La costilla de Adán	1917
Esta noche es nochebuena	1917
El Zorro	1917
Abejas y zánganos	1918
La bella persa	1918
Tras Tristán	1918
La España de la alegría	1919
El gran Olavide	1919
Soleares	1919
La cortesana de Omán	1920

Federico Moreno Torroba (1891–1982)

La mesonera de Tordesillas	1925
La pastorella	1925
La marchenera	1929
Baturra de Temple	1929
Maria la tempránica	1930
Luisa Fernanda	1932
Xuanón	1933
La caravana de Ambrosio	1934
La chulapona	1934
Paloma Moreno	1936
Monte Carmelo	1936
Sor Navarra	1936
Oro de Ley	1938
Cascabeles	1940

Maravilla	1941
Polonesa	1941
La caramba	1942
La ilustra moza	1943
Baile de Trajes	1944
La canción del organillo	1945
Orgullo de Jalisco	1947
La niña del Polisón	1948
El diablo en Sierra Morena	1952
La boda del Señor Bringas	1953
Hola Ciqui	1953
Maria Manuela	1953

Pablo Sorozábal (1897–1988)

Katiuska	1931
La guitarra de Fígaro	1931
La isla de las perlas	1933
Adiós a la bohemia	1933
El alguacil rebolledo	1934
Sol en la cumbre	1934
La del manojo de rosas	1934
No me olvides	1935
La casa de las tres muchachas	1935
La tabernera del puerto	1936
La Rosario, o La Rambla de fin de siglo	1941
Cuidado con la pintura	1941
Black, el payaso	1942
Don Manolito	1943
La eterna canción	1945
Los burladores	1948
Entre Sevilla y Triana	1950
La ópera del mogollón	1954
Brindis	1955
Las de Caín	1958

Amadeu/Amadeo Vives (1871–1932)

La primera del barrio	1898
Don Lucas del Cigarral	1899
La balada de la luz	1900
Euda d'Uriach	1900
Los amores de la Inés (with de Falla)	1902
Bohemios	1904
El húsar de la guardia	1904
El arte de ser bonita	1905
La gatita blanca	1906
Juegos malabares	1909
Colomba	1910
El carro del sol	1911
La generala	1912
Maruxa	1914
La balada de Carnaval	1919
Doña Francisquita	1923
La villana	1927
Talismán	1932

APPENDIX B

"Top 10" and "Top 40" Lists of Light Opera

This "Top 10" list includes the most frequently performed operettas across the world, according to statistics by Operabase and Opera America.

1. *Die Fledermaus*

   The obvious choice for the number one operetta, *Die Fledermaus* earns its top spot thanks to the amusing disguises of its characters and the musical appeal of the Watch Duet, the Laughing Song, the *csárdás*, and the Strauss waltzes.

2. *The Merry Widow*

   Franz Lehár's classic comes in a close second. With its mature romance (exemplified in the delayed denouement of "Lippen schweigen") and irresistible can-can, *The Merry Widow* provides ample variety in its tuneful music and colorful costuming.

3. *The Pirates of Penzance*

   The best-known Gilbert and Sullivan (G&S) show, *Pirates'* amusing story of pilot/pirate confusion features the Modern Major-General's famous patter song (which includes a joke about *HMS Pinafore*) and the ever-popular "Poor Wandering One" (which even figured prominently in the 1992 thriller *The Hand That Rocks the Cradle*).

4. *HMS Pinafore*

Perhaps the most quintessentially British of the G&S canon, *Pinafore* charms with its nautical theme and endearing romance while satirizing class distinctions. The patriotic "A British Tar" and the catchy trio "Never Mind the Why and Wherefore" are among its greatest hits.

5. *The Mikado*

Despite the challenge of presenting it in the twenty-first century, *The Mikado* is perhaps the most-quoted G&S show (parodied in everything from *The Simpsons* to *The Muppet Show*). "Three Little Maids," "A Wandering Minstrel I," "I've Got a Little List," and "Tit-willow" are the top songs that live on beyond the context of the show and fuel its continued popularity despite its cultural insensitivities.

6. *Orphée aux enfers*

Jacques Offenbach's mythological farce offers opportunities for many singers in its numerous roles, but its greatest delights are the absurdly clever Fly Duet and, of course, the Infernal Galop's signature can-can, which lives on at the Moulin Rouge.

7. *Die Csárdásfürstin*

The Gypsy Princess maintains immense popularity, outranking Verdi's *Otello* and *Un ballo in maschera* in Operabase's 2016 global listing. Although not as familiar to American audiences, Emmerich Kálmán's operetta has been a star vehicle for both Anna Moffo and Anna Netrebko.

8. *Candide*

Leonard Bernstein's version of Voltaire showcases sharp satire with memorable musical moments such as the coloratura tour de force "Glitter and Be Gay"; the inspiring ensemble finale "Make Our Garden Grow"; and the witty "We Are Women" (added in 1958) with lyrics by Bernstein himself.

9. *La Périchole*

The title role in Offenbach's opera has been a signature one for singers like Frederica von Stade and Teresa Berganza. The show depends on an endearing leading lady, as epitomized in the charming Tipsy Waltz.

10. *Babes in Toyland*

Victor Herbert's nursery rhyme–themed operetta has found a niche in children's theater and on film thanks to its kid-friendly songs and scenarios. Its familiar tunes include "I Can't Do the Sum," "March of the Toys," and, of course, "Toyland."

Completing the "Top 40," the remainder of this list is categorized by country, and the categories could easily be in a different order depending on one's preferences.

British Operetta:

11. *Trial by Jury*

   The only G&S opera without dialogue, *Trial by Jury* remains incredibly relevant as a satire of the legal system. With only one female principal role, it requires a strong cast of male singers, although modern productions are starting to cast mezzo-sopranos in the traditionally baritone role of Angelina's Counsel.

12. *The Gondoliers*

   My favorite G&S show, *The Gondoliers* contains some of Sullivan's most appealing music, featuring Italianate touches, mocking of the monarchy, and two strong quartets of characters.

13. *The Yeomen of the Guard*

   Thought by many critics to be the most refined musical score of the G&S oeuvre, *The Yeomen of the Guard* has some of Gilbert's most droll song titles: "I've Jibe and Joke," "Is Life a Boon?" and "Oh! A Private Buffoon Is a Light-Hearted Loon."

14. *Iolanthe*

   This G&S fairy operetta parodies parliamentary politics while celebrating fairyland. The Lord Chancellor's so-called Nightmare Song, "When You're Lying Awake," is one of their best patter songs.

15. *Ruddigore*

   With a cast of witches and ghosts, *Ruddigore* is the perfect G&S Halloween opera. Lampooning melodrama, it features the plum mezzo-soprano role of Mad Margaret.

16. *Bitter Sweet*

   Although it is set primarily in London, Noël Coward's *Bitter Sweet* pays homage to France with cabaret singer Manon's song "Bonne nuit, merci" and to Austro-Hungary in Sarah's aria, "Zigeuner," and the Bitter Sweet Waltz.

French *opéra bouffe*:

17. *La Grande-Duchesse de Gérolstein*
    Offenbach's playful satire of the military demands a grand presence for its title character, and recently Susan Graham has fit the bill. The Duchess sings the show's highlights, "Ah! Que j'aime les militaires" and "Dites-lui."

18. *La belle Hélène*
    As with his *Orphée*, Offenbach turns another set of mythological characters into a plethora of comedic parts. The arias sung by Hélène ("Amours divins") and Paris ("Au mont Ida") figure prominently, as does the "Trio Patriotique" of Ménélas, Agamemnon, and Calchas.

19. *La vie parisienne*
    With its supremely Parisian style and setting, this Offenbach operetta portrays Second Empire "Gay Paree" with its cast of dandies, valets, and demimondaines. Among its memorable musical moments are the patter piece "Je suis Brésilien, j'ai de l'or" and Gabrielle's *couplets* "On va courir, on va sortir."

American Operetta:

20. *The New Moon*
    Sigmund Romberg's operetta has the appeal of a New Orleans setting along with some of the genre's most romantic music: "Lover, Come Back to Me," "One Kiss," and "Softly, as in a Morning Sunrise."

21. *The Desert Song*
    Inspired by *Lawrence of Arabia*, Romberg's *The Desert Song* embodies light opera's predilection for exotic locales. It is probably best known for the beautiful ballad "One Alone."

22. *The Student Prince*
    One of Romberg's most popular works, *The Student Prince* is performed annually at Heidelberg Castle. It features the lyrical tenor serenade "Overhead the Moon Is Beaming," as well as the obligatory drinking song "Drink! Drink! Drink!"

23. *Naughty Marietta*
    Herbert's *Naughty Marietta* is famous for Marietta's show-pieces "Italian Street Song" and "Ah! Sweet Mystery of Life." Set

in the Big Easy, the show makes the most of its lively aspects, including pirates, marionettes, and voodoo.

24. *Rose-Marie*

Later parodied in the musical *Little Mary Sunshine*, Rudolf Friml's *Rose-Marie* is set in the Rocky Mountains, making it ideal for outdoor summer theater venues. It includes what is often considered Jeanette MacDonald and Nelson Eddy's most famous duet, "Indian Love Call."

25. *The Vagabond King*

Friml's other notable work, *The Vagabond King*, bears a markedly more serious tone than most light opera, with Renaissance Paris under attack by Burgundy. Still, it has typical operetta elements, such as a drinking song ("A Flagon of Wine"), a waltz ("Never Try to Bind Me"), and a march ("Song of the Vagabonds").

26. *El Capitain*

So-called March King John Philip Sousa found success with this story of the Viceroy of Peru disguised as a rebel leader. The El Capitain March remains popular, as does Isabel's waltz aria, "Oh, Warrior Grim," with its refrain of "boom a boom."

Viennese Operetta:

27. *Gräfin Mariza*

Kálmán's *Countess Maritza* is full of Hungarian gypsy touches and country charm, with a feigned engagement to a pig farmer and allusion to Strauss's *Der Zigeunerbaron*. "Hör ich Zigeunergeigen" is Mariza's famous entrance aria.

28. *Das Land des Lächelns*

The Land of Smiles, Lehár's depiction of a Viennese countess who marries a Chinese prince, remains a staple of the repertory, as does the famous *Tauberlied* "Dein ist mein ganzes Herz."

29. *Der Graf von Luxemburg*

In Lehár's *The Count of Luxembourg*, the Grand Duke pays a penniless Count to marry and divorce opera singer Angèle so she can attain the rank to marry him. But of course, she and the Count fall for each other, declaring their love in the duet "Es duftet nach Trèfle incarnat/Was ich im Traum nur ersah."

30. *Im weißen Rößl*

The *White Horse Inn* is known for its Austrian alpine setting, not to mention the well-known numbers "Es muß was wunderbares sein" (by Ralph Benatzsky) and "Die ganze Welt ist himmelblau" (by Robert Stolz).

31. *Der Zigeunerbaron*

Hungarian influences permeate Strauss's *The Gypsy Baron*, from Saffi's *Zigeunerlied* "So elend und so treu" to Homonay's *csárdás* "Wir alle wollen lustig sein."

32. *Die Dollarprinzessin*

The charm of Leo Fall's *The Dollar Princess* is in notable numbers such as the opening chorus of Die Schreibmaschinenmädel typing in unison; Fredy's romantic waltz, "Will sie dann lieben treu und heiß"; and Hans and Daisy's playful duet, "Paragraf Eins." An American version added two songs by Jerome Kern.

33. *Der Vogelhändler*

Carl Zeller's operetta follows the romance between Tyrolean birdseller Adam and postmistress Christel, characterized by his melodious waltz "Wie mein Ahnl zwanzig Jahr."

34. *Der tapfere Soldat*

Based on George Bernard Shaw's *Arms and the Man*, *The Chocolate Soldier* is set in Bulgaria. Its greatest hits by Oscar Straus include Nadina's aria "Komm, komm! Held meiner Träume" and her duet with Bumerli "Ach, du kleiner Praliné-Soldat."

Spanish Zarzuela (ranking by Christopher Webber):

35. *La verbena de la Paloma*

In Tomás Bretón's one-act *sainete lírico*, Julián wins back the love of Susana, overcoming the interference of the old apothecary Don Hilarión. Its most famous music is Julián's habanera, "¿Dónde vas con mantón de Manila?" Zarzuela expert Christopher Webber calls *La verbena* "the brightest jewel of the repertoire."

36. *La revoltosa*

Ruperto Chapí wrote his popular one-act in response to his rival's success with *La verbena de la Paloma*. The so-called troublemaker of the zarzuela's title is the spirited Mari-Pepa. Her passionate duet with Felipe "¿Por qué de mis ojos los tuyos retiras?" is one of its musical highlights.

37. *Doña Francisquita*

This romantic zarzuela by Amadeo Vives has reached an international audience thanks to recordings by Plácido Domingo and Alfredo Kraus. Francisquita wins over her lover, Fernando, with her seductive coloratura *Canción del ruiseñor* "Era una rosa que en un jardín."

38. *El barberillo de Lavapiés*

Barber Lamparilla is the star of Francisco Asenjo Barbieri's *zarzuela grande*. With the help of his girlfriend, Paloma, he overcomes conspirators, reminding us of Rossini's Figaro with his spirited seguidilla "En el templo de Marte."

39. *Luisa Fernanda*

The title role in Federico Moreno Torroba's zarzuela has been a showcase for singers such as Verónica Villarroel and Nancy Herrera. *Luisa Fernanda* centers on the love triangle between Luisa, Javier (a military officer), and Vidal (a wealthy landowner), depicted in their trio "¡Cuánto tiempo sin verte, Luisa Fernanda!"

40. *La del manojo de rosas*

The Girl with the Roses is Pablo Sorozábal's heroine florist Ascensión, who has a complicated romance with the mechanic Joaquín. The zarzuela soars in their noteworthy duet "Hace tiempo que vengo al taller" and the habanera "Qué tiempos aquellos!"

APPENDIX C

Audition Aria Lists by Voice Type

Soprano

Audran, Edmond	Allons, petit serpent	*Le grand mogol*	Irma
	Mon Dieu, sait-on jamais	*La poupée*	Alésia
Barbieri, Francisco	De qué me sirve	*Los diamantes de la*	Catalina
		corona	
Bernstein, Leonard	Glitter and Be Gay	*Candide*	Cunegonde
Caballero, Manuel	Ésta es su carta	*Gigantes y cabezudos*	Pilar
Chapí, Ruperto	Mi tio se figura	*El rey que rabió*	Rosa
Coward, Noël	The Call of Life	*Bitter Sweet*	Sarah
	Zigeuner	*Bitter Sweet*	Sarah
Fall, Leo	Ein echtes Selfmade-	*Die Dollarprinzessin*	Alice
	Mädel		
Friml, Rudolf	Giannina mia	*The Firefly*	Nina
	Love Is like a Firefly	*The Firefly*	Nina
	Pretty Things	*Rose-Marie*	Rose-Marie
	Some Day	*The Vagabond King*	Katherine
Giménez, Gerónimo	Me llaman la primosoa	*El barbero de Sevilla*	Elena
	Sierras de Granada	*La tempranica*	Maria
Herbert, Victor	A Legend	*Babes in Toyland*	Gertrude
	Barney O'Flynn	*Babes in Toyland*	Mary
	Go to Sleep, Slumber	*Babes in Toyland*	Fairy
	Deep		
	He Won't Be Happy	*Babes in Toyland*	Jane
	Always Do as People Say	*The Fortune Teller*	Irma
	If I Were on the Stage	*Mlle. Modiste*	Fifi
	The Nightingale and	*Mlle. Modiste*	Fifi
	the Star		

Composer	Aria	Opera	Character
	Ah! Sweet Mystery of Life	Naughty Marietta	Marietta
	Italian Street Song	Naughty Marietta	Marietta
	Mignonette	The Red Mill	Tina
	Cupid and I	The Serenade	Yvonne
	Mother Goose	Sweethearts	Sylvia
	Sweethearts	Sweethearts	Sylvia
	There Is Magic in a Smile	Sweethearts	Liane
Kálmán, Emmerich	Heia, in den Bergen	Die Csárdásfürstin	Sylva
	Was in der Welt geschieht	Die Zirkusprinzessin	Fedora
	Hör ich Zigeunergeigen	Gräfin Mariza	Mariza
Lecocq, Charles	Je vous dois tout	La fille de Madame Angot	Clairette
	Père adoré, c'est Giroflé	Giroflé-Girofla	Giroflé
	Petit papa, c'est Girofla	Giroflé-Girofla	Girofla
Lehár, Franz	Im heimlilchen Dämmer	Eva	Eva
	Meine Lippen, sie küssen so heiß	Giuditta	Giuditta
	Heut' meine Herr'n war ein Tag	Das Land des Lächelns	Lisa
	Es lebt' eine Vilja	Die lustige Witwe	Hanna
	Liebe, du Himmel auf Erden	Paganini	Maria
	Einer wird kommen	Der Zarewitsch	Sonja
	Hör' ich Zimbalklänge	Zigeunerliebe	Ilona
Lortzing, Albert	Die Eifersucht ist eine Plage	Zar und Zimmermann	Marie
Messager, André	Le jour sous le soleil béni	Madame Chrysanthème	Madame Chrysanthème
Moreno Torroba, Federico	La petenera	La marchenera	Valentina
Offenbach, Jacques	Au chapeau je porte	Les brigands	Fiorella
	La femme dont le coeur rêve	Orphée aux enfers	Eurydice
	La mort m'apparaît souriante	Orphée aux enfers	Eurydice
	Quand Diane descend	Orphée aux enfers	Diane
	On va courir, on va sortir	La vie parisienne	Gabrielle
	Je suis nerveuse	Le voyage dans la lune	Princess Fantasia
Romberg, Sigmund	French Military Marching Song	The Desert Song	Margot
	Romance	The Desert Song	Margot
	Lover, Come Back to Me	The New Moon	Marianne
	One Kiss	The New Moon	Marianne
Sorozábal, Pablo	Noche hermosa	Katiuska	Katiuska
Sousa, John Philip	Oh, Warrior Grim	El Capitan	Isabel
	When the Gallant Fight Is O'er	El Capitan	Estrelda
Stolz, Robert	Spiel' auf deiner Geige	Venus in Seide	Jadja

Composer	Aria	Opera	Character
Straus, Oscar	Komm! Held meiner Träume	*Der tapfere Soldat*	Nadina
	G'stellte Mädeln, resch und fesch	*Ein Walzertraum*	Franzi
Strauss, Johann	Frutti di mare	*Eine Nacht in Venedig*	Annina
	Was mir der Zufall gab	*Eine Nacht in Venedig*	Annina
	Csárdás: Klänge der Heimat	*Die Fledermaus*	Rosalinda
	Mein Herr Marquis	*Die Fledermaus*	Adele
	Spiel ich die Unschuld vom Lande	*Die Fledermaus*	Adele
	So elend und so treu	*Der Zigeunerbaron*	Saffi
Sullivan, Arthur	Kind Sir, You Cannot Have the Heart	*The Gondoliers*	Gianetta
	Thank You, Gallant Gondolieri	*The Gondoliers*	Gianetta
	How Would I Play This Part	*The Grand Duke*	Julia
	So Ends My Dream	*The Grand Duke*	Julia
	A Simple Sailor Lowly Born	*HMS Pinafore*	Josephine
	Sorry Her Lot	*HMS Pinafore*	Josephine
	Good Morrow, Good Lover!	*Iolanthe*	Phyllis
	For Riches and Rank	*Iolanthe*	Phyllis
	The Sun, Whose Rays	*The Mikado*	Yum-Yum
	Ah! If There Be Pardon	*Patience*	Patience
	I Cannot Tell What This Love	*Patience*	Patience
	Poor Wandering One	*The Pirates of Penzance*	Mabel
	A Lady Fair of Lineage High	*Princess Ida*	Lady Psyche
	I Built upon a Rock	*Princess Ida*	Ida
	Oh, Goddess Wise	*Princess Ida*	Ida
	'Neath My Lattice	*The Rose of Persia*	Rose-in-Bloom
	If Somebody There Chanced to Be	*Ruddigore*	Rose
	Dear Friends, Take Pity on My Lot	*The Sorcerer*	Constance
	Happy Young Heart	*The Sorcerer*	Aline
	Let Us Fly to a Far-Off Land	*The Sorcerer*	Aline
	When He Is Here	*The Sorcerer*	Constance
	'Tis Done! I Am a Bride	*The Yeomen of the Guard*	Elsie
Suppé, Franz von	Leise bebt	*Die schöne Galathée*	Galathée
Vives, Amadeu	Era una rosa que en un jardín	*Doña Francisquita*	Francisquita
Zeller, Carl	Ich bin die Christel von der Post	*Der Vogelhändler*	Christel

Composer	Aria	Opera	Character
Mezzo-soprano			
Barbieri, Francisco	Como nací en la calle de la Paloma	El barberillo de Lavapiés	Paloma
	Romanza de la Duquesa	Jugar con fuego	Duquesa
Bernstein, Leonard	I Am Easily Assimilated	Candide	Old Lady
Caballero, Manuel	Balada y Alborada	El señor Joaquín	Trini
	Al espejo al salir me miré	La viejecita	Carlos
Chapí, Ruperto	Cuando está tan hondo	El barquillero	Socorro
	Carceleras	Las hijas del Zebedeo	Luisa
Coward, Noël	If Love Were All	Bitter Sweet	Manon
Friml, Rudolf	Never Try to Bind Me	The Vagabond King	Huguette
Giménez, Gerónimo	La tarántula e un bicho mu malo	La tempranica	Grabié
Herbert, Victor	'Neath the Southern Moon	Naughty Marietta	Adah
	A Widow Has Ways	The Red Mill	Bertha
Lecocq, Charles	Marchande de marée	La fille de Madame Angot	Amaranthe
	Pauvres victimes	Giroflé-Girofla	Aurore
Lehár, Franz	Alles mit Ruhe geniessen	Der Graf von Luxemburg	Countess Kokozow
Offenbach, Jacques	Amours divins	La belle Hélène	Hélène
	On me nomme Hélène la blonde	La belle Hélène	Hélène
	Là, vrai, je ne suis pas coupable	La belle Hélène	Hélène
	Examinez ma figure	La fille du Tambour-Major	Duchesse
	Ah! Que j'aime les militaires	La Grande-Duchesse de Gérolstein	Duchesse
	Je passe sur mon enfance	Madame Favart	Madame Favart
	Ah! Quel dîner je viens de faire	La Périchole	La Périchole
	Tu n'es pas beau, tu n'es pas riche	La Périchole	La Périchole
	C'est ici l'endroit redouté	La vie parisienne	Métella
	Vous souvient-il, ma belle	La vie parisienne	Métella
Romberg, Sigmund	Song of the Brass Key	The Desert Song	Clementina
Sousa, John Philip	This Barbarous Land Uncouth	El Capitan	Princess Marghanza
Straus, Oscar	Ein Mädchen, das so lieb und brav	Ein Walzertraum	Friederike
Strauss, Johann	Chacun à son goût	Die Fledermaus	Prince Orlofsky
	Bald wird man dich viel umwerben	Der Zigeunerbaron	Czipra
	Just sind es vierundzwanzig Jahre	Der Zigeunerbaron	Mirabella
Sullivan, Arthur	On the Day When I Was Wedded	The Gondoliers	Duchess of Plaza-Toro

Composer	Aria	Opera	Character
	When a Merry Maiden Marries	*The Gondoliers*	Tessa
	Come Bumpers-Aye Ever So Many	*The Grand Duke*	Baroness of Krakenfeldt
	Take Care of Him	*The Grand Duke*	Lisa
	A Many Years Ago	*HMS Pinafore*	Buttercup
	I'm Called Little Buttercup	*HMS Pinafore*	Buttercup
	My Lord, a Suppliant at Your Feet	*Iolanthe*	Iolanthe
	Oh Foolish Fay	*Iolanthe*	Queen of the Fairies
	Alone and Yet Alive	*The Mikado*	Katisha
	Silvered Is the Raven Hair	*Patience*	Lady Jane
	When Fredric Was a Lad	*The Pirates of Penzance*	Ruth
	Come Mighty Must!	*Princess Ida*	Lady Blanche
	Cheerily Carols the Lark	*Ruddigore*	Mad Margaret
	Sir Rupert Murgatroyd	*Ruddigore*	Dame Hannah
	There Grew a Little Flower	*Ruddigore*	Dame Hannah
	Bold-Faced Ranger	*Utopia, Limited*	Lady Sophy
	When But a Maid of Fifteen Year	*Utopia, Limited*	Lady Sophy
	Were I Thy Bride	*The Yeomen of the Guard*	Phoebe
	When Maiden Loves	*The Yeomen of the Guard*	Phoebe
	When Our Gallant Norman Foes	*The Yeomen of the Guard*	Dame Carruthers
Suppé, Franz von	Eine Frau darf wolbedacht	*Boccaccio*	Isabella
	Ich sehe einen jungen Mann	*Boccaccio*	Boccaccio
	So oft man mich nach Neum fragt	*Boccaccio*	Boccaccio

Tenor

Composer	Aria	Opera	Character
Audran, Edmond	Oui, la raison guidant son coeur	*La cigale et la fourmi*	Frantz
	Par tout le pays je chemine	*La grand mogol*	Mingapour
Barbieri, Francisco	En el templo de Marte	*El barberillo de Lavapiés*	Lamparilla
Bernstein, Leonard	It Must Be So	*Candide*	Candide
Chapí, Ruperto	No extrañéis, no, que se escapen	*La bruja*	Leonardo
	Salve, costa de Bretaña	*La tempestad*	Beltrán
Coward, Noël	If You Could Only Come with Me	*Bitter Sweet*	Carl
Fall, Leo	Ein Röslein auf der Haide war ja	*Die Dollarprinzessin*	Fredy
	Hans Heinrich Baron	*Die Dollarprinzessin*	Hans

Composer	Aria	Opera	Character
Friml, Rudolf	A Woman's Smile	*The Firefly*	Jack
	Rose-Marie	*Rose-Marie*	Jim
Herbert, Victor	When Heroes Have Fallen in Vain	*The Fortune Teller*	Captain Ladislas
	Love Me, Love My Dog	*Mlle. Modiste*	Gaston
	The Time, and the Place and the Girl	*Mlle. Modiste*	Etienne
	Ze English Language	*Mlle. Modiste*	Gaston
	Falling in Love with Someone	*Naughty Marietta*	Dick
	I Envy the Bird	*The Serenade*	Lopez
	The Game of Love	*Sweethearts*	Lt. Karl
Hervé	Oh! Je suis un joyeux viveur!	*Le petit Faust*	Faust
Kálmán, Emmerich	Aus ist's mit der Liebe	*Die Csárdásfürstin*	Boni
	Auch ich war einst ein feiner Csárdáskavalier	*Gräfin Mariza*	Tassilo
	Wenn ich in den Zirkus gehe	*Die Zirkusprinzessin*	Toni
	Zwei Märchenaugen	*Die Zirkusprinzessin*	Mister X
Lecocq, Charles	Certainement, j'aimais Clairette	*La fille de Madame Angot*	Ange-Pitou
	Elle est tellement innocente	*La fille de Madame Angot*	Pomponnet
Lehár, Franz	Octave, gesteh' dir's ein	*Eva*	Octave
	O Mädchen, mein Mädchen	*Friederike*	Goethe
	Dein ist mein ganzes Herz	*Das Land des Lächelns*	Prince Sou-Chong
	Von Apfelblüten einen Kranz	*Das Land des Lächelns*	Prince Sou-Chong
	Gern hab' ich die Frau'n geküßt	*Paganini*	Paganini
	Allein, wieder allein	*Der Zarewitsch*	Der Zarewitsch
	Ich bin ein Zigeunerkind	*Zigeunerliebe*	Józsi
Moreno Torroba, Federico	De este apacible rincón de Madrid	*Luisa Fernanda*	Javier
Offenbach, Jacques	Au mont Ida	*La belle Hélène*	Paris
	O mes amours, ô mes maitresses	*Les brigands*	Antonio
	Adieu, mes chers enfants	*Orphée aux enfers*	Orphée
	Eh hop! Eh hop!	*Orphée aux enfers*	Mercure
	Heureuses divinités	*Orphée aux enfers*	Pluton
	Moi, je suis Aristée	*Orphée aux enfers*	Pluton
	Pour découper adroitement	*La vie parisienne*	Le Major
Romberg, Sigmund	One Alone	*The Desert Song*	Robert
	Overhead the Moon Is Beaming	*The Student Prince*	Karl
Sorozábal, Pablo	No puede ser	*La tabernera del puerto*	Leandro

Composer	Aria	Opera	Character
Straus, Oscar	Ich hab' mit Freuden angehört	Ein Walzertraum	Lt. Niki
	Ich hab' mit Freuden angehört	Ein Walzertraum	Lt. Niki
Strauss, Johann	Der Herzog von Urbino	Eine Nacht in Venedig	Caramello
	Sei mir gegrüsst, du holdes Venezi	Eine Nacht in Venedig	Guido
	Als flotter Geist	Der Zigeunerbaron	Barinkay
Sullivan, Arthur	Take a Pair of Sparkling Eyes	The Gondoliers	Marco
	Were I a King	The Grand Duke	Ernst
	A Maiden Fair to See	HMS Pinafore	Ralph
	Spurn Not the Nobly Born	Iolanthe	Lord Tolloller
	A Wandering Minstrel I	The Mikado	Nanki-Poo
	Oh Is There Not One Maiden Breast?	The Pirates of Penzance	Frederic
	Today We Meet	Princess Ida	Hilarion
	They Intend to Send a Wire	Princess Ida	Hilarion
	Would You Know the Kind of Maid?	Princess Ida	Cyril
	Our Tale Is Told	The Rose of Persia	Yussuf
	I Shipped, D'Ye See	Ruddigore	Richard
	Love Feeds on Many Kinds	The Sorcerer	Alexis
	Thou Hast the Power	The Sorcerer	Alexis
	Oh, Gentlemen, Listen, I Pray	Trial by Jury	Edwin
	When First My Old, Old Love	Trial by Jury	Edwin
	A Tenor, All Singers Above	Utopia, Limited	Fitzbattleaxe
	Free from His Fetters Grim	The Yeomen of the Guard	Fairfax
	Is Life a Boon?	The Yeomen of the Guard	Fairfax
Vives, Amadeu	Por el humo se sabe	Doña Francisquita	Fernando
Zeller, Carl	Wie mein Ahnl zwanzig Jahr	Der Vogelhändler	Adam

Baritone/Bass

Composer	Aria	Opera	Character
Audran, Edmond	Vous allez quitter	La poupée	Le Père Maximin
Chapí, Ruperto	La lluvia ha cesado	La tempestad	Simón
Friml, Rudolf	A Flagon of Wine	The Vagabond King	Guy
	Song of the Vagabonds	The Vagabond King	Villon
Herbert, Victor	Floretta	Babes in Toyland	Alan
	Migonette	Babes in Toyland	Tom Tom
	Song of the Poet	Babes in Toyland	Alan
	Toyland	Babes in Toyland	Tom Tom

Composer	Aria	Opera	Character
	Ho! Ye Townsmen	The Fortune Teller	Sandor
	Slumber On, My Little Gypsy	The Fortune Teller	Sandor
	Marry a Marionette	Naughty Marietta	Etienne
	Every Day Is Ladies Day with Me	The Red Mill	Governor of Zeeland
	Woman, Lovely Woman	The Serenade	Duke
	Every Lover Must Meet His Fate	Sweethearts	Prince Franz
	Pretty as a Picture	Sweethearts	Von Tromp
Lecocq, Charles	Pour un tendre père	Giroflé-Girofla	Boléro
Lehár, Franz	Mein Ahnherr war der Luxemburg	Der Graf von Luxemburg	René
	Da geh' ich zu Maxim	Die lustige Witwe	Danilo
Lortzing, Albert	O sancta justitia	Zar und Zimmermann	Van Bett
	Verraten!	Zar und Zimmermann	Czaar
Moreno Torroba, Federico	Luche la fe por le triunfo	Luisa Fernanda	Vidal
Offenbach, Jacques	À cheval sur la discipline	La Grande-Duchesse de Gérolstein	General Boum
	Pardieu! C'est un amiable charge	La jolie parfumeuse	Germain
	Dans une cave obscure	Madame Favart	Favart
	Quand du four on le retire	Madame Favart	Favart
	Quand il cherche dans sa cervelle	Madame Favart	Favart
	Elles sont tristes les marquises	La vie parisienne	Bobinet
	Je suis Brésilien	La vie parisienne	Le Brésilien
	V'lan, V'lan, je suis V'lan	Le voyage dans la lune	King V'lan
Romberg, Sigmund	Let Love Go	The Desert Song	Ali Ben Ali
	Marianne	The New Moon	Robert
Sorozábal, Pablo	Madrileña bonita	La del manojo de rosas	Joaquín
Sousa, John Philip	If You Examine Humankind	El Capitain	Don Medigua
	When Some Serious Affliction	El Capitain	Don Medigua
Sullivan, Arthur	I Stole the Prince	The Gondoliers	Don Alhambra
	In Enterprise of Martial Kind	The Gondoliers	Duke of Plaza-Toro
	Rising Early in the Morning	The Gondoliers	Giuseppe
	About a Century Since	The Grand Duke	Notary
	A Pattern to Professors	The Grand Duke	Rudolph
	When You Find	The Grand Duke	Rudolph
	Ten Minutes Since I Met a Chap	The Grand Duke	Ludwig
	Fair Moon, to Thee I Sing	HMS Pinafore	Captain Corcoran

Composer	Aria	Opera	Character
	He Is an Englishman	HMS Pinafore	Boatswain
	I Am the Monarch of the Sea	HMS Pinafore	Sir Joseph
	Good Morrow, Good Mother!	Iolanthe	Strephon
	The Law Is the True Embodiment	Iolanthe	Lord Chancellor
	When All Night Long	Iolanthe	Private Willis
	When Britain Really Ruled	Iolanthe	Lord Mountararat
	When I Went to the Bar	Iolanthe	Lord Chancellor
	When You're Lying Awake	Iolanthe	Lord Chancellor
	As Someday It May Happen	The Mikado	Ko-Ko
	On a Tree by the River (Titwillow)	The Mikado	Ko-Ko
	Am I Alone, and Unobserved?	Patience	Bunthorne
	If You Want a Receipt	Patience	Colonel
	When I First Put This Uniform On	Patience	Colonel
	I Am the Very Model of a Modern Major-General	The Pirates of Penzance	Major-General
	Oh, Better Far to Live and Die	The Pirates of Penzance	Pirate King
	When a Felon's Not Engaged	The Pirates of Penzance	Sergeant
	If You Give Me Your Attention	Princess Ida	King Gama
	Whene'er I Spoke	Princess Ida	King Gama
	Let a Satirist Enumerate	The Rose of Persia	Sultan
	My Boy, You May Take It from Me	Ruddigore	Robin
	My Name Is John Wellington Wells	The Sorcerer	Mr. Wells
	Oh, My Voice Is Sad and Low	The Sorcerer	Dr. Daly
	Time Was When Love and I	The Sorcerer	Dr. Daly
	When I, Good Friends	Trial by Jury	Learned Judge
	First, You're Born	Utopia, Limited	King Paramount
	A Wonderful Joy Our Eyes to Bless	Utopia, Limited	Mr. Goldbury
	I've Jibe and Joke	The Yeomen of the Guard	Jack Point
	Oh! A Private Buffoon	The Yeomen of the Guard	Jack Point
Suppé, Franz von	Fassbinder Lied	Boccaccio	Lotteringhi
	Um des Fürsten Zorn zu meiden	Boccaccio	Lambertuccio

APPENDIX D

Selected Discography and Filmography

LIGHT OPERA EXCERPTS ON CD (CATEGORIZED BY ARTIST)

Bonney, Barbara. *Im Chambre séparée: The Operetta Album.* Ronald Schneider. Decca, 2003.

Bostridge, Ian. *The Noël Coward Songbook.* Jeffrey Tate, Sophie Daneman. EMI Classics, 2002.

Caballé, Montserrat, and Bernabé Martí. *Zarzuela Arias & Duets.* Sony Classical, 1995.

Carreras, José, and Isabel Bey. *Zarzuelas: The Passion of Spain.* English Chamber Orchestra, Enrique Ricci. Erato, 1994.

De los Angeles, Victoria. *Zarzuela Arias.* Spanish National Orchestra, Rafael Frühbeck de Burgos. Angel Records, 1990.

Domingo, Plácido. *Romanzas de Zarzuelas.* Orquesta Sinfónica de Madrid, Manuel Moreno-Buendia. Angel Records, 1990.

Domingo, Plácido, and Pilar Lorengar. *Zarzuela Arias & Duets.* ORF-Symphonieorchester, Garcia Navarro. Sony Classical, 2012.

Eddy, Nelson, and Jeanette MacDonald. *Song of Love: The Best of Nelson Eddy and Jeanette MacDonald.* Dynamic, 2011.

Ford, Bruce. *Bruce Ford Sings Viennese Operetta.* London Philharmonic Orchestra, Walter Weller. Chandos, 2003.

Furtral, Elizabeth, and Steven White. *Sweethearts: A Collection of Operetta Favorites of Jeanette MacDonald and Nelson Eddy*. Palmer Chorus, Robert Tweeten. Newport Classic, 1999.

Gedda, Nicolai. *My Favorite Operetta Heroes*. Warner Classics, 2015.

Graham, Susan. *C'est ça la vie, c'est ça l'amour: French Operetta Arias*. City of Birmingham Symphony Orchestra, Yves Abel. Erato Disques, 2002.

Hadley, Jerry. *The World Is Beautiful: Viennese Operetta Arias*. Munich Radio Orchestra, Richard Bonynge. RCA Red Seal, 2003.

Hampson, Thomas. *Operetta Arias*. London Philharmonic, Franz Welser-Most. EMI Classics, 2006.

Hendricks, Barbara, and Gino Quilico. *Operetta Arias and Duets*. Orchestre de l'Opéra National de Lyon, Lawrence Foster. Warner Classics, 2007.

Kaufmann, Jonas, and Julia Kleiter. *You Mean the World to Me*. Rundfunk-Sinfonieorchester Berlin, Jochen Rieder. Sony Classical, 2014.

Keenleyside, Simon, and Angelika Kirchschlager. *My Heart Alone: Favorite Operetta Arias and Duets*. Sony Classical, 2008.

Lanza, Mario. *Mario Lanza Sings Songs from "The Student Prince" and "The Desert Song."* Sony Masterworks, 1989.

Lott, Felicity. *Champagne: Operetta Arias*. Orchestre de la Suisse Romande, Armin Jordan. Virgin France, 2005.

Migenes, Julia. *Vienna*. Symphonie Orchester der Wiener Volksoper, Lalo Schifrin. Erato, 1993.

Moffo, Anna. *Songs from the Great Operettas*. Flare, 2013.

Popp, Lucia. *Wiener Operettenarien*. Academy of St. Martin-in-the-Fields, Neville Marriner. EMI, 1996.

Romberg, Sigmund. *Romberg Conducts Romberg—1*. Naxos, 2003.

———. *Romberg Conducts Romberg—2*. Naxos, 2004.

Rothenberger, Anneliese. *Operettenlieder*. EMI, 1988.

Schwarzkopf, Elisabeth. *Elisabeth Schwarzkopf Sings Operettas by Lehár, Suppé and Strauss*. Haenssler Classic, 2000.

Tauber, Richard. *The Gentleman Tenor: Opera and Operetta Arias and Songs*. Warner Classics, 2009.

———. *Operetta Arias*. Berlin State Opera Orchestra. Naxos, 2004.

Villazón, Rolando. *Gitano*. Orquesta de la Comunidad de Madrid, Plácido Domingo. Virgin Classics, 2007.

Von Otter, Anne Sofie. *Anne Sofie von Otter Sings Offenbach*. Choeur des Musiciens du Louvre, Musiciens du Louvre, Marc Minkowski. Deutsche Grammophon, 2002.

Wunderlich, Fritz. *Operetta Arias*. Arts Music, 2004.

LIGHT OPERAS ON CD (CATEGORIZED BY COMPOSER)

Audran, Edmond. *Gillette de Narbonne/La mascotte*. Orchestre lyrique de l'Orte, Pierre Tellier, Robert Benedetti. Musidisc, 1957.

———. *La mascotte*. Michel Dens, Liliane Berton, Nadine Renaux, Duvaleix, Claude Devos. EMI, 1954.

———. *Le grand mogol*. Orchestre lyrique de l'Orte, Annick Simon, Lina Dachary, Bernard Plantey. Musidisc, 1992.

———. *Miss Helyett/La poupée*. Orchestre lyrique de l'Orte, Marcel Cariven. Musidisc, 1993.

Barbieri, Francisco. *El barberillo de Lavapiés*. Coro de Cámara del Orfeón Donostiarra, Ana Maria Olaria, Teresa Bergenza, Ataúlfo Argenta. Sony, 1990.

———. *Los diamantes de la corona*. Coro Cantares de Madrid, Gran Orquesta Sinfónica, Ataúlfo Argenta, Pilar Lorengar, Dolores Alite, Gerardo Monreal, Rafael Campos. RCA, 2009.

Bernstein, Leonard. *Candide*. Original Broadway Cast, Barbara Cook, Leonard Bernstein. Sony, 1956.

———. *Candide*. London Symphony Orchestra and Chorus, Jerry Hadley, June Anderson, Christa Ludwig, Adolph Green, Leonard Bernstein. Deutsche Grammophon, 1991.

Bretón, Tomás. *La verbena de la Paloma*. Ohio Light Opera, J. Lynn Thompson. Albany Records, 2000.

Chapí, Ruperto. *La revoltosa*. Coro Cantares de Madrid, Anna M. Iriarte, Manuel Ausensi, Ataúlfo Argenta. Sony, 1996.

Fall, Leo. *Der liebe Augustin*. Kölner Rundfunkchor, Kölner Rundfunk Orchester, Brigitte Mira, Anny Schlemm, Franz Fehringer, Willy Schneider, Franz Marszalek. Sony, 2010.

———. *Die Kaiserin*. Chor des Lehár Festivals Bad Ischl, Franz-Lehár Orchester, Miriam Portmann, Jevgenij Taruntsov, Verena Barth-Jurca, Gerhard Balluch, Marius Burkert. CPO, 2015.

———. *Paroli*. WDR Rundfunkchor Köln, WDR Funkhausorchester Köln, Anke Krabbe, Andrea Bönig, Jörg Dürmüller, Michael Roider, Ralf Lakas, Axel Kober. CPO, 2015.

———. *The Rose of Stambul*. Chicago Folks Operetta: Kimberly McCord, Alison Kelly, Erich Buchholz, Gerald Frantzen, Robert Morrissey, John Frantzen. Naxos, 2013.

Friml, Rudolf. *The Firefly*. Ohio Light Opera, Jason Altieri. Albany Records, 2006.

———. *The Vagabond King*. Ohio Light Opera, Steven Byess. Albany Records, 2006.

Herbert, Victor. *Dream City & The Magic Knight*. Ohio Light Opera, Steven Byess. Albany Records, 2015.

———. *Eileen*. Ohio Light Opera, James Stuart. Albany Records, 1998.

———. *Eileen*. Orchestra of Ireland, David Brophy. New World Records, 2012.

———. *The Fortune Teller*. Ohio Light Opera, Steven Byess. Albany Records, 2011.

———. *Mlle. Modiste*. Ohio Light Opera, Michael Borowitz. Albany Records, 2009.

———. *Naughty Marietta*. Ohio Light Opera, Steven Byess. Albany Records, 2001.

———. *The Only Girl*. Light Opera of New York, Gerald Steichen. Albany Records, 2015.

———. *Orange Blossoms*. Light Opera of New York, Evans Haile. Albany Records, 2014.

———. *The Red Mill*. Ohio Light Opera, J. Lynn Thompson. Albany Records, 2001.

———. *Sweethearts*. Ohio Light Opera, J. Lynn Thompson. Albany Records, 2002.

Kálmán, Emmerich. *Autumn Maneuvers*. Ohio Light Opera, Steven Byess. Albany Records, 2003.

———. *The Bayadere*. Ohio Light Opera, J. Lynn Thompson. Albany Records, 1999.

———. *The Carnival Fairy*. Ohio Light Opera, Steven Byess. Albany Records, 2012.

———. *Countess Maritza*. Ohio Light Opera, Steven Byess. Albany Records, 2003.

———. *Der Zigeunerprimas*. Ohio Light Opera, J. Lynn Thompson. Albany Records, 2002.

———. *Der Zigeunerprimas*. Münchner Rundfunkorchester, Edith Lienbacher, Gabrielle Rossmanith, Zoran Todorovich, Claus Peter Flor. CPO, 2005.

———. *Die Csárdásfürstin*. Slovak Philharmonic Choir and Radio Symphony Orchestra, Yvonne Kenny, Richard Bonynge. Naxos, 2005.

———. *Die Csárdásfürstin*. Graunke Symphony Orchestra, Anneliese Rothenberger, Nicolai Gedda, Olivera Miljakovic, Willy Mattes. EMI Classics, 2012.

———. *Die Herzogin von Chicago*. Berlin Rundfunk Symphony, Endrick Wollrich, Monica Groop, Deborah Riedel, Brett Polegato, Richard Bonynge. Decca, 1999.

———. *Gräfin Mariza.* Chor der Bayerischen Staatsoper, Symphonie-Orchester Graunke, Anneliese Rothenberger, Nicolai Gedda, Willi Brokmeier, Olivera Miljakovic, Willy Mattes. EMI Classics, 2012.

———. *The Violet of Montmartre.* Ohio Light Opera, Steven Byess. Albany Records, 2008.

Lecocq, Charles. *Giroflé-Girofla.* Orchestre lyrique de l'Orte, Marcel Cariven, Jean Doussard. Musidisc, 1991.

———. *La fille de Madame Angot.* Orchestre lyrique de l'Orte, Colette Riedinger, Suzanne LaFaye, Gabriel Bacquier, Georgette Spanellys, Richard Bladeau. Musidisc, 2000.

———. *La fille de Madame Angot.* Orchestre du Théâtre National de l'Opéra-Comique, Mady Mesplé, Bernard Sinclair, Christiane Stutzmann, Charles Burles, Jean Doussard. EMI, 2002.

———. *Le coeur et la main.* Orchestre lyrique de l'Orte, Marcel Hamel, Claude Bergeret. Musidisc, 1992.

———. *Le petit duc.* Elaine Thibault, Denise Benoit, André Jobin, Jean Giraudeau, André Grassi. Decca, 1969.

Lehár, Franz. *Das Fürstinkind.* Chor des Bayerischen Rundfunks, Münchner Rundfunkorchester, Chen Reiss, Mary Mills, Matthias Klink, Ralf Simon, Ulf Schirmer. CPO, 2013.

———. *Das Land des Lächelns.* Philharmonia Orchestra, Elisabeth Schwarzkopf, Nicolai Gedda, Otto Ackermann. EMI Classics, 1953.

———. *Der Rastelbinder.* ORF Symphonieorchester, Fritz Muluiar, Elfie Hobarth, Helga Papouschek, Hans Graf. CPO, 2004.

———. *Der Zarewitsch.* Chor des Bayerischen Rundfunks, Münchner Rundfunkorchester, Alexandra Reinprecht, Christina Landshamer, Matthias Klink, Andreas Winkler, Ulf Schirmer. CPO, 2010.

———. *Die lustige Witwe.* Chor des Bayerischen Rundfunks, Symphonie-Orchester Graunke, Anneliese Rothenberger, Nicolai Gedda, Willy Mattes. EMI Classics, 1967.

———. *Die lustige Witwe.* Monteverdi Choir, Wiener Philharmoniker, Cheryl Studer, Boje Skovhus, Barbara Bonney, Bryn Terfel, John Eliot Gardiner. Deutsche Grammophon, 1994.

———. *Eva.* Chor des Lehár Festivals Bad Ischl, Franz-Lehár, Orchester, Morenike Fadayomi, Zora Antonic, Reinhard Alessandri, Thomas Malik, Wolfgang Bozic. CPO, 2006.

———. *Frasquita.* Chor des Lehár Festivals Bad Ischl, Franz-Lehár, Orchester, Rupert Bergmann, Laura Scherwitzl, Vincent Schirrmacher, Ronbert Maszl, Vinzenz Praxmarer. CPO, 2011.

————. *Giuditta.* Chor des Bayerischen Rundfunks, Münchner Rundfunkorchester, Christiane Libor, Nikolai Schukoff, Laura Scherwitzl, Ralf Simon, Ulf Schirmer. CPO, 2016.

————. *Schön ist die Welt.* Chor des Bayerischen Rundfunks, Münchner Rundfunkorchester, Elena Mosuc, Zoran Todorovich, Ulf Schirmer. Alliance, 2006.

————. *Wiener Frauen.* WDR Rundfunkchor, WDR Rundfunkorchester, Anke Hoffmann, Anneli Pfeffer, Peter Minich, Thomas Dewald, Helmut Froschauer. CPO, 2007.

————. *Wo die Lerche singt.* Chor des Lehár Festivals Bad Ischl, Franz-Lehár, Orchester, Gerhard Ernst, Sieglinde Feldhofer, Jevgenij Taruntsov, Wolfgang Jerold, Marius Bukert. CPO, 2014.

————. *Zigeunerliebe.* NDR-Chor, NDR Radiophilharmonie, Johanna Stojkovic, Dagmar Schellenberger, Zoran Todorovich, Bernhard Schneider, Frank Beermann. CPO, 2005.

Messager, André. *Véronique.* Ohio Light Opera, J. Lynn Thompson. Albany Records, 1998.

Moreno Torroba, Federico. *Luisa Fernanda.* Orquesta Sinfonica de Madrid, Plácido Domingo, Veronica Villarroel, Antoni Ros-Marbà. Auvidis-Valois, 1960.

Mozart, Wolfgang Amadeus. *Bastien und Bastienne.* Soloisten der Wiener Sängerknaben, Wiener Kammerorchester, Edouard Lindenberg. Membran, 1957.

————. *Bastien und Bastienne.* Franz Liszt Chamber Orchestra, Edita Gruberova, Vinson Cole, László Polgár, Raymond Leppard. Sony, 1990.

————. *Bastien und Bastienne/Der Schauspieldirektor.* Bayerisches Staatsorchester, Nicolai Gedda, Mady Mesplé, Peter Ustinov, Brigitte Lindner, Kurt Moll, Eberhard Schoener. EMI Classics, 1993.

————. *Der Schauspieldirektor.* Wiener Philharmoniker, Kiri Te Kanawa, Edita Gruberova, Manfred Jungwirth, John Pritchard. Decca, 1991.

————. *Der Schauspieldirektor.* Deutsches Symphonie-Orchester, Noëmi Nadelmann, Ofelia Sala, Lothar Odinius, Carsten Sabrowski, Neville Marriner. Phoenix, 2008.

Offenbach, Jacques. *Bluebeard.* Ohio Light Opera, Michael Borowitz. Albany Records, 2007.

————. *The Brigands.* Ohio Light Opera, J. Lynn Thompson. Albany Records, 2004.

————. *La belle Hélène.* Choeur des Musiciens du Louvre, Les Musiciens du Louvre-Grenoble, Felicity Lott, Marc Minkowski. EMI Classics, 2001.

————. *La belle Hélène.* Choeur et Orchestre du Capitole de Toulouse, Jessye Norman, John Aler, Michel Plasson. EMI, 2009.

———. *La Grande-Duchesse de Gérolstein*. Choeur des Musiciens du Louvre, Les Musiciens du Louvre-Grenoble, Felicity Lott, Marc Minkowski. Erato, 2005.

———. *La Périchole*. Orchestre et Choeurs du Capitole de Toulouse, Teresa Berganza, José Carreras, Michel Plasson. EMI, 1989.

———. *La Périchole*. Chor de l'Opéra du Rhin, Orchestre Philharmonique de Strasbourg, Régine Crespin, Alain Lombard. Alliance, 1992.

———. *La vie parisienne*. Orchestre et Choeurs du Capitole de Toulouse, Régine Crespin, Mady Mesplé, Michel Plasson. EMI Classics, 1976.

———. *Les brigands*. Choeur et Orchestre de l'Opéra de Lyon, Ghislaine Raphanel, Colette Alliot-Lugaz, François Le Roux. EMI, 2009.

———. *Orphée aux enfers*. Choeur et Orchestre de l'Opéra National de Lyon, Marc Minkowski, Natalie Dessay, Véronique Gens, Laurent Naouri, Ewa Podleś. EMI Classics, 1998.

———. *Orphée aux enfers*. Choeur et Orchestre du Capitole de Toulouse, Mady Mesplé, Jane Rhodes, Jane Berbié, Michel Plasson. Erato, 2009.

Romberg, Sigmund. *Blossom Time*. Ohio Light Opera, Steven Byess. Albany Records, 2013.

———. *The Desert Song*. Studio Cast Recording, Giorgio Tozzi, Kathy Barr. RCA Legacy, 1957.

———. *Maytime*. Ohio Light Opera, Steven Byess. Albany Records, 2005.

———. *The New Moon*. 2003 Encores! Revival Concert Cast, Christiane Noll. Ghostlight, 2005.

———. *The Student Prince*. WDR Rundfunkchor Köln, WDR Funkhausorchester Köln, John Mauceri. CPO, 2017.

Schubert, Franz. *Das Dreimäderlhaus*. Ohio Light Opera, Steven Byess. Albany Records, 2003.

Sorozábal, Pablo. *Black, el payaso*. Coros y Gran Orquesta de Conciertos de Madrid, Leda Barclay, Enriqueta Serrano, Luisa Espinosa, Alfredo Kraus, Pablo Sorozábal. Vocación Records, 2010.

———. *La del manojo de rosas*. Coro Cantares de Madrid, Isabel Penagos, Manuel Ausensi, Pablo Sorozábal. Sony, 1996.

Sousa, John Philip. *El Capitain*. Ohio Light Opera, Steven Byess. Albany Records, 2010.

Straus, Oscar. *The Chocolate Soldier*. Ohio Light Opera, J. Lynn Thompson. Albany Records, 1999.

Strauss, Johann, II. *Der Zigeunerbaron*. Wiener Symphoniker, Arnold Schoenberg Chor, Nikolaus Harnoncourt. Elektra, 1995.

———. *Der Zigeunerbaron*. Philharmonica Orchestra and Chorus, Elisabeth Schwarzkopf, Nicolai Gedda, Hermann Prey, Otto Ackermann. ZYX, 2012.

————. *Die Fledermaus*. Bayerischen Staatsorchester, Julia Varady, Lucia Popp, Hermann Prey, Carlos Kleiber. Deutsche Grammophon, 1999.

————. *Die Fledermaus*. Wienerstaatsopernchor, Wiener Philharmoniker, André Previn, Kiri Te Kanawa, Edita Gruberova. Decca, 2012.

————. *Karneval in Rom*. Chor und Orchester des Wiener Rundfunks, Max Schönherr. Cantus Classics, 2010.

————. *A Night in Venice*. Ohio Light Opera, Steven Byess. Albany Records, 2000.

————. *A Night in Venice*. Coro Notturno, Stockholm Strauss Orchestra, Mika Eichenholz. Naxos, 2009.

Sullivan, Arthur. *The Gondoliers*. D'Oyly Carte Opera Company, John Pryce-Jones. Sony Classical, 1991.

————. *The Gondoliers*. Ohio Light Opera, J. Lynn Thompson. Albany Records, 2007.

————. *The Grand Duke*. D'Oyly Carte Opera Company, Royston Nash. Decca, 1998.

————. *The Grand Duke*. Ohio Light Opera, J. Lynn Thompson. Albany Records, 2003.

————. *HMS Pinafore*. D'Oyly Carte Opera Company, Isidore Godfrey. Decca, 1959.

————. *HMS Pinafore*. Ohio Light Opera, J. Lynn Thompson. Albany Records, 2013.

————. *HMS Pinafore*. Welsh National Opera, Richard Suart, Thomas Allen, Rebecca Evans, Felicity Palmer, Charles Mackerras. Telarc, 2006.

————. *Iolanthe*. D'Oyly Carte Opera Company, Royston Nash. Decca, 2015.

————. *The Mikado*. Welsh National Opera, Anthony Rolfe Johnson, Marie McLaughlin, Charles Mackerras. Telarc, 2006.

————. *The Mikado*. Ohio Light Opera, J. Lynn Thompson. Albany Records, 2008.

————. *The Mikado*. D'Oyly Carte Opera Company, John Pryce-Jones. Jay Records, 2014.

————. *Patience*. D'Oyly Carte Opera Company, Isidore Godfrey. Decca, 1989.

————. *Patience*. Ohio Light Opera, Michael Borowitz. Albany Records, 2010.

————. *The Pirates of Penzance*. D'Oyly Carte Opera Company, Royal Philharmonic Orchestra, Isidore Godfrey. Decca, 2003.

————. *The Pirates of Penzance*. Welsh National Opera, John Mark Ainsley, Rebecca Evans, Richard Van Allen, Charles Mackerras. Telarc, 2006.

————. *The Pirates of Penzance*. Ohio Light Opera, J. Lynn Thompson. Albany Records, 2011.

————. *Princess Ida*. Ohio Light Opera, J. Lynn Thompson. Albany Records, 2000.

———. *Princess Ida/Pineapple Poll*. D'Oyly Carte Opera Company, Malcolm Sargent, Charles Mackerras. Decca, 2007.

———. *Ruddigore*. Ohio Light Opera, Michael Borowitz. Albany Records, 2009.

———. *Ruddigore/Cox and Box*. D'Oyly Carte Opera Company, Isidore Godfrey. Decca, 2003.

———. *The Sorcerer*. Ohio Light Opera, Steven Byess. Albany Records, 2005.

———. *The Sorcerer/The Zoo*. D'Oyly Carte Opera Company, Isidore Godfrey. Decca, 1993.

———. *Utopia, Limited*. Ohio Light Opera, J. Lynn Thompson. Albany Records, 2001.

———. *Utopia, Limited*. D'Oyly Carte Opera Company, Royston Nash. Decca, 2003.

———. *The Yeomen of the Guard/Trial by Jury*. D'Oyly Carte Opera Company, Isidore Godfrey. Decca, 1989.

———. *The Yeomen of the Guard*. Ohio Light Opera. J. Lynn Thompson. Albany Records, 2004.

Suppé, Franz von. *Boccaccio/Die schöne Galathée*. Berliner Symphoniker, Ursula Schirrmacher, Rudolf Schock, Renate Holm, Anna Moffo. Sony, 2015.

Vives, Amadeu. *Doña Francisquita*. Coro Titular del Gran Teatro de Córdoba, Orquesta Sinfónica de Sevilla, Plácido Domingo, Ainhoa Arteta, Miguel Roa. Sony, 1995.

Zeller, Carl. *The Birdseller*. Ohio Light Opera, Nathaniel Motta. Albany Records, 2008.

LIGHT OPERAS ON DVD

Benatzky, Ralph. *Im weißen Rößl*. Rainhard Fendrich, Zabine Kapfinger. Videoland, 2014.

Bernstein, Leonard. *Candide*. New York Philharmonic, Kristin Chenoweth, Patti LuPone, Paul Groves, Thomas Allen. Image Entertainment, 2005.

Coward, Noël. *Bitter Sweet*. 1940 film. Nelson Eddy, Jeanette MacDonald. Warner Archive, 2012.

Fall, Leo. *Die Dollarprinzessin*. Tatjana Iwanow, Horst Niendorf, Gabriele Jacoby. Arthaus Musik, 2012.

Friml, Rudolf. *The Firefly*. 1937 film. Jeanette MacDonald, Allan Jones. Warner Archive, 2012.

———. *Rose-Marie*. 1936 film. Nelson Eddy, Jeanette MacDonald. Warner Archive, 2012.

Herbert, Victor. *Disney's Babes in Toyland*. 1961 film. Ray Bolger, Tommy Sands, Annette Funicello, Ed Wynn. Disney, 2002.

———. *Naughty Marietta.* 1955 telecast. Patrice Munsel, Alfred Drake. Video Artists International, 2003.

———. *Naughty Marietta.* 1935 film. Nelson Eddy, Jeanette MacDonald. Warner Archive, 2011.

———. *Sweethearts.* 1938 film. Nelson Eddy, Jeanette MacDonald. Warner Archive, 2011.

Kálmán, Emmerich. *Die Csárdásfürstin.* Anna Moffo, René Kollo. Deutsche Grammophon, 2006.

———. *Die Zirkusprinzessin.* Ingeborg Hallstein, Rudolf Schock, Peter Frankenfeld. Arthaus Musik, 2017.

———. *Giuditta.* Natalia Ushakova, Mehrzad Montazeri. Videoland, 2016.

———. *Gräfin Mariza.* Dagmar Schellenberger, Nikolai Schukoff. Videoland, 2003.

Lehár, Franz. *Das Land des Lächelns.* Stuttgart Opera, René Kollo, Birgit Pitsch-Sarata. Deutsche Grammophon, 2005.

———. *Der Graf von Luxemburg.* Michael Suttner, Gesa Hoppe. ORF, 2015.

———. *Der Graf von Luxemburg.* Eberhard Wächter, Lilian Sukis, Erich Kunz. Arthaus Musik, 2017.

———. *Der Zarewitsch.* Teresa Stratas, Wieslaw Ochman. Deutsche Grammophon, 2007.

———. *Die lustige Witwe.* Zurich Opera, Rodney Gilfry, Dagmar Schellenberger. Arthaus Musik, 2005.

———. *Die lustige Witwe.* 1934 film. Jeanette MacDonald, Maurice Chevalier. Warner Archive, 2013.

———. *Die lustige Witwe.* Metropolitan Opera, Renée Fleming, Nathan Gunn, Kelli O'Hara, Alek Shrader, Thomas Allen. Decca, 2015.

———. *Paganini.* Antonio Theba, Teresa Stratas. Arthaus Musik, 2017.

———. *Zigeunerliebe.* Janet Perry, Iona Buzea, Adolf Dallapozza, Colette Lorand. Arthaus Musik, 2012.

Millöcker, Carl. *Der Bettelstudent.* Cornelia Zink, Milko Milev, Mirko Roschkowski. Videoland, 2014.

Moreno Torroba, Federico. *Luisa Fernanda.* Teatro Real Madrid, Plácido Domingo, Nancy Herrera. Opus Arte, 2007.

Mozart, Wolfgang Amadeus. *Bastien und Bastienne/Der Schauspieldirektor.* Salzburg Marionettentheater, Benhard Berchtold, Aleksandra Zamojska, Evmorfia Metaxaki, Radu Cojocariu. Deutsche Grammophon, 2007.

Offenbach, Jacques. *La belle Hélène.* Zurich Opera, Vesselina Kasarova, Deon Van Der Walt, Carlos Chausson, Volker Vogel, Oliver Widmer. Kultur, 2004.

———. *La belle Hélène.* Hamburg Philharmonic, Jennifer Larmore, Jun-Sang Han, Peter Galliard, Viktor Rud. Naxos, 2015.

———. *La Grande-Duchesse de Gérolstein*. Théâtre du Châtelet, Felicity Lott, Sandrine Piau, Yann Beuron, François Le Roux. Erato, 2006.

———. *La vie parisienne*. Opéra National de Lyon, Laurent Naouri, Jean-Paul Fouchecourt, Marie Devellereau, Sebastian Roulan. Erato, 2008.

———. *Les brigands*. Opéra National de Lyon, Michel Trempont, Valérie Chevalier, Colette Alliot-Lugaz. Image Entertainment, 2002.

———. *Orphée aux enfers*. Opéra National de Lyon, Natalie Dessay, Yann Beuron, Jean-Paul Fouchecourt, Laurent Naouri. Arthaus Musik, 2009.

———. *Orphée aux enfers*. Théâtre Royal de la Monnaie, Elizabeth Vidal, Alexandro Badea. Arthaus Musik, 2014.

———. *Orpheus in der Unterwelt*. Hamburg Philharmonic State Orchestra, Liselotte Pulver, Inge Meysel, Franz Grundheber, Elisabeth Steiner, Kurt Marschner. Arthaus Musik, 2007.

———. *Orpheus in der Unterwelt*. Deutsche Oper Berlin, Donald Grobe, Julia Migenes-Johnson, Astrid Varnay, George Shirley. Arthaus Musik, 2013.

Romberg, Sigmund. *The Desert Song*. 1953 film. Kathryn Grayson, Gordon MacRae. Warner Archive, 2014.

———. *Maytime*. 1937 film. Nelson Eddy, Jeanette MacDonald. Warner Archive, 2012.

———. *New Moon*. 1940 film. Nelson Eddy, Jeanette MacDonald. Warner Archive, 2012.

———. *The Student Prince*. 1954 film. Ann Blyth, Edmund Purdom. Warner Archive, 2014.

Straus, Oscar. *The Chocolate Soldier*. 1941 film. Nelson Eddy, Risë Stevens. Warner Archive, 2012.

Strauss, Johann, II. *Der Zigeunerbaron*. Wolfgang Brendel, Siegfried Jerusalem, Martha Mödl, Ellen Shade. Deutsche Grammophon, 2008.

———. *Die Fledermaus*. Kiri Te Kanawa, Hermann Prey, Hildegard Heichele, Dennis O'Neill. Kultur, 2003.

———. *Die Fledermaus*. Gundula Janowitz, Eberhard Wächter, Renate Holm, Erich Kunz. Deutsche Grammophon, 2008.

———. *Eine Nacht von Venedig*. Anton De Ridder, Sylvia Geszty, Trudeliese Schmidt, Julia Migenes, Erich Kunz. Deutsche Grammophon, 2009.

———. *Wiener Blut*. Ingeborg Hallstein, René Kollo, Dagmar Koller, Benno Kusche. Deutsche Grammophon, 2008.

Sullivan, Arthur. *Gilbert & Sullivan: "The Gondoliers."* Opera World, Eric Shilling, Anne Collins, Francis Egerton, Tom McConnell, Fiona Kimm. Acorn Media, 2002.

———. *Gilbert & Sullivan: "HMS Pinafore."* Opera World, Peter Marshall, Frankie Howerd, Meryl Drower, Michael Bulman. Acorn Media, 2002.

————. *Gilbert & Sullivan: "The Mikado."* Opera World, William Conrad, Clive Revill, Kate Flowers, John Stewart, Anne Collins. Acorn Media, 2002.

————. *Gilbert & Sullivan: "Patience."* Opera World, Donald Adams, Derek Hammond-Stroud, John Fryatt, Sandra Dugdale, Anne Collines. Acorn Media, 2002.

————. *Gilbert & Sullivan: "Princess Ida."* Opera World, Frank Gorshin, Neil Howlett, Laurence Dale, Bernard Dickerson, Richard Jackson. Acorn Media, 2002.

————. *Gilbert & Sullivan: "Ruddigore."* Opera World, Vincent Price, Keith Mitchell, John Treleaven, Donald Adams, Sandra Dugdale. Acorn Media, 2002.

————. *Gilbert & Sullivan: "The Sorcerer."* Opera World, Clive Revill, David Kernan, Donald Abrams, Nuala Willis. Acorn Media, 2002.

————. *Gilbert & Sullivan: "The Yeomen of the Guard."* Opera World, Alfred Marks, Joel Grey, Elizabeth Gale, Claire Powell. Acorn Media, 2002.

————. *The Gondoliers.* Opera Australia, David Hobson, Roger Lemke, Suzanne Johnston. Kultur, 2006.

————. *The Gondoliers/HMS Pinafore/Trial by Jury.* Stratford Festival, Eric Donkin, Michael Burgess, Douglas Campbell, Eric Christmas, Dennis Dowling. CBC Home Video, 1984.

————. *HMS Pinafore/Trial by Jury.* Opera Australia, David Hobson, Anthony Warlow, Celeste Mann. Kultur, 2006.

————. *Iolanthe/The Mikado/The Pirates of Penzance.* Stratford Festival, Maureen Forrester, Eric Donkin, Marie Baron, Paul Massel, Brent Carver. Acorn Media, 2000.

————. *The Mikado.* English National Opera, Eric Idle, Lesley Garrett. A&E Home Video, 2005.

————. *The Mikado.* Opera Australia, Mitchell Butel, Karen Breen, Taryn Fiebig. Opera Australia, 2012.

————. *Patience.* Opera Australia, Christine Douglas, Heather Begg, Anthony Warlow, Dennis Olsen. Kultur, 2008.

————. *The Pirates of Penzance.* Opera Australia, John Bolton Wood, Anthony Warlow, David Hobson, Taryn Fiebig. Kultur, 2008.

————. *The Pirates of Penzance.* 1983 film. Kevin Kline, Angela Lansbury, Linda Ronstadt, Rex Smith. Universal, 2010.

————. *"The Pirates of Penzance": Broadway Theatre Archive.* Delacorte Theatre, Kevin Kline, Linda Ronstadt, Rex Smith, Patricia Routledge. Kultur, 2002.

————. *The Yeomen of the Guard.* 1957 telecast. Celeste Holm, Barbara Cook, Alfred Drake, Bill Hayes. Video Artists International, 2012.

Zeller, Carl. *Der Vogelhändler.* Sebastian Reinthaller, Ute Gfrerer. Videoland, 2014.

APPENDIX E

Where to Sing (and See) Light Opera

Unfortunately, a number of light opera companies have folded over the years, including Light Opera of Manhattan (LOOM), Los Angeles Civic Light Opera, Washington Savoyards, and Light Opera Oklahoma, while others have rebranded themselves; for instance, Light Opera Works in Evanston, Illinois, has become Music Theater Works. But there are still companies producing light opera across North America and Europe. Quotes about the companies listed below come from their respective websites.

NORTH AMERICA

Chicago Folks Operetta
Chicago, IL
The goal of CFO is the "nurturing of live operetta through articulate and dynamic productions," with a focus on Viennese and American operettas from the early twentieth century.

College Light Opera Company
Cape Cod, MA

CLOC is the largest resident theater company in the United States, presenting a summer season of nine shows (light opera and music theater) with a full pit orchestra and a company of thirty-two singers.

Durham Savoyards
Durham, NC

This company is dedicated to "producing the topsy-turvy musical comedies" of Gilbert and Sullivan.

Gilbert & Sullivan Austin
Austin, TX

GSA was founded with the goals of entertaining and educating Central Texas residents and "preserving the works of Gilbert and Sullivan."

Gilbert & Sullivan Very Light Opera Company
Minneapolis, MN

This Twin Cities theater company presents an annual production in addition to assisting "schools and community organizations looking to perform the works of Gilbert and Sullivan, bringing these operettas to new generations."

Gilbert & Sullivan Yiddish Light Opera Company
Long Island, NY

This unique company has produced Yiddish versions of Gilbert and Sullivan favorites, including *Der Yiddisher Pinafore*, *Di Yam Gazlonim*, and *Der Yiddisher Mikado*.

Greensboro Light Opera and Song
Greensboro, NC

Under the aegis of the University of North Carolina at Greensboro, GLOS typically presents two summer productions, a Gilbert and Sullivan show and a musical.

Lamplighters Music Theatre
San Francisco, CA

Lamplighters is dedicated to "the comic operas of Gilbert & Sullivan and other works of comparable wit, literacy and musical merit."

Light Opera of New York
New York, NY
LOONY lists its mission as "bringing light opera out of the dark." Besides productions and concerts, they have released three recordings of lesser-known shows by Victor Herbert and Jerome Kern.

New York Gilbert & Sullivan Players
New York, NY
NYGASP is "the leading custodian of the G&S classics" in the United States, with all thirteen shows in its repertory.

Ohio Light Opera
Wooster, OH
OLO is inarguably "America's premier lyric theater festival." Although they have added music theater in recent seasons, they have been devoted to creating English-language productions and recordings of American, British, French, and Viennese operetta.

Toronto Operetta Theatre
Toronto, ON
TOT is "Canada's only professional operetta company." Besides presenting standard light opera repertoire, they have revived the work of Canadian operetta composer Oscar Telgmann.

Utah Festival Opera & Musical Theatre
Logan, UT
UFOMT has expanded their original focus on operetta to add musicals and mainstream opera to their summer seasons.

While the only operettas the Metropolitan Opera has produced recently are *Die Fledermaus* and *The Merry Widow*, other opera companies have previously included light opera beyond these two standard shows in their performance seasons. Here are a few examples:

- Arizona Opera (*Arizona Lady, HMS Pinafore, The Mikado, The Pirates of Penzance*)
- Central City Opera (*Candide, Naughty Marietta, Orpheus in the Underworld, La Périchole, The Isle of Tulipatan, The Desert Song, The New Moon, The Student Prince, The Gypsy Baron, The*

Gondoliers, HMS Pinafore, Iolanthe, The Mikado, The Pirates of Penzance, Trial by Jury, The Yeomen of the Guard, The Beautiful Galatea, Rose-Marie, The Vagabond King)

- Glimmerglass Opera (*The Gypsy Baron, The Mikado, The Student Prince, The Pirates of Penzance, The Grand Duchess of Gerolstein, The Yeomen of the Guard, Iolanthe, The Mikado, Patience, Orpheus in the Underworld, Candide*)
- Santa Fe Opera (*Countess Maritza, La belle Hélène, The Grand Duchess of Gerolstein, Orpheus in the Underworld, The Gondoliers, HMS Pinafore, The Pirates of Penzance, Candide*)
- Wolf Trap Opera (*Candide, Cox and Box, Fleurette, The Gondoliers, The Island of Tulipatan*)

EUROPE

Budapest Operetta Theatre
Budapest, Hungary
Budapesti Operettszínház presents Hungarian operettas with German subtitles and contemporary musicals with English subtitles.

English National Opera
London, United Kingdom
ENO is committed to opera in English with a belief that "singing in our own language connects the performers and the audience to the drama onstage, and enhances the experience for all."

Festival d'Opérettes de Lamalou-les-Bains
Hérault, France
This summer operetta festival features primarily French composers such as Jacques Offenbach, Edmond Audran, and Charles Lecocq.

Festivalul de Operă și Operetă în aer liber (Open-Air Opera and Operetta Festival)
Timișoara, Romania
In August, the Opera Națională Română Timișoara presents outdoor opera and operetta productions.

Gärtnerplatztheater
Munich, Germany
This company in Munich offers a mix of musicals and bread-and-butter Viennese operetta.

Hamburger Engelsaal
Hamburg, Germany
This historic theater hosts the Theater der leichten Muse (Theatre of Light Entertainment), featuring classic operetta and contemporary concerts.

Komische Oper Berlin
Berlin, Germany
Opera, operetta, and musicals are part of the programming of this German company.

Lehár Festival
Bad Ischl, Austria
Franz Lehár is celebrated in his hometown by this summer festival of his work, dubbed the "Bayreuth der Operette."

The National Gilbert & Sullivan Opera Company
Halifax, United Kingdom
Begun at the International Gilbert & Sullivan Festival in Buxton, this is "the UK's leading professional opera company dedicated to performing the works of Gilbert & Sullivan."

Seefestspiele Mörbisch
Mörbisch am See, Austria
This music festival presents operettas and musicals on its scenic lakeside stage.

Staatsoperetten Dresden
Dresden, Germany
This company follows the paradigm of a balanced mix of operetta, opera, and music theater productions.

Teatro de la Zarzuela
Madrid, Spain
At this Spanish theater, "where the Spanish musical comedy has always been cultivated, the best works of the zarzuela repertoire are still sung and performed."

Volksoper Wien
Vienna, Austria
They present Viennese operetta as well as concerts and musicals.

GLOSSARY

A cappella: Sung without accompaniment. In light opera, some musical numbers include a cappella sections. Examples include "A Nice Dilemma We Have Here" from *Trial by Jury*.

Action: In acting, the approach or response taken in order to achieve one's character objective. For example, in *Die Fledermaus*, Eisenstein takes the action of going to the ball while pretending to go to jail.

***Alborada*:** A Spanish term for a serenade, typically taking place at dawn. Examples include "Noche pura y serena" from *El señor Joaquín* and "Clavellina de la huerta" from *La dolorosa*.

Ballad: In music theater, a song with a slow tempo, usually with a dramatic or romantic nature. Examples include "The Impossible Dream" from *Man of La Mancha* and "Bill" from *Show Boat*.

Barihunk: A colloquial term for a handsome baritone, especially one who often appears shirtless onstage. Examples include Nathan Gunn and Erwin Schrott.

Belting: A term used to describe an approach to vocal technique and registration associated with music theater, typically involving chest voice or speech-like singing. Examples of famous belters include Ethel Merman and Patti LuPone.

Bolero: A Spanish dance in slow triple time, typically performed in pairs and with castanets. It occurs as a musical form in zarzuela. Examples include "Bolero a dos" from *Los diamantes de la corona.*

***Bon vivant*:** A French term used to describe a "life of the party" person who enjoys good food and drink. It is also used as a label for the leading tenor role in Viennese operetta. Examples include Eisenstein in *Die Fledermaus* and Danilo in *Die lustige Witwe.*

***Cachucha*:** A solo Spanish dance in triple time. Besides appearing in zarzuela, it is featured in "Dance a Cachucha" from *The Gondoliers.*

Cameo: A short, featured role that is small in duration but has significant impact. Examples include the Countess Kokozow in *Der Graf von Luxemburg* and Zineco in *Black, el payaso.*

Can-can: A French dance characterized by high kicks and splits still performed at the Moulin Rouge and Folies Bergères. Examples in light opera include the "Galop Infernal" from *Orphée aux enfers* and the Grisetten-Lied from *Die lustige Witwe.*

***Canción*:** A Spanish term for song, typically strophic in form. Examples in zarzuela include "¡Gol!" from *Don Manolito* and "Pues señor, este era un rey" from *La bruja.*

***Cantables*:** A Spanish term for the sung portion of zarzuela. In zarzuela, *cantables* alternate with *hablados* or spoken dialogue.

Chiaroscuro: A bel canto ideal of vocal resonance with a timbral balance of bright and dark. In light opera, the tonal ideal is usually demonstrated in the singing of the leading romantic couple, such as Margot and Pierre in *The Desert Song* and Sylva and Edwin in *Die Csárdásfürstin.*

Choreography: A sequence of dance steps coordinated with music. In light opera, choreography can play a major role not just in dance numbers but in both solo songs and ensemble pieces.

Coaching: A one-on-one session with a vocal coach/pianist who helps the singer with diction and musical details. Coachings typically include work on style, interpretation, and performance practice.

Coloratura: An Italian term for an elaborate and ornamented musical line. It is also used in the *Fach* designation coloratura soprano, describing a singer who excels at florid runs and high notes.

***Commedia dell'arte*:** An Italian term for a sixteenth-century improvisational theatrical form involving stock characters such as Arlecchino

(Harlequin), Colombina, and Pantalone. Its influence on character archetypes continues in light opera.

Comprimario: An Italian term meaning "with the principal," it is a supporting operatic role, typically of comedic quality. Examples include Dr. Blind and Ida/Sally in *Die Fledermaus.*

Coplas: A Spanish term for strophic, rhyming verses, typically of a satirical nature. Examples include the *coplas* de Don Hilarión from *La verbena de la Paloma.*

Couplets: A French term for an aria with rhyming verses, typically witty in nature. Examples include the "Couplets du sabre" from *La Grande-Duchesse de Gérolstein.*

Crossover: A term describing when singers move across genre designations to sing a different musical style. Examples include opera star Renée Fleming recording a jazz album or Broadway star Kelli O'Hara singing in Wolfgang Amadeus Mozart's *Così fan tutte* at the Metropolitan Opera.

Csárdás: A traditional Hungarian folk dance with gypsy influences, typically featuring a violin solo. The *csárdás* plays a prominent role in Viennese operetta. Examples include "Klänge der Heimat" from *Die Fledermaus* and "Hör' ich Zimbalklänge" from *Zigeunerliebe.*

Double entendre: A French-derived term for a word or saying with a double meaning. For instance, in *Trial by Jury*, the chorus calls Angelina a "broken flower," implying she is a beautiful, blooming young woman but also one who has been "deflowered."

Duo: A Spanish term for duet in zarzuela. Examples include "¡Cállate, corazón!" from *Luisa Fernanda* and "Chinochilla de mi Charniqué" from *La del manojo de rosas.*

Drinking song: A common feature in light opera, it is a celebratory song involving toasting. Examples include "Drink! Drink! Drink!" from *The Student Prince* and the Tea-Cup Brindisi ("Eat, Drink, and Be Gay") from *The Sorcerer.*

En travesti: A French term for an actor playing a character of the opposite sex. Examples include pants roles such as the mezzo title role in *Boccaccio* and skirt roles, like when a tenor sings the Witch in *Hansel and Gretel.*

Fach: A German term for a specific voice category or voice type. In opera, the *Fach* system is used in the casting of singers, especially in Germany.

Foxtrot: A ballroom dance step in duple time. In light opera, examples include "Student Life" from *The Student Prince* and the French foxtrot from *Im weißen Rößl*.

Grand opéra: A French term for a serious, large-scale opera, typically having five acts and a ballet. Examples include *Les Huguenots* and *La Juive*.

Grapevine: A basic dance step involving side-stepping footwork crossing forward and back. In light opera, it is a common step used in choreography.

Graustarkian: A term for an overly romanticized and/or melodramatic scenario. Its origin is the imaginary Eastern European country of Graustark, which is featured in a series of novels by George Barr McCutcheon.

Grisette: A French term for nineteenth-century Parisian Bohemian women, typically identifying artsy, independent women with progressive sexual mores. Examples include the Grisettes in *Die lustige Witwe* and the Prater girls in *Bitter Sweet*.

Hablados: A Spanish term for spoken dialogue in zarzuela. In zarzuela, *hablados* alternate with *cantables* (or sung portions).

Ingénue: A young, sweet-natured female character typically played by a light soprano. Examples include Josephine in *HMS Pinafore* and Marianne in *The New Moon*.

Intermezzo: An Italian term for a short, one-act *opera buffa*, typically performed in between the acts of a longer opera. A notable example is Giovanni Battista Pergolesi's *La serva padrona*.

Jazz square: A basic dance step involving footwork in a box-step pattern. In light opera, it is a common step used in choreography.

Kitsch: A German term used to describe "cheesiness." It is often used in relation to the corny or garish aspects of operetta, such as its melodrama and sentimentality.

Legato: An Italian term for a line calling for smooth, connected phrasing without any breaks between notes. In light opera, it features prominently in the singing style.

Madrigalesque: A term used to describe a piece of music that resembles a madrigal. An example is "Strange Adventure" from *The Yeomen of the Guard.*

March: A term for a musical genre in duple time with a steady beat. Examples include the El Capitan March and "March of the Toys" from *Babes in Toyland.*

Mazurka: A Polish folk dance in a triple meter. Examples include the opening mazurka from *Maytime* and "The Blue Mazurka" from *Die blaue Mazur.*

Melisma: A term used to describe an ornamented vocal line or elaborate cadenza. Examples include the vocal lines in "La canción del ruiseñor" from *Doña Francisquita* and "Glitter and Be Gay" from *Candide.*

Modal voice: A term used to describe the male chest voice. In light opera, it is the vocal register used by patter baritones such as Major-General Stanley in *The Pirates of Penzance.*

Monologue: In theater, a speech given by a single character. In theatrical auditions, performers are often required to present a monologue from memory.

Novelty song: A theatrical musical number involving a comedic gimmick or novel feature. An example is "Jeanette and Her Wooden Shoes" from *Sweethearts.*

Objective: In acting, what the character wants or hopes to achieve. For example, in *HMS Pinafore*, Josephine's objective is to marry Ralph.

Obstacle: In acting, the impediment to achieving a character's objective. For example, in *HMS Pinafore*, the obstacle to Josephine marrying Ralph is that he is a sailor and thus beneath her station.

Onomatopoeia: A poetic term that refers to words that sound like what they mean. Examples include the words *hiss* in English and *plouf* in French.

Opéra bouffe: A French term for comic opera. Examples include *Chilpéric* and *Orphée aux enfers.*

Opera buffa: An Italian term for comic opera. Examples include *Le nozze di Figaro* and *Il barbiere di Siviglia.*

Opéra comique: A French term for operas written to be performed at the Opéra-Comique in Paris. Examples include *Carmen* and *Fra Diavolo.*

Operetta: A term used to describe any light opera, typically a humorous work with spoken dialogue. In a narrower sense, the waltz-based Viennese flavor of light opera, exemplified most famously in *Die Fledermaus* and *Die lustige Witwe*. Many American operettas—particularly those by Sigmund Romberg—were also influenced by this distinctly Viennese flavor.

Pants role: A male character meant to be played by a female singer. Examples include Prince Orlofsky in *Die Fledermaus* and Cupidon in *Orphée aux enfers*.

Patter song: A song requiring quick delivery of text and agile articulation, often sung by comic baritones, especially in Gilbert and Sullivan operas. Examples include "I Am the Very Model of a Modern Major-General" from *The Pirates of Penzance* and the Nightmare Song from *Iolanthe*.

Polka: A Czech folk dance in a duple meter. Examples include the Peasant Polka from *Friderike* and the "Polka de l'arrestation" from *Madame l'archiduc.*

Refrain: A term for the chorus or recurring musical section of a song, as opposed to the introductory, expository verse. Examples include the refrain of the Vilja-Lied from *Die lustige Witwe.*

Romanza: A Spanish term for romantic aria. Examples include "Esta es su carta" from *Gigantes y cabezudos* and "Por el humo se sabe donde está el fuego" from *Doña Francisquita.*

Rondalla: A Spanish term for a traditional street band often including lute and/or mandolin players. This type of band is associated with festive occasions.

Rubato: An Italian term meaning "robbing" that describes a flexible tempo with give and take or a balance of ritardando and accelerando. It is a common musical practice in light opera.

Salida: A Spanish term for entrance aria. Examples include "Mi aldea" from *Los gavilanes* and "Dice la gente del barrio" from *La del manojo de rosas.*

Scena: An Italian term for scene. In light opera, it implies an extended scene with several dramatic sections. Examples include "The Hours Creep On Apace" from *HMS Pinafore*.

Schmaltz: A Yiddish term for melted animal fat, which in theater and opera describes the use of overdone sentimentality. It is a common trait of operetta style.

Singspiel: A German term for a light opera that includes spoken dialogue and sung musical numbers. Examples include Hiller's *Der verwandelten Weiber* and Mozart's *Bastien und Bastienne.*

Skirt role: A female character meant to be played by a male singer. Examples include the tenor and baritone roles Madame Poiretapée, Madame Madou, and Madame Beurrefondu in *Mesdames de la Halle.*

Sostenuto: An Italian term for sustained singing usually involving a slowing of tempo. In light opera, *sostenuto* typically takes place at climactic moments, such as the conclusion of "Lippen schweigen" from *Die lustige Witwe.*

Soubrette: A stock character type who is typically a sassy, coquettish young woman and is often a maid or best friend to another leading lady. Examples include the soprano role of Adele in *Die Fledermaus* and the mezzo part of Paquette in *Candide.*

Spieltenor: A voice category describing a comedic tenor, typically in a supporting role. Examples include Zsupán in *Der Zigeunerbaron* and Boni in *Die Csárdásfürstin.*

Spinto: An Italian term meaning "pushed" used to describe heavier lyric voices not quite as heavy as full dramatic voice types. Examples of *spinto* soprano roles in operetta include the title roles in *Gräfin Mariza* and *Die Csárdásfürstin.*

Staccato: An Italian term for rapid, detached musical articulation, or the opposite of legato or *sostenuto* phrasing. In light opera, songs requiring staccato singing include Adele's Laughing Song from *Die Fledermaus* and "Poor Wandering One" from *The Pirates of Penzance.*

Stock character: A stereotypical character type found throughout the theatrical tradition. In light opera, examples include the ingénue and the comic baritone.

Strophic: A song form with repeated musical strophes involving multiple verses set to the same music. Examples include "On a Tree by the River" (a.k.a. "Titwillow") from *The Mikado.*

Subtext: In acting, the underlying thought or inner monologue of the character, which may not be the same as the perceived intent of the spoken text. For example, when Valencienne sings "I Am a Dutiful Wife" in *The Merry Widow*, she is actually flirting with her lover Camille.

Tauberlied: A song written by Franz Lehár for tenor Richard Tauber. Examples include "Dein ist mein ganzes Herz" from *Das Land des Lächelns* and "Gern hab' ich die Frau'n geküßt" from *Paganini*.

Terceto: A Spanish term for trio or musical number for three singers in zarzuela. Examples include "Mi amor, mi bien, mi dueño" from *El rey que rabío* and "Diamantes brasileños" from *La tempestad*.

Tessitura: A term used to describe the primary pitch area where a vocal part lies instead of its full vocal range or compass. For example, the roles of Rosalinda and Adele in *Die Fledermaus* have a similar vocal range but Adele's tessitura is slightly higher.

Timbre: A term used to describe vocal quality. Subjective adjectives are often used, such as bright, dark, warm, and metallic, among others.

Tiple: A Spanish term for a light soprano in zarzuela. Examples of *tiple* roles include Mari-Pepa in *La revoltosa* and Asia in *Agua, azucarillos y aguardiente*.

Triple-threat: A term used to describe a performer with multiple talents as a singer, actor, and dancer. Examples include Amy Adams and Hugh Jackman.

Up-tempo: In music theater, a song with a fast tempo and typically an up-beat or cheerful nature. Examples include "A Cockeyed Optimist" from *South Pacific* and "On a Wonderful Day like Today" from *The Roar of the Greasepaint, the Smell of the Crowd*.

Verismo: An Italian term meaning "realism." In opera, it is associated with the works of Mascagni, Leoncavallo, and Puccini.

Vibrance: A term used to describe vibrato, or an oscillation in pitch. In light opera, it is usually present in the singing style while not as much in music theater.

Waltz: A ballroom dance in triple time. Waltzes play a prominent role in operetta. Examples include the *Merry Widow* waltz and the *Wiener Blut* waltz.

Yellowface: A term used to describe when Asian characters are portrayed by Caucasian performers. Most often associated with *The Mikado*, this practice has become less common due to increasing awareness of racism and cultural insensitivity.

Zarzuela: The Spanish form of light opera typically including musical numbers and spoken dialogue. The term comes from La Zarzuela, a name for the palace of King Philip IV of Spain.

Zarzuelero: A Spanish term for someone who performs or composes zarzuela. Examples include Plácido Domingo and Pablo Sorozábal.

Zigeuner: The German word for gypsy. Gypsy influences and characters are found throughout Viennese operetta. Examples include *Zigeunerliebe* and *Der Zigeunerbaron*.

Zwischenfach: A German term meaning "between" used to describe voices that fall in between standard vocal *Fach* categories. In Viennese operetta, some leading male roles are *Zwischenfach*.

INDEX

ABOUT THE CONTRIBUTORS

Matthew Hoch is associate professor of voice and coordinator of voice studies at Auburn University. He is the author of several books, including *A Dictionary for the Modern Singer, Welcome to Church Music and The Hymnal 1982,* and *Voice Secrets: 100 Performance Strategies for the Advanced Singer,* coauthored with Linda Lister. Hoch is president of the New York Singing Teachers Association (NYSTA) and is the 2016 winner of the Van L. Lawrence Fellowship, awarded jointly by the Voice Foundation and the National Association of Teachers of Singing (NATS). He holds a BM from Ithaca College, MM from the Hartt School, DMA from the New England Conservatory, and a certificate in vocology from the National Center for Voice and Speech (NCVS). He actively performs art song, chamber music, and opera, as well as in professional choral settings.

Wendy LeBorgne is a voice pathologist, speaker, author, and master-class clinician. She actively presents nationally and internationally on the professional voice and is the clinical director of two successful private practice voice centers: the ProVoice Center in Cincinnati and the Blaine Block Institute for Voice Analysis and Rehabilitation (BBIVAR) in Dayton. Dr. LeBorgne holds an adjunct professorship at University of Cincinnati College–Conservatory of Music as a voice consultant, where she also teaches voice pedagogy and wellness courses. She completed a

BFA in musical theater from Shenandoah Conservatory and her graduate and doctoral degrees from the University of Cincinnati. Original peer-reviewed research has been published in multiple journals, and she is a contributing author to several voice textbooks. Most recently, she coauthored *The Vocal Athlete* textbook and workbook with Marci Rosenberg. Her patients and private students currently can be found on radio, television, film, cruise ships, Broadway, off-Broadway, national tours, commercial music tours, and opera stages around the world.

Scott McCoy is a noted author, singer, conductor, and pianist with extensive performance experience in concert and opera. He is professor of voice and pedagogy, director of the Swank Voice Laboratory, and director of the interdisciplinary program in singing health at Ohio State University. His voice science and pedagogy textbook, *Your Voice: An Inside View*, is used extensively by colleges and universities throughout the United States and abroad. McCoy is the associate editor of the *Journal of Singing* for voice pedagogy and is a past president of the National Association of Teachers of Singing (NATS). He also served NATS as vice president for workshops, program chair for the 2006 and 2008 national conferences, chair of the voice science advisory committee, and as a master teacher for the intern program. Deeply committed to teacher education, McCoy is a founding faculty member in the New York Singing Teachers Association (NYSTA) Professional Development Program (PDP), teaching classes in voice anatomy, physiology, acoustics, and voice analysis. He is a member of the distinguished American Academy of Teachers of Singing.

Christopher Webber is a British actor, writer, and stage director. As the author of *The Zarzuela Companion* and curator of Zarzuela.net, he has written widely on the genre and lectured in the United States, Britain, Spain, and throughout Europe. He is an advisory editor for Oxford University Press's *Dictionary of National Biography*, was a major contributor to the *Oxford Companion to Music*, and is part of *Opera Magazine*'s regular reviewing team. Zarzuela aside, his special interests include Czech, Russian, and British opera; Jacobean drama; and thoroughbred horse racing. His first published book was *Bluff Your Way at the Races* for the famous Bluffer's Guide series. As an actor, he has been closely associated with Sir Alan Ayckbourn and the plays of Alan Bennett, though his chief claim to fame was creating Owl in the first-ever stage play of *Winnie the Pooh* in London's West End.

ABOUT THE AUTHOR

Linda Lister is author of *Yoga for Singers: Freeing Your Voice and Spirit through Yoga* and coauthor of *Red Rock Mantras* (with Gianni Becker) and *Voice Secrets: 100 Performance Strategies for the Advanced Singer* (with Matthew Hoch). In the realm of light opera, she has directed and choreographed *Die Fledermaus, Orpheus in the Underworld, The Merry Widow, Bastien and Bastienne, The Impresario, Trial by Jury, The Gondoliers*, and *HMS Pinafore* and has performed in *Babes in Toyland* (Mary), *Bitter Sweet* (Jane/Toni), *The Mikado* (Peep-Bo), *Utopia, Limited* (Phylla), *The Gondoliers* (Casilda), *The Merry Widow* (Olga/Lolo), and *Die Fledermaus* (Adele). A Phi Beta Kappa graduate of Vassar College, she received her MM degree from the Eastman School of Music and her DMA degree from the University of North Carolina at Greensboro. Her solo credits include performances with the Washington Symphony Orchestra, Buffalo Philharmonic, Evansville Philharmonic, Las Vegas Philharmonic, Piedmont Opera Theatre, Opera Theatre of Rochester, Long Leaf Opera, Sin City Opera, Greensboro Oratorio Society, Cambridge Gilbert and Sullivan Society, and Maine State Music Theatre. She created the role of Madge in the world premiere of Libby Larsen's opera *Picnic* (2009) and sang Savannah in the world-premiere concert version of *The Prince of Tides* (2010) with the Carolina Master Chorale. She is the soprano soloist with the Prague

Radio Symphony on the Centaur Records release *Moments of Arrival* (2016), as well as the Albany Records releases *The American Soloist* and *Midnight Tolls*. Winner of the 2014 American Prize in Directing, she directed UNLV Opera to two first-place awards in the 2015 National Opera Association (NOA) Collegiate Opera Scenes Competition in both musical theater and graduate opera divisions and a second-place award in the 2015–2016 NOA Opera Production Competition for her pairing of *Trial by Jury* with Dan Shore's *The Beautiful Bridegroom*. She has been a stage director for the Druid City Opera Workshop and Emerald City Opera Institute. Also a composer, she has written a number of vocal works including *Pleas to Famous Fairies*, *Bring Me the Wine of Love*, *Flags: Summer of 2015*, and a chamber opera about the Brontë sisters titled *How Clear She Shines!* Dr. Lister is associate professor of music and director of opera theater at the University of Nevada, Las Vegas.